SLAVERY AND PROTESTANT MISSIONS IN IMPERIAL BRAZIL

"The Black Does Not Enter the Church, He Peeks in from Outside"

José Carlos Barbosa

Translated with an introduction by
Fraser G. MacHaffie and Richard K. Danford

University Press of America,® Inc.
Lanham · Boulder · New York · Toronto · Plymouth, UK

Copyright © 2008 by
University Press of America,® Inc.
4501 Forbes Boulevard
Suite 200
Lanham, Maryland 20706
UPA Acquisitions Department (301) 459-3366

Estover Road
Plymouth PL6 7PY
United Kingdom

Library of Congress Control Number: 2008932348
ISBN-13: 978-0-7618-4300-9 (paperback : alk. paper)
ISBN-10: 0-7618-4300-0 (paperback : alk. paper)
eISBN-13: 978-0-7618-4301-6
eISBN-10: 0-7618-4301-9

⊖™ The paper used in this publication meets the minimum
requirements of American National Standard for Information
Sciences—Permanence of Paper for Printed Library Materials,
ANSI Z39.48—1984

FOR DUDU AND ZEQUINHA, DEAREST CHILDREN

FOR RACHEL, THE WIFE OF JACOB

TABLE OF CONTENTS

TRANSLATORS' INTRODUCTION

B
razil has the dubious honor of being defined as the first true slave society in the Americas and also the last nation of the New World to abolish slavery. The timeframe of Dr. José Carlos Barbosa's book, *Negro não Entra na Igreja, espia da banda de fora: Protestantismo e Escravidão no Brasil Império*,[1] is the imperial age in Brazil, extending from 1808, when the Portuguese Court fled to Brazil in the face of Napoleon's invading army, until 1888, when slavery was finally abolished (to be followed by abolition of the monarchy the following year).

The principal human subjects in this volume are the Protestant missionaries who were active in Brazil during the nineteenth century. The majority of these individuals hailed from the United States of America, more specifically from states that formed part of the Confederate States of America during the time of the U.S. Civil War. They were drawn to Brazil by the promise of generous land grants and an economy based largely on single-crop cultivation carried out by slave labor from Africa. Slavery was not abolished in Brazil until 1888, and Barbosa examines the attitudes and actions of Protestant missionaries in Brazil regarding slavery during the waning days of this institution. He argues that the missionaries' relatively public silence on the slavery issue is a consequence of political expediencies related to the more urgent imperative of implanting in Brazil a variety of Christianity that directly challenged the authority of the Roman Catholic Church. The principal strategy employed in this endeavor was to first make inroads among the country's elites, particularly in what are today the states of Rio de Janeiro and São Paulo, the centers of political and economic power. This was achieved by gaining entrance into the homes of such families in order to preach reformed doctrine, and also through the establishment of private schools for educating their children—schools that fostered the liberal education in vogue at that time among society's elites in Europe and the Americas. Largely ignored during these early Protestant efforts were the non-elites of Brazilian society, particularly the slaves of African origin. This directly contradicted Protestant ideology of the times, particularly as it developed in the United States.

Barbosa's analysis begins by examining the socio-political realities faced by Protestant missionaries who labored in Brazil, drawing on the metaphor of the country as a 'closed garden which wild animals cannot enter,' meaning that the presence of the Roman Catholic Church was such that Protestantism faced great challenges in making any inroads into Brazilian social life. Of particular interest is Barbosa's examination of historical documents that reveal the harsh criticism

leveled at Protestant missionaries by Ultramontanist clergy in Brazil, attacks that
frequently address the issue of the Protestants' focused efforts on Brazilian elites
that ignored other segments of the country's populace. Barbosa then examines
the specific strategies carried out by the Protestant missionaries, who hoped to
implant their faith among Brazil's strongly Catholic populace.

Barbosa then proceeds to examine U.S. Protestantism and its stance on the
issue of slavery, bringing to bear the differences in opinion that mirrored the
North-South divide leading up to the Civil War. This provides the necessary
context for Barbosa's discussion of abolitionist activity by Protestant missionaries in Brazil, which did in fact exist, although it was limited by the aforemen-
tioned political expediencies and by the personal experiences and ideals of individual missionaries. Such endeavors included preaching to encourage slaveholders to free their slaves; conformity with Brazilian proposals to approach abolition gradually so as to minimize the impact on slaveholders' personal fortunes;
and arguments presented publicly to view blacks as brothers and sisters in
Christ, as a means of fostering racial democracy. Protestant publications were
particularly important in these efforts, as a means of educating the Brazilian
populace.

Barbosa also draws attention to the fact that the same Protestant missionaries who advocated abolition often spoke of slavery as a 'necessary evil' because
it would provide the means of allowing Protestantism to be glorified over
Roman Catholicism when Protestants led the way in the abolition of slavery in
Brazil. What is noted by their critics, however, is that the move towards abolition was already well under way in Brazilian society, with no real influence on
that trend exerted by Protestant preaching or conversions. The Protestant missionaries also saw an important role for Protestantism in Brazil in transforming
freed blacks into 'non-dangerous' members of Brazilian society, through their
conversion to Protestantism and their education at the hands of Protestant
teachers.

Barbosa concludes that ultimately the temerity of Protestant missionaries in
Brazil regarding slavery was a function of: 1) the difficulties of establishing
Protestantism in an almost exclusively Roman Catholic country, where Church
and State were closely linked; 2) a strong conservative tendency among many of
the missionaries regarding slavery that favored the spiritual salvation of blacks
over their corporal emancipation; 3) Protestant concern for moral regeneration
of Brazilian society, which focused more on the integration, conversion and
education of blacks within Protestantism than on challenging Brazilian political
structures; and 4) the preconceived notion that Protestantism would be the
bearer and representative of a new era of progress in Brazil, a role that required
them to address concerns above and beyond the issue of slavery.

A desire to make his research available to non-Portuguese-speaking readers has motivated the translators. While there are several accessible
English-language texts that describe aspects of slavery in Brazil,[2] a
strength of the book lies in the range of sources used. Not only does Barbosa
bring to our attention impressions of slavery recorded by travelers and letters

sent home by the missionaries, but he makes extensive use of Portuguese-language newspapers to develop several themes. Access to these newspapers remains almost impossible for non-Brazilians, and especially useful are the extracts from the evangelical press represented by *Imprensa Evangélica* (founded in 1864 by Presbyterian missionary Ashbel Green Simonton) and *O Novo Mundo* (established in 1870 by José Carlos Rodrigues and edited in New York).

Education became a particular focus of the mission enterprise, both serving denominational needs and also responding to the concerns of a minority of abolitionists, such as Joaquim Nabuco and Tavares Bastos, who saw abolition as only one of several reforms needed to create a truly enlightened society in Brazilian.[3] Nearly all the freed slaves were illiterate, with no training other than that of working on the plantations. Illiteracy was also prevalent among the population at large, and the work of the missionaries (Methodist and Presbyterian) led to the establishment of schools (at first Sunday schools and then regular schools) that have grown to be institutions of national renown, offering kindergarten through doctoral programs. An example of this is the Educational Institute of Piracicaba, which had its origins in a kindergarten, the Colégio Piracibano, founded in 1884 by Martha Hite Watts, born in Kentucky and sent to Brazil by the Woman's Missionary Society of the Methodist Episcopal Church, South. The Educational Institute of Piracicaba now includes the Universidade Metodista de Piracicaba (UNIMEP), whose press, the Editora UNIMEP, published the Portuguese edition of this book as part of a series on Protestantism and Education.[4]

Some general observations about Protestantism and slavery in Brazil are needed to illuminate and contextualize Barbosa's conclusions. Unlike the United States, where a movement toward the abolition of slavery had gathered momentum by early in the nineteenth century, it was beyond mid-century before agitation against the institution gained any strength in Brazil. Again, in contrast to the United States, Brazil's (Roman Catholic) ecclesiastical establishment was silent and the abolitionists did not look to the pulpit for support in their cause. Shifts in the Brazilian agrarian economy away from cotton in the northern provinces toward coffee in the central and southern provinces, with an accompanying movement of slaves from the north to the south, was seen by some as creating a divide similar to that of the contemporary United States. In the 1860s Brazil's republican movement grew in strength, and implicit in the movement was the expectation of a weak centralized government with power residing in the provincial legislatures, thus allowing each province to determine its own way of dealing with slavery. The possibility of a Brazil divided into slave provinces and non-slave provinces was recognized.[5] The specter of replicating in Brazil the horrendous conflict unleashed in the American Civil War was a factor in the growing recognition that slavery was becoming more and more untenable. But accompanying this realization was the concern that any gradual move toward emancipation could dash hopes for an early resolution and so provoke a bloody uprising such as had been experienced in the French Colony of Santo Domingo (Haiti) and some thirty years later in Jamaica in 1833, two years after the Nat Turner uprising in Virginia. The result was disagreement about how to bring about change. In the meantime, the institution was disintegrating beyond recovery and was accelerating toward final abolition in 1888.

For readers familiar with the forms of slavery in the South of the United States, it is necessary to point out that Brazilian slavery presents a more complex face. Laird Bergad describes the scene as Brazil approached its imperial epoch thus:

> By the second half of the eighteenth century, Brazil had developed the largest and most diversified slave labor system in all of the Americas. Urban slavery, with its varied occupational structures, was well-entrenched; slaves labored in mines and small scale cottage industries; and a wide array of rural activities, from export-oriented sugar production to local food-crop cultivation, used slave labor extensively in nearly every region of the colony.
>
> Additionally, Brazil developed the largest free black and mulatto populations in all of the Americas over the seventeenth and eighteenth centuries. . . . This diversified racial structure, where to be black or mulatto was not necessarily to be a slave, was in sharp contrast with the British- and French-controlled Caribbean and North America, where free peoples of African descent were few and far between.[6]

The progress toward the eventual abolition of slavery in Brazil is marked by several pieces of legislation. For reference, the principal items are listed here.

March 1826	In a Convention with Great Britain, Brazil agreed to abolish the African slave trade within four years. (Ineffective to a large degree.)
November 1831	Law passed declaring the freedom of all slaves entering Brazil. (Law was largely unenforced, which meant that by the 1880's it is estimated about half of the slaves in Brazil were held illegally.)
January 1851	Brazilian government forced by Britain to implement suppression of the African trade. (Marks effective end of importation of slaves.)
September 1871	Law of the Free Womb (Rio Branco Law). Provided for freedom of children born to slave women. From the age of eight until the age of twenty-one, the children (the *ingênuos*) were obliged to provide free labor for their mothers' masters.
September 1885	Sexagenarian Law (Saraiva-Cotegipe Law). Provided for freedom of slaves sixty years and older. Slaves had to serve masters for three more years.
May 1888	The "Golden Law," which abolished slavery in Brazil.

On a technical note, the translators have remained faithful to the original text and have made little use of the editorial pen, though a handful of obvious errors have been corrected. Occasionally, the translators have added notes to explain historical context or theological terms. Also, some sources not included in the original text have been added to the bibliography. Where an English-language text has been translated into the Portuguese for the original book, an effort has been made to include here the original text with the English-language source cited in endnotes and bibliography. In a few cases it has not been possible to locate the original English source and the translators have retranslated from Portuguese to English and such instances are so identified. When tracing monographs and books long out of print, the assistance provided by the program books.google.com is acknowledged with gratitude.

A word of thanks must go to the staff of the Legacy Library of Marietta College, especially Professor J. Peter Thayer and Ms. Mary E. Zimmer, who have gone the extra mile to locate material for this translation. Our thanks also go to Marietta College for financial support of this project.

Fraser G. MacHaffie
Richard K. Danford
Marietta, Ohio

NOTES

1. The first section of the book's title, *Negro não Entra na Igreja, espia da banda de fora* [The Black Does not Enter the Church: He peeks in From Outside] is derived from a fragment of a slave's prayer, the "Padre-Nosso do Negro" [The Black's 'Our Father'], recorded by the folklorist Celso de Magalhães (1849-1879). Sílvio Romero, *Estudos Sobre a Poesia Popular do Brasil*, 2nd ed. (Petrópolis: Editora Vozes Ltda., 1977), 85.

2. For example, Robert Edgar Conrad, *Children of God's Fire: A Documentary History of Black Slavery in Brazil* (University Park, Pennsylvania: The Pennsylvania State University Press, 1984), Conrad, *The Destruction of Brazilian Slavery* (Berkeley: University of California Press, 1972), Mary C. Karasch, *Slave Life in Rio de Janeiro 1808-1850* (Princeton: Princeton University Press, 1987), Katia M. de Queirós Mattoso, *To Be a Slave in Brazil 1550-1888*, trans. Arthur Golhammer (New Brunswick: Rutgers University Press, 1986), Robert Brent Toplin, *The Abolition of Slavery in Brazil* (New York: Atheneum, 1975.)

3. Writing in 1870, Bastos declared, "To emancipate and to instruct are two intimately linked tasks." (A.C. Tavares Bastos, *A Provincia*, 2nd ed. (São Paulo, 1937), quoted in Conrad, *The Destruction of Brazilian Slavery*, 158.)

4 . Over a hundred years later, public education remains a controversy in Brazil, where federal funding provides for a tuition-free university system at, some claim, the expense of primary and secondary education. Another concern of the reformers—"democratization of the soil" or land reform—apparently remains an intractable problem.

5. In the House of Deputies in March 1879, Martim Francisco Robeiro de Andrada spoke in threatening tones, "We, the representatives of the southern provinces of the Empire, appreciate the integrity of this vast country, but not so much that, in order to preserve it, we are willing to tolerate the general liquidation of fortunes and the violent destruction of slave property." (Robert Conrad, *The Destruction of Brazilian Slavery*, 136.)

6 . Laird W. Bergad, *The Comparative Histories of Slavery in Brazil, Cuba, and the United States* (New York: Cambridge University Press, 2007), 61.

PREFACE

A PAINFUL CONFESSION

DUNCAN ALEXANDER REILY [1]

It is with much pleasure that I write the preface to this excellent study on Protestantism in Imperial Brazil. This pleasure of mine is linked to four factors, which I will now explain. First, the book discusses a subject which has been only fleetingly examined and for that very reason brings new information and supplies clues for future research. Second, as a Methodist and historian of Brazilian Christianity, I see in the work of Professor Barbosa a valuable contribution toward our understanding of religion in Brazil and, in particular, of Methodism and Protestantism in general. Third, the author's conclusions bring to light with perception, honesty, courage and, perhaps, penitence the near silence of Brazilian Methodism, as well as Protestantism generally, when faced with what was called an "execrable villainy" by John Wesley a few days before his death, in a letter to William Wilberforce. Fourth and finally, because it was my privilege to have José Carlos Barbosa as a student in the Department of Theology at the Methodist University of São Paulo, I am proud to recognize him as a competent researcher in the area of ecclesiastical history and Wesleyan studies.

I had not personally studied the topic of slavery deeply, but the author brings to our attention three books in which I presented facets of the question. The first was my doctoral thesis about William Capers (1790-1855), son of aristocratic landowners in South Carolina. Even in his infancy, Capers possessed as his own personal property a young slave who was his servant and companion. Barbosa recounts (see page 51) the unfortunate experience of Capers, once an adult and Methodist preacher, of giving to the slaves on his plantation all the freedom permitted at that time by state law. The experience convinced the young pastor and slave owner that the blacks were a race of children and as such required the protection of whites for their own good. The concern of Capers with the spiritual well-being of the slaves caused him to initiate and supervise missions to the slaves on the plantations. The numerical success of the conversion of these slaves was, without a doubt, an important factor in his election as a bishop of the Methodist Episcopal Church, South in the first General Conference of this church after its separation from the Methodist Episcopal Church.

In my book *Metodismo Brasileiro e Wesleyano* [Brazilian and Wesleyan Methodism], there is an essay about the characteristics of North American Christianity in the missionary era. I affirm that at the time the main American denominations were establishing their missions in Brazil, the United States was "a nation and a religion deeply divided because of slavery." Among other things, I attempted to show that in the South (where the people strongly believed that society would disintegrate if slavery was abolished) the sophistic *Pro-Slavery Argument* was developed (which attempted to show through use of history, philosophy, and even the Bible, that slavery was not an evil, but was indeed a positive good for the slaves themselves). In the North, meanwhile, the abolitionist movement was growing. In time, this dichotomy led to the terrible Civil War.

In the third book, *História Documental do Protestantismo no Brasil* [A Documentary History of Protestantism in Brazil], the first period covers the years 1808 to 1880, in other words, from the beginning of a permanent Protestantism up to abolition and the proclamation of the Republic, most of the period of Imperial Brazil. I endeavored to describe the beginning of the main denominations, their doctrines, and the nature of their work. I saw the book as an instrument to facilitate the study and teaching of Brazilian Protestantism in its entirety rather than conforming to the denominational loyalty of the instructor or the institution where the teaching was taking place, daring to dream that it would stimulate research in the general area of Protestantism, and even Christianity in Brazil.

História Documental do Protestantismo no Brasil, however, is weak in the area of Protestantism and slavery. Fortunately, Professor José Carlos Barbosa's book, the fruit of research much deeper than mine in this area, brings to light an abundance of information about the topic

I have already referred to the honesty and courage of Barbosa's research. These characteristics may shock many Protestant readers due to the timidity or even silence of their respective denominations in the battle for abolition. But a careful reading will help the readers to understand the reasons why the main "missionary" Protestant churches showed little concern for the abolitionist movement. Their top priority was the establishment and development of their work in a territory that was predominately Roman Catholic. The natural disposition of these churches was individualistic and their theological orientation was toward a "spiritual church." This required that owners treat their slaves well and that the Church take care of the spiritual needs of both slaves and owners, leaving the destiny of the institution of slavery in the hands of "Caesar" (the properly constituted government).

The book before us tells also of many *individuals* who were concerned not only with the soul but also with the body of the slave. One of these people was the educator Martha Watts, who purchased the slave Flora in order to give her freedom. Flora, in turn, became one of the first members of the Methodist Church of Piracicaba and worked in the Colégio Piracicabano for many years.[2] Dr. Robert Kalley went so far as to exclude Bernardino de Oliveira from the Rio de Janeiro Evangelical Church for refusing to free his slaves. The layman Júlio

Ribeiro saw to it that one of his slaves, named Joaquim, was baptized. Later, this same Ribeiro gave a certificate of freedom to the young man and his mother, who had also accepted the faith. The repudiation of the institution of slavery by missionaries such as Justin Spaulding and Ashbel Green Simonton, among others, is well known. But Barbosa tells that, despite all this, the "first protest [against slavery] by a Brazilian Protestant pastor was "A Religião Christã e suas relações com a escravidão" [The Christian Religion as it Relates to Slavery], published in 1886 by the Presbyterian pastor Eduardo Carlos Pereira. Barbosa brings a gift to his readers in the form of a transcription of this entire manifesto as an appendix. Throughout the entire book, however, he insists that as far as churches are concerned, the denominations contributed little or nothing to the cause of abolition in Brazil! Let us hope that this painful confession alerts us to the silences of the churches today.

NOTES

1. Duncan Alexander Reily (1924-2004) was born in the United States and was an ordained minister of the Methodist Church. He earned the degree of Master of Theology in 1947, and came to Brazil the following year. In 1972 he received the degree of Doctor of Theology from Emory University. In 1969 he was appointed to the Chair of Ecclesiastical History in the School of Theology of the Methodist Church [in Brazil]. Dr. Reily was professor in the Ecumenical Master's in Religious Studies at the Methodist University of São Paulo and was the author of several books, including *História Documental do Protestantismo no Brasil* (São Paulo: Associação de Seminários Teológicos Evangélicos (ASTE), 1984), and *Metodismo Brasileiro e Wesleyano* (São Paulo: Imprensa Metodista, 1981).

2. See *Evangelizar e Civilizar: cartas de Martha Watt, 1881-1908,* ed. Zuleica Mesquita. (Piracicaba: Editora UNIMEP, 2001).

INTRODUCTION

It is very probable that many Protestants, crossing paths with a group of slaves, heard the customary greeting "*Vassum Crisso.*" We do not understand the meaning of these strange words. They, the Protestants of yesteryear, didn't understand them either. The article/poem published in *Revista Illustrada* in the same year as the official proclamation of the abolition of slavery, explains for us that the blacks shouted to listening Christians ears, crying out for help, but they went unheeded. The text reads:

> What barbaric words are these, which our readers do not know and which affect us so much?
>
> They belong to our history and summarize a world of bitter recollections.
>
> They are, neither more or less, a corruption of those greetings of the patriarchs with which, since the time of the birth of Christianity, men have promised to love one another. In this century of enlightenment [nineteenth century] in our fatherland, until just four months ago the *Vassum Crisso* was a respectful and fearful greeting which, along the dark highways, the slave would direct at the traveler, addressing him in the name of God, as if saying to him: "I am your brother in Christ. . . . Help me!" But he would hear in response to this singular unthinking and automatic reply, "For ever!"
>
> The *Vassum Crisso*, which will have assaulted the delicate ears of our readers with its African roughness, is yet a synthesis, an abbreviation, a more simple expression of that gentle greeting which the peasants of Catholic countries still use today among themselves. It is "Praised be our Lord Jesus Christ," [*Louvado seja nosso Senhor Jesus Cristo*] mutilated by three centuries of slavery, simplified by the human tendency to abbreviate everything, reduced to four dominant syllables by the demands of constant repetition.
>
> The *Vassum Crisso* today has a nostalgic poetic quality; it represents the pain of so many innocent victims; it is the flight of souls to the consolations of religion; it sums up the traditions of the sad life of the slave. The *Vassum Crisso*, for he who meditates upon it, for he who repeats it, will be like a dark legend from a world of hardship and misfortune— which happily today is no more than a bad memory.
>
> Whether it be at the hour of the soft twilight that precedes the dark night, or the shining moon with its gentle light, throughout that whole

hinterland, in the midst of nature's splendid creation, there was not a traveler who did not encounter groups of slaves, subdued and out of breath, returning to their quarters from work, being led by the overseer. They came from making the earth bloom and were walking to their mansard-roofed huts, a hoe on their shoulders, but stooped under the weight of their innumerable bruises. The sad and resigned band, on meeting the traveler, in turn removed their miserable straw hats, and on every impassioned mouth, made even darker by life's bitterness, hovered a smile and a greeting. One by one, the slaves said to the traveler, "*Vassum Crisso.*"

And the latter, mechanically, repeated just as many times,

"For ever!" Or "May He be praised for ever!"

The civilized man, moved to offer his greeting to this melancholy group, sometimes fearfully, walked on not even reflecting that he the citizen and the flock of slaves had offered their greetings as one power to another, both equal by having evoked the same divinity, equal in the eyes of God, who had created both to be free and to venerate His holy name.

The *Vassum Crisso*, familiar to all traveling in the interior, was a word of peace bringing calm to the excited heart of the passer-by.

Seeing this silent and bowed-down group passing through the darkness of the night, the traveler could just as easily be encountering a group of poor fatigued workers as a group in revolt, incited by the heroism of liberty.

The *Vassum Crisso* was a sweet-smelling, miraculous balm that instilled in the soul the sweet tranquility of peace and trust. . .

It was the branch of the olive tree, extended to the untamed fears unconquered by sudden dread that everyone feels when, in the middle of the night, the footfalls of a crowd announce a mysterious encounter.

It was a cordial and friendly greeting, a brotherhood of hearts, somewhat distressed, remembering the name of God, the supreme comforter to those who were unable to have any other on earth.

The *Vassum Crisso* was the "Hail!", the "Welcome!", the "God help you!" of the civilized peoples, placed in the mouths of those wretched, ragged slaves.

Hearing it, what a sweet sensation bathed the slightly frightened souls of so many travelers on our roads and in our forests.

Poor slaves! Your pain, acute and resigned, did not even have the great release of invoking the name of God in full!

The *Vassum Crisso* was more a solution than a true expression of feeling.

You may not find picturesque this abbreviation, this mutilation if you will, of a poetic form of greeting.

I, however, become ecstatic when confronted with these two words. When I read them a torrent of memories passes before my eyes in. I see the dramas of slavery painful to my sight, I remember the gentleness of the race which, in its suffering, suckled us, and which today is free. I see nameless misfortunes, I see the infinite goodness of the slaves and their long suffering as martyrs. I think, I ponder and, compassionately, the *Vassum Crisso* makes me weep.[1]

So ends the text of the journalist, a sensitive poet who wept over the pain of the enslaved blacks.

Just like the persistent old steam engine, which runs along the tracks making the same phrase ring out, a sign of its strength in carrying the heavy load, so too repeated the black slaves throughout all the fields of Brazil: *Vassum Crisso!* *Vassum Crisso! Vassum Crisso!*

Just like the foolish and almost extinct *tsiu*, that little black hopping bird that I and many other lads from another age tried to hit with our slingshots, which insisted on repeating indefinitely the same litany, thus repeated the black slaves throughout all the fields of Brazil: *Vassum Crisso! Vassum Crisso! Vassum Crisso!*

Just like the Catholic Christians who colluded with the conquistadors and were protected by their weapons and favors, pretending that they were presenting the radical Jesus of Nazareth to the inhabitants of the Land of the Holy Cross but turned a deaf ear to the pitiful appeals of the blacks, so too, the Protestants failed to hear the insistent supplications coming from the blacks scattered across all the fields of Brazil as they proclaimed: *Vassum Crisso! Vassum Crisso! Vassum Crisso!*

To the sad and resigned blacks, who reverentially removed their miserable straw hats, white Christendom repeated mechanically and slightly irritated, "Forever!"

Once more the truth of the parable told by Jesus was shown. Catholics and Protestants received the staff of the priests and Levites and offered the same response by hiding from the victim lying on the ground. Jesus proclaimed: The Samaritan was the fellow man and brother of the oppressed.

An impoverished chorus, sad and indicting, appears in the history of the Church with startling frequency, and the role of brother persists in being occupied by the Samaritan. "What great shame is ours," regrets pastor Eduardo Gomes Pereira. What a great perplexity to recognize that it is the unbelievers/Samaritans who free their slaves. "What a great sadness to see that those who profess faith in the Redeemer of captives do not break the bonds of mercilessness nor allow the oppressed to go free!" [2]

The Protestants, just like the priests and the Levites, did not attend to the enslaved blacks because they had more important and pressing obligations to fulfill. Faithful followers of European rationalism, they developed a strategy aimed at success in the face of a task that was challenging, difficult and almost impossible to achieve. They became busy and blinded by the task of implanting a new religion in an impermeable country, a "closed garden," protected, difficult to enter. The "heretical and worldly" newspaper that called itself *Voz do Escravo*, and which proclaimed that the liberation of a million and a half slaves was a more important topic than business or industry or agriculture or religion or government, was not taken seriously by the zealous missionaries. They had another mission to achieve, much more "important and spiritual." They came to construct temples, cathedrals, schools and great buildings. They came to publish books and newspapers, to distribute Bibles, to undertake proselytism, to convert an idolatrous and ignorant population.

"Give to Caesar what is Caesar's, and to God what is God's" (Mark 12:17) was the phrase pulled out of the Bible and steadfastly brandished when convenient by the fundamentalist Americans who were transplanted to Brazil. Lulled by this motto, they devoted themselves zealously and foremost to the task of strengthening the establishment of Protestantism. The concern for moral principles and ethical values would come later, when the institution was more solid, visible and structured. The first outline was emerging of the rough notion that argued that the dough must first rise before it can be divided.

The Protestants, just like the last-minute abolitionists, only responded to the laments of the blacks after movements were popping up in every corner of the country in support of emancipation. It was at this point that they joined the movement, filling the last coaches on the train, almost alongside the slave masters who always wanted to protect their physical and material well-being.

Vassum Crisso! Vassum Crisso! That tearful and thundering lament continued to echo for a long time. But the Christians did not hear. Their ears were closed tight, just like the crew of Ulysses' boat, so as not to be seduced by the tender song of the sirens. The Christians did not hear.

Vassum Crisso! The Protestant Christians did not hear either because they were blinded by the embittered struggle searching for religious space within Brazilian society, the subject of the first two chapters of this book. They were extremely courageous and creative, capable of constructing primary and secondary schools, founding newspapers, developing an aggressively proselytical catechism, and establishing interminable polemics with the defenders of the official religion. They simply did not have the courage to address the most uncomfortable question of the time.

In the third chapter we will show in a more detailed fashion this "politics" of non-involvement, this effort to place some distance between them and the slavery issue. And this is why the blacks do not enter the Church: they peek in from outside. May our Lord Jesus Christ be praised! May He be praised for ever!

NOTES

1. "Vassum Crisso," *Revista Ilustrada,* (29 September 1888): 6.
2. See Appendix.

CHAPTER I

"A CLOSED GARDEN WHICH WILD ANIMALS CANNOT ENTER": THE IMPLANTATION OF PROTESTANTISM IN BRAZIL

NO WOLF DARED TO APPROACH

> *Until now the Catholic Church was a closed garden into which no wild animal could enter, it was a sheepfold enclosed on all sides so that no wolf dared to approach who was not detected and put to flight by its vigilant shepherds.*[1]

The system of patronage established in Brazil by the Portuguese crown bound Brazilian society to Roman Catholicism and attempted to make the struggles and attempts at establishing Protestantism as difficult as possible. The indelible presence of the Catholic Church in the history of the colonization of Brazil did not allow the inclusion within Brazilian culture of any space whatsoever for the presence of another religion. The bellicosity of the confrontation between the Reformation and the Counter-Reformation was transplanted in its most extreme form to the Portuguese colony.

Many Catholic theologians interpreted the conquest of America as a divine gift, a recompense in the face of the losses occasioned by the reform movement started by the former Augustinian monk [Martin Luther]. Since in Europe it had not been possible to restrain the growth of the opposing religion, in Brazil vigilance would be redoubled. The newspaper *A Reação*, published by the Catholic Student Organization of the Law Academy of São Paulo, in the issue of 13 June 1880, reproduced in an editorial an article opposing the presence of American missionaries in Brazil. It said that the "invasion of a mob of Protestant ministers" was explained by the fact that, in the United States, the Catholic Church was regaining lost ground. It pointed out that the Protestant ministers, "far from seeking out the regions where barbarity ruled, far from burying themselves in the arid interior remote from civilization, instead seek out peoples who have already heard the preaching of the good news. It seems that the Protestant sects only have soldiers to combat the Catholic Church."[2]

Several important and thwarted attempts to introduce Protestantism into Brazil reinforced the conviction that the Portuguese colony was a "closed garden" and that it should continue being protected. The first attempt occurred in the mid-sixteenth century, at the exact time when the Counter-Reformation was at its height, when the French-controlled Rio de Janeiro and Calvin himself collaborated in this effort at implantation, sending a group of Protestant pastors. There was another attempt in the following century, with considerable repercussion, through the presence of the Dutch in the north and northeast of Brazil. The Political Council of the Dutch Company declared that its principal objective was political-economic and it was not considering in the least imposing reformed doctrine on the Portuguese, "alsoo het gelvoow een gave Godts was" (because faith was a gift from God).

But several pastors were sent to Brazil, until in 1635 it was decided to maintain a permanent group of eight to nine clergy. There was an introduction of the Calvinist ecclesiastical regime, the maintenance of strict discipline in the Church, the propagation of religious books, a careful registry of marriages, births and deaths and the insistence upon the participation of the community in the celebrations of the Eucharist. All these elements combined so that, in Recife, Fredericopólis and other smaller locations, religious life took on a spirited development and a great number of faithful took part in Sunday services.[3]

Protestantism was looked upon as an interloper during the nineteenth century, not only by the missionaries who struggled to overcome difficult barriers, but principally by the representatives of the Roman Church. The most active vigilance was the responsibility of the Ultramontanist clergy, who not only sought to impede the catechetical work carried out by the Protestants, but also denounced the liberal position of the Jansenists. By way of example we can point to Father Luis Gonçalves dos Santos, nicknamed Padre Perereca ("Father Toad"), who expounded an embittered polemic against Father Diogo Antônio Feijó about the legislative proposal to permit the marriage of Brazilian priests.[4]

It was not only the Jansenist Feijó who became the target of the virulent insults of Father Perereca. At this time of increased radicalism and invective, there were two Protestant missionaries, friends of Feijó's, in Rio de Janeiro, and they became the target of the keenly sharpened quill of the journalist priest. These two missionaries were Daniel P. Kidder and Justin Spaulding.

Naturally, the presence in Brazil of Protestant missionaries carrying out religious activities was of extreme concern, as can be confirmed by considering the positions taken by the radical Ultramontanist Father Perereca, who ultimately wrote three books against the presence of the Methodist missionaries in Rio de Janeiro. The first two are *Desagravos do Clero e do Povo Católico Fluminense; ou Refutacão das Mentiras e Calúnias do Impostor que se Entitula Missionário do Rio de Janeiro, e Enviado pela Sociedade Metodista Episcopal de New York para Civilizar e Converter ao Cristianismo os Fluminenses* [The Redress of the Clergy and the People of the Province of Rio de Janeiro, or Refutation of the Lies and Calumnies of the Imposter Calling Himself the Missionary of Rio de Janeiro, Sent by the Methodist Episcopal Society of New York to Civilize and Convert to Christianity the People of the Province of Rio de Janeiro] and *O Católico e o Metodista; ou Refutação das Doutrinas Heréticas que os Intitulados Missionários do Rio de Janeiro, Metodistas de New York têm vulgarizado nessa Corte.*[5] [Catholic and Methodist, or Refutation of the Heretical Doctrines which the Self-Named Missionaries of Rio de Janeiro, Methodists of New York, Popularized in our Imperial Court.] The third book was written in 1839 in partnership with Father Guilherme Paulo Tilbury, an English Catholic cleric who emigrated to Brazil,[6] and it is titled *Antídoto Católico Contra o Veneno Metodista, ou Refutação do Segundo Relatório do Entitulado Missionário do Rio de Janeiro* [The Catholic Antidote for the Methodist Poison, or Refutation of the Self-Named Missionary of Rio de Janeiro]. According to Father Perereca, the Brazilian Catholic Church "was an enclosed garden into which no wild animal could enter, it was a sheepfold enclosed on all sides so that no wolf dared to approach who was not detected and put to flight by its vigilant shepherds."[7]

The pioneer Kidder explained this feeling of intruding and affirmed that the catechetical model of proselytism used in the United States and Europe did not suit Brazil. "The stranger, therefore, and especially the supposed heretic, who would labor for the promotion of true religion, must expect to avail himself of providential openings" and leave aside the approaches used elsewhere. "The romantic notions which some entertain of a mission field, may become chastened and humbled by contact with the cold reality of facts."[8]

The bold Robert R. Kalley, who carried out extraordinary work on the Island of Madeira, also showed considerable constraint and caution when faced with the new reality. Kalley pointed out the need for greater care to the inexperienced Presbyterian missionary Ashbel Green Simonton, who disembarked at Rio de Janeiro, fearless in carrying out his task.[9]

Even some of the innumerable European Protestant travelers who were in the country, especially in the nineteenth century, agreed with Father Perereca's notion of a closed garden, an enclosed sheepfold, and admitted that Brazil would never be able to shelter the austere and cold Protestant religion. They revealed that the society itself was completely adapted to the Catholic religion and, consequently, impenetrable to the Protestant catechism. For them, the possibility of successful implantation of a new religion was quite limited, considering mainly the absence of any concern for conversion shown by the Protestant immigrants settled in Brazil at that time.

Right from the beginning of his ministry in Brazil, Simonton expressed his disbelief in the possibility of initiating a mission of evangelism starting with the foreigners there. For him, the foreigners, "nominal Protestants," impeded the missionary task because they rejected the Gospel and did not believe in it. He concludes, "There is no hope for Brazil, with the foreigners who now mingle with the natives. A belief that is superficial, unreflective and unreasoning affects them all."[10]

Implanting Protestantism in Brazil was an arduous task that was difficult to achieve. The closed garden continued to be preserved, in terms of the rigorous control exercised by the partnership between the Portuguese monarchy and the Vatican, through the innumerable legal obstacles which made impossible the installation of a new religion and, particularly, the impenetrability of the society regarding Protestantism. The existence of this impermeability—the touted incompatibility between the character of the Brazilian people and the Protestant religion—was highlighted repeatedly by innumerable individuals.

Richard Francis Burton points to the existence of deep personality differences between the Brazilian Catholics and the European Protestants. He observes that English immigrants had regular attendance at the Anglican Church only in times of dry weather, and the canticles and music "were those of the country church in Great Britain" and were chanted only during worship services. There was no inserting of Protestant religiosity into the very concrete day-to-day life of the faithful as occurred in Catholicism. He claims he spent many days without "hearing the English Litany" and this fact caused him to reflect upon the following question: "Why should these men, who cannot sing a song, sing psalms and hymns?" This Protestantism, he concludes, holds no attraction to arouse the interest of Brazilians. And he goes further in agreeing with the observation of the Oratorian Dr. Henry Newman, whom he cites saying that Protestantism "is the dreariest of possible religions, and that the thought of an Anglican service makes man shudder." [11]

The German Thomas Davatz, a school master who also served as pastor of the Lutheran church formed by German immigrants who settled in Ibicaba, characterized the whole of Brazilian society as strongly rooted in Catholicism. According to him, even the black slaves, despite "forced conversion to the Catholic Church" and the scanty religious concepts they understood, did not offer any space whatsoever for the Protestant religion, because "they think so poorly of followers of other sects," just like their masters. [12]

Henry Koster, author of *Travels in Brazil*, who was in the country in 1815 and 1816 (and therefore at the time of the arrival of the first Protestant immigrants), expresses the same view in suggesting that Brazilian culture, impregnated by Catholicism, completely precluded any possibility of accepting, or even tolerating, the Protestant presence. He states that the slaves inevitably and without any room for contradiction, adopted the same religion as their masters. There was not the least chance of an alternative. He notes that even the slaves themselves took the initiative in integrating into the official religion because otherwise they would be subjected to insults from their own companions.

> The slave himself wants likewise to be made a Christian for his fellow bondsmen will in every squabble or trifling disagreement with him, close their string of opprobrious epithets with the name of *pagão* (pagan). The unbaptized negro feels that he is considered as an inferior being, and although he may not be aware of the value which the whites place upon baptism, still he knows that the stigma for which he is upbraided will be removed by it; and therefore he is desirous of being made equal to his companions. [13]

Thomas Ewbank, another visitor in the middle of the same century, reveals deep questions about the possibility of some day establishing in Brazil more rigorous forms of worship. He noted that the more he got to know Brazil, the more he was convinced of the limited possibility of success in the implantation of Protestantism in Brazil. Among the obstacles, one of the greatest was the inordinate fondness of the population for Catholic religious festivals. The

Brazilian gentlewomen laughed openly at the seriousness and the alleged long faces of the English families in Rio de Janeiro, who went to church as if they were going to a funeral. The Protestant pastors were avoided, thus there was no opportunity whatsoever for encounters between them and the population. The gentry considered it disreputable to be seen in the company of a Protestant minister. He adds that the climate itself "is against the severities of northern sects. Neither stringent Methodism nor Puritanism can ever flourish in the tropics." [14]

It was not only the Europeans who found Brazilian customs very strange, especially regarding the relative intimacy between domestic slaves and their masters. The American Daniel Kidder was frightened by what he saw in the homes of the rich in the Rio de Janeiro region, where dirty children, completely naked, "are allowed the run of the house and the amusement of seeing visitors." Kidder elaborates that one of his friends regularly dined in the home of a general, a member of high society, and that there he saw amazing things. Before and during the meal, black children would hang on to "father" (for this is what they called the master), insisting on food and expecting him to feed them with his own hands.

According to Kidder, the children were also accustomed to accompanying their mistresses wherever they went. When they were not allowed into their carriages, "these pets" felt insulted. The missionary points out that in the homes of families with "some tincture of European manners, these unsightly little bipeds are kept in the background." [15] And he made countless comparisons between the blacks of Brazil and those of the United States, concluding that Brazilian blacks feel a deep tie to Catholicism because of this intimacy and, relative to his own country, they have fewer shackles imposed on them.

Further, Father Perereca sensed that the "closed garden" was being attacked and that the "vigilant pastors" were no longer concerned or obligated with the task of putting the "Protestant wolves" to flight. According to him, "These self-named missionaries have been among us for almost two years pursuing the demons' work of perverting Catholics, attacking their faith with public preaching in their homes, with weekday and Sunday schools, distributing Bibles that are truncated and without notes, . . . in sum, inviting one and all to Protestantism."

What was most startling, added the Ultramontane father, was that this activity was taking place "in the Imperial Court of the Land of the Holy Cross, right under the very nose of the emperor himself, and of all the ecclesiastical and secular authorities." And this tolerance was not to be permitted, given the countless legal impediments contained in the country's constitution. He expressed his surprise that there was no police authority willing to interrogate the missionaries, asking them, "Who are you? Why are you here? If your doctrine is the same as ours, we don't need you; and if not, the oath we take under our constitution to maintain the Catholic religion, Roman and Apostolic, obliges me to bid you farewell. Get out!" [16]

THE WOLVES APPEAR

> *The only hope for this place lies in immigration and continuing missionary work. If we can get a few thousand of our countrymen to this beautiful and adorable country, we will be able to succeed quickly.*[17]

Protestantism, of the variety dedicated to catechizing Brazilians, was implanted in Brazil in the middle of the nineteenth century, at a moment in history when the nation's socio-economic structure was solidly based on the use of slave labor. Moreover, this implant was achieved principally by way of American Protestantism, with a coming together of missionaries from the North and South of the United States. The former were opposed to slavery and the latter in favor, and in their native land they had entered into conflict as part of the schism that occurred in all Protestant denominations in that country.

In this phase of implanting Protestantism in Brazil, we find two distinct periods. The first is geared basically toward immigrants of Protestant origin, and religious ministry is carried out through the services of chaplains using the native language of the immigrants. In the second period, concern is focused on the task of proselytizing among the Brazilians, that is, an effort is made by way of preaching and other practices to win over and convince the Catholics to adhere to Protestant doctrines.

The present account aims to touch upon only what is considered missionary Protestantism, leaving aside the Protestantism associated with immigration, which had other characteristics. In this manner, it is possible to frame within Protestantism the activities developed by missionaries linked to the Presbyterian, Methodist, Baptist and Congregational churches. Daniel P. Kidder and James C. Fletcher, of the American Bible Society, were precursors to the establishment of the Protestant missions and worked to distribute Bibles and religious pamphlets. Robert R. Kalley, a Scottish physician and missionary, provided an important impetus. He arrived in Rio de Janeiro in 1855, fleeing religious persecution on the Island of Madeira. Kalley began proselytizing activity in Portuguese in Petrópolis and, in 1858, organized the Evangelical Church of the Province of Rio de Janeiro, which later came to be called the Congregational Church, with a small number of Brazilian proselytes in addition to immigrants from Madeira.

In 1859, the missionary Ashbel Green Simonton, of the Presbyterian Church in America, arrived in Brazil. At Kalley's suggestion, he showed great interest in beginning to preach in Portuguese and becoming involved with the Brazilians in order to gain followers among them. In 1865, with the arrival of two other missionaries, Alexander L. Blackford and F.J.C. Schneider, a Presbyterian church was organized in Brotas, Province of São Paulo, with eleven people, all of them Brazilian. Present at this event was José Manoel da Conceição, a former priest and the ex-vicar of Brotas who was the first Brazilian to become a Protestant pastor. In 1868, a mission of the Presbyterian Church in the U.S., the "southern branch" of Presbyterianism in the United States, was established in Campinas. This church was concerned with the religious needs of the Confederate immigrants who in 1866 settled in Santa Bárbara, in the vicinity of Campinas, in the interior of the Province of São Paulo. These same Confederates drew the attention of the Baptists and Methodists who in 1871, established churches in the same community.

The system of patronage implanted in Brazil established a close relationship between the State and the Catholic Church, placing many obstacles in the path of Protestant penetration.[18] What resulted was a tense confrontation between Protestantism and Catholicism. Some missionaries, and the national denominational leaders in particular, led the discussion into axiological disputes, talking of truth and untruth, thereby replicating the arguments of the Reformation. At the same time, a large faction of missionaries was concerned with the ideas of democracy and republicanism raised by Protestantism. The debate established at the beginning of Protestantism in Brazil would characterize it in an almost definitive manner, and it would accompany Brazilian Protestantism throughout its history. Among the missionaries, the debate was measured and careful, perhaps due to political reasons; among the national leaders, the debate was frank and aggressive, starting with the first generation of Brazilian pastors. From one side is seen a concern for converting Catholics to Protestantism, from the other the cultural transplant, exporting the "American Way of Life" in obedience to Manifest Destiny.

For the missionaries and national Protestant leaders, Brazilian Catholicism displayed the same traits as pre-Reformation Christianity, aggravated by local practices that more closely followed folklore than a true Christian religion. To the classic points of controversy of the sixteenth century were added the popular festivals and ceremonies that resulted from local syncretism under the complacency of a religion that was superficial and unconcerned, probably because of its absolute hegemony. The dogged missionary efforts to implant Protestantism in Brazil were justified, in large part, by the Monroe Doctrine and its notion that the Catholic Church was the bearer and legitimizer of political regimes that were antagonistic to North American ideals.

The effective and definitive participation of Protestant denominations in Brazilian society became possible only in the nineteenth century. Socio-political conditions arose within this period that enabled this effective participation. The principal elements were the signing of a trade agreement between Portugal and Britain in 1810, the national liberation movements that resulted in political independence in 1822, the spread of liberal beliefs, the leadership of the global capitalist system assumed by Britain and the increasing influence of the United States, and the flow of migrants from a variety of countries.

In addition to the attractive land, especially for the agrarian southerners and their slavery, and the intensification of commerce, which was of interest to the northerners who were expanding their industries, there were also the aspirations of the different Protestant denominations to spread themselves in a nation which had been Catholic from its very beginning. The enthusiastic article of José Carlos Rodrigues, editor of the New York-based *O Novo Mundo* newspaper, reveals some of the more marked characteristics of the messianism to be found in the concept of Manifest Destiny adopted by the evangelical churches in the United States that were interested in expanding to Brazil.

> Just as in days gone by when the Jews served to guard the Law of the Ever-
> lasting until the time came when it was to be spread among the nations, so now
> America is chosen to be the depository for Christian Law as it applies to the
> governance of peoples and to display the likeness of the one people which all
> peoples of the future will come to form.[19]

The enterprising and previously planned strategy of the pastors representing the different denominations who set out on similar journeys of exploration demonstrated the missionary character of these religious institutions.

The War of Secession, which involved northerners and southerners in a confrontation without precedent in the history of the United States, was settled decisively, prompting a willingness to migrate. Simultaneous with this impetus, a deep disquiet was created in Brazil by the knowledge of the speed at which the division between North and South occurred. There was fear that a migratory wave of southerners to Brazil would create the conditions for producing the same type of confrontation there. F. Biard, in *Deux Années au Brésil*, reported witnessing countless political discussions claiming that Brazil "would one day be the prey of American adventurers . . . and that the North would quickly separate itself from the South." [20]

The editor of *O Novo Mundo* emphasized that such a conflict was not possible since things were quite different in Brazil, with none of the radical antagonism found in the United States. He claimed that Brazilian society as a whole had shown itself to be in favor of abolition. The pressing question was to find a means of bringing about abolition without hurting the slave owners economically.

At the conclusion of the American conflict, the South wound up with considerable debt, bankruptcy, misery, desolation, hunger, destruction and plundering. This society in shambles faced two options: submission to the North, with the appeal of starting over on a new foundation, or self-imposed exile. Emigration, as a response to the damage to morale provoked by the war, was one solution.

After the War of Secession, a good number of southerners emigrated to Brazil, as well as to Mexico, Venezuela, Peru, Australia and New Zealand. In the Province of São Paulo alone it is possible to count more than a hundred settled families, almost all in Santa Bárbara and its environs, where they founded a village named Americana in homage to their homeland.[21] These immigrants who settled in Brazil were mainly Protestants with links to the Presbyterian, Methodist and Baptist Churches. Nevertheless, the first *missionary* church implanted in Brazil would not be American, but English, as will be shown in what follows.

The wolf who came from the Island of Madeira

The first *missionary* church implanted in Brazil was started by Robert R. Kalley (1809-1888). He is known as the missionary who organized the oldest Protestant church in Brazil with church services in the Portuguese language. The work of

Kalley can be differentiated from other missionary denominations established in the country, which can be characterized as offshoots of churches already firmly established in other countries. The Evangelical Church of Rio de Janeiro established by Kalley had no direct affiliation with any Protestant denomination.[22]

A native of Mount Florida [now a suburb of Glasgow], Scotland, Kalley graduated with a degree in medicine and, after converting to Christianity, entered seminary and was admitted to the ministry of the Free Church of Scotland. His wish was to serve as a missionary in China, but because of the poor health of his wife, Sara Poulton Kalley, he went to live on the Island of Madeira, which at that time was a place of quiet rest for well-to-do English.[23]

Along with providing charitable medical attention, Kalley engaged in intense evangelical missionary activity. This religious work was well received, and in a few years he succeeded in bringing together a significant number of followers. This success provoked a negative reaction from the authorities and a campaign ensued aimed at discrediting him as a doctor. As a consequence of this campaign, Kalley was imprisoned and a violent persecution of his adherents ensued.[24]

So, after being released from prison, Kalley was forced to leave Madeira along with some three thousand followers who refused to renounce their faith. The great majority of his converts sought refuge in the United States, especially in Illinois, and later in Massachusetts and New Jersey. Kalley himself went to Brazil with a small number of followers to work at spreading Congregational Protestantism.[25]

Established in Rio de Janeiro, Kalley initiated a new phase in terms of the evangelical Protestant endeavor in Brazil. In contrast to the activities carried out by missionaries who, up to that time, had committed themselves simply to the distribution of Bibles, Kalley began the work of proselytism.[26] João Gomes da Rocha explains that Kalley's missionary work was relatively moderate and distinct from what he had done on Madeira. Undoubtedly contributing to this were the bitter experiences he had suffered there. Thus, Kalley became scrupulous in his concern for preventing his adherents from being exposed to similar difficulties. Caution, he constantly urged his collaborators, "Be wise as serpents, and gentle as doves." [27]

Kalley himself concentrated foremost on establishing contacts with the authorities and members of Brazilian society. His primary objective was to secure support and avoid possible problems.[28] Kalley knew that his experiences on Madeira had been made public and were followed attentively by the Ultra-montanists of Brazil and that his new activities in this country would be examined with even greater scrutiny.[29]

The Evangelical Church ("of Rio de Janeiro" was added later) officially came into being on 11 July 1858, when Kalley baptized Pedro Nolasco de Andrade, the first Brazilian at that time to join a Protestant church. The Evangelical Church began its activities with fourteen members: Kalley and his wife, three Americans, eight Portuguese and the Brazilian Pedro Nolasco de Andrade.

The following year (January of 1859) public attention in Brazil was drawn to the missionary work of Kalley when two ladies of the Imperial Court were baptized and received as members of the Church: Dona Gabriela Augusta Carneiro Leão, sister of the Marquis of Paraná and of the Baron of Santa Maria, and her daughter Henriqueta.[30] This event provoked a great controversy and Kalley was told by the Minister for Foreign Affairs, at the request of the Papal Nuncio, that "religious tolerance, guaranteed by the Brazilian Constitution, is not so wide as to allow the spread of doctrines contrary to the religion of the State." When Kalley appealed to three of the greatest Brazilian jurists of the day—José Tomaz Nabuco do Araujo, Caetano Alberto Soares, and Urbano Sabino Pessoa de Melo—he received a judgment confirming that he had broken no Brazilian laws.[31]

The pioneering missionary work carried out by Kalley in the implantation of Protestantism in Brazil was of great relevance and stimulated the activities of other missionaries and denominational groups. Before Kalley, other Protestant efforts existed in Brazil that are worthy of recording, such as the Methodist mission, which left marks so profound as to make the term "Methodist" synonymous with "Protestant" in nineteenth century Brazil.

The Methodist Fanatics

The first Methodist mission in Brazil lasted only five years, from 1836 to 1841, with the work of the missionaries Fountain E. Pitts, Justin Spaulding and Daniel P. Kidder, the latter two coming to Brazil as chaplains with the American Seamen's Friend Society and with the support of the Methodist Missionary Society. The Rev. Fountain E. Pitts was sent by the Methodist Episcopal Church of the United States to conduct missionary work and investigate the possibility of implanting Protestantism in Brazil and in other Latin American countries.[32]

Pitts managed to organize small groups of Methodists in Rio de Janeiro and Buenos Aires. In a report given to the Missionary Society of the Methodist Episcopal Church, claiming the necessity of establishing a Methodist mission in Brazil, Pitts spoke of his welcome, "I have held several meetings and preached eight times in different dwelling houses, where I have been respectfully invited and kindly received by the dear people." He demonstrated further that there was a need to begin a broader and more permanent activity by sending another missionary to attend to the work already started. He continues, "Several appear concerned for their souls. . . . Our little band of Methodists will greatly need an experienced Christian to lead them. . . . The missionary who is sent to this place should come immediately—and should commence the study of the Portuguese language forthwith." [33]

In response to Pitts' request, the Methodist Episcopal Church sent to Brazil another missionary, Rev. Justin Spaulding who organized a small Sunday school starting with a group assembled by Pitts.[34] Soon thereafter, the same missionary society agreed to send the Rev. Daniel P. Kidder to help Spaulding in the religious endeavor. As an agent of the American Bible Society, Kidder was especially involved in the distribution of Bibles and pamphlets among the

Brazilian population. Kidder left an interesting account of his travels to the Province of São Paulo and to the northeast of Brazil.[35]

This first missionary effort in Brazil by the Methodist Episcopal Church lasted only seven years, coming to an end in 1841.[36] The work done by the two pastors was watched closely and with great vigilance by the Catholic Ultramontantist clergy, especially Father Perereca, who wrote several works denouncing the missionaries' activities. Protesting the Methodist presence, he said

> These self-named missionaries have been among us for nearly two years, seeking with the work of the demons to pervert Catholics, attacking their faith with public preaching in their homes, with weekday and Sunday schools, distributing truncated Bibles without notes . . . in sum, inviting one and all to Protestantism, and most especially to embrace the sect of the Methodists, who are the most modern, troublemaking, loose, fanatical, hypocritical and ignorant of all Protestants.[37]

According to Duncan A. Reily, the main factors bringing about the closing of the Methodist mission were: 1) lack of missionary staff; 2) difficulty of direct access to the Brazilian people, because of superstition and limitations on religious freedom; and 3) financial constraints following the Panic of '37, the economic depression in the United States.[38]

The return to Methodist missionary work in Brazil did not occur until August 1867 with the arrival of Rev. Junius E. Newman, of the Methodist Episcopal Church, South. Previously, between the first missionary attempt and the beginning of the second, the Methodist Church in the United States experienced serious conflicts involving particularly the question of slavery. As a result of this conflict, the Methodist Church divided in 1844, creating the Methodist Episcopal Church, South, which was responsible for the re-opening of Methodist missions in Brazil.[39]

Newman organized the first Methodist congregation in Saltinho, in the vicinity of Santa Bárbara, in the Province of São Paulo, close to where immigrants from the southern United States had settled.[40] In addition to Newman, other missionaries were sent to Brazil by the Southern Methodist Church in following years. Another Methodist pastor, Rev. Richard Henington, also came to Brazil at this time. But we note that he did not come exactly as a missionary but as an immigrant, as was the case with thousands of others.

Henington served as a chaplain with the Confederate Army from the beginning of the War of Secession. After the war's conclusion, he remained for a time in the United States, but later became enthusiastic about the idea of emigrating to Brazil after considering the offers made by the Imperial government, which he considered quite generous, especially with regard to religion.

Henington and his family arrived in Pará on 16 August 1868. After traveling to nearly all the Southerners' "colonies" of Brazil, his choice was the Hastings colony, in what was at that time the unknown city of Santarém, in the province of Pará. He tells in a letter published in the 22 August 1869 issue of *The Copiahan*, of Crystal Springs, Mississippi, of organizing a church and beginning to preach to a small congregation of immigrants. Fifteen American families lived in the region and there were good prospects of holding monthly services to tend to this group.

> By 1869, some fifteen American and English families had gathered in the area. The children showed a desire for the reverend to minister to them the teachings of the Bible in the Portuguese language, which they quickly learned. We found amusing the difficulties the poor reverend had with Portuguese vowels. In truth, this was the principal reason why he never managed to deliver effectively the message of the gospel to the people of the region, even though he spent his whole life serving as pastor of the American community. He officiated at weddings and later obtained permission from the authorities to celebrate civil marriages.[41]

Henington was a popular and highly respected figure in the city. The people of Santarém referred to him as the "American priest." In 1874, he visited the United States and appealed to Dr. Marvin Summers and Bishop Holland MacIntyre to send a missionary to the Amazon region, but in vain. In 1877 Henington wrote to J.J. Ransom, the Methodist missionary in Rio de Janeiro, asking him to visit the colony.[42] By all indications, the Methodist congregation continued active under the direction of Henington, usually meeting in the store of a Mr. Rhome, a well-to-do immigrant.

Innumerable itinerant Protestant pastors visited the colony. In 1888, the Methodist pastor H.C. Tucker was visiting, and over seven consecutive evenings Tucker himself reported that he preached to an "eager multitude" that filled the parlor of Dr. Pitts' house and gathered outside to hear him. Tucker confirmed that Dr. Pitts was the son of the late Rev. Fountain Pitts of Tennessee, who, as was said earlier, had been in missionary service in Brazil in 1835. Henington became a naturalized Brazilian citizen on 5 September 1891, and was the only pastor to stay with a congregation until his death, which occurred in 1894.[43] Another Methodist pastor, Rev. Harvey, who came to Brazil with the Hastings group, founded a school for the children of immigrants but stayed for only a brief time, since his name no longer appears in the registers after 1869.

It is important to note that the Methodist mission in Brazil was organized primarily by the Methodist Episcopal Church, South, of the United States. The activity of the Northern Methodist Episcopal Church was quite small, limited principally to the work carried out by Justus Nelson, a missionary of independent means who was active in the north and northeast of Brazil. Nelson was recruited by William Taylor, who was responsible for the establishment of missions in India, South America and Africa.

The Abolitionist Simonton and the Presbyterians

The Presbyterian Church was organized in Brazil by means of the work of the missionary Ashbel Green Simonton, who was sent in 1859 by the Board of Foreign Missions of the Presbyterian Church in the United States of America, the "Northern branch of Presbyterianism."[44] During the eight years he spent in Brazil, Simonton worked vigorously, with important results: in January 1862, he organized the first Presbyterian Church in Rio de Janeiro; in 1864, he founded the newspaper *Imprensa Evangélica*; and in 1867, he also organized the first Protestant theological seminary in Rio de Janeiro.

The Presbyterian endeavor developed by Simonton was augmented by the arrival in July 1860 of the new missionaries A.L. Blackford and F.J.C. Schneider. In March 1865, Blackford organized a second Presbyterian church, in São Paulo. Moving outward from the capital of the province, the Presbyterians developed missionary activity in the interior of São Paulo, organizing a third Presbyterian church in November 1865 in Brotas.[45]

The formation of this church in Brotas was of fundamental importance to the advancement of the Presbyterian endeavor in Brazil. This was the first time that a church was organized in which all members were Brazilian. In addition, participating in the ceremonies, which were under the direction of the missionary Blackford, was José Manoel da Conceição, the former priest and ex-vicar of Brotas who joined the Presbyterian Church on 2 October 1864 and became the first Protestant Brazilian pastor when he was ordained on 16 December 1865.[46]

The labor of José Manoel da Conceição was very important for the expansion of the Presbyterian effort. As a Protestant pastor, Conceição began to travel through his former parishes, proclaiming his new beliefs and creating openings for the missionary endeavor. The church at Brotas, mainly because of the work of Conceição, was seen as providing great help in the evangelization of the interior of that province. There was great interest in the Gospel in neighboring locations and this created strategic advantages and made the work of evangelization easier.[47]

After being ordained as a Presbyterian pastor, José Manoel da Conceição never came to occupy a pastorate in the conventional sense. He dedicated himself only to proclaiming the message of salvation through faith in Jesus Christ, in the same way in which he had accepted it. He went from house to house, place to place, city to city, without any concern for creating denominational proselytes or in any organized way leading people to join the Presbyterian rolls.

Another factor that contributed considerably to the expansion of the Presbyterian Church was the establishment of a mission of the Presbyterian Church of the U.S. in Campinas, São Paulo Province, in 1868. In that year, the Presbyterian synod of South Carolina sent the missionaries Edward Lane and George Nash Norton, who settled in Campinas.[48] The arrival of these two missionaries shows that this church of the southern United States was concerned about the religious situation of the Confederate immigrants who had settled in 1866 in Santa Bárbara, in close proximity to Campinas. In addition to these missionaries, who came to give religious aid to the Confederates of Santa Bárbara, this same Church also sent two more missionaries in 1873 to work in Recife: William Leconte and J. Rockwell Smith.

The first Presbyterian missionaries sent by the Presbyterian Church in the northern states were openly opposed to slavery, but they never carried out activity geared toward the abolitionist movement.[49] On the contrary, there is no record that adherence to Presbyterianism implied that new converts would need to free their slaves. What can be verified is simply the adoption of a more paternalistic attitude focusing only on improvement in treatment and work conditions.

Between 1859 (the date of the beginning of the Presbyterian effort) and 1889, the two Presbyterian missions, northern and southern, sent to Brazil a total of forty-five evangelists and educators. Immediately after Brazil had officially decreed the abolition of slavery, the Synod of the Presbyterian Church in Brazil was organized in Rio de Janeiro, on 6 September 1888, resulting in the union of two Presbyterian factions in a single church. Within the synod were joined sixty churches and thirty-two pastors, of whom twelve were Brazilian. Of these sixty churches, forty-two were located in the Province of São Paulo and the adult members totaled 2,947.[50]

The Confederate General and the Baptists

The first attempt by the Baptist Church to organize a mission in Brazil was the arrival of Thomas Jefferson Bowen and his wife, missionaries who had worked in western Africa. They settled in Rio de Janeiro in mid-1859 and started missionary work. This first Baptist mission lasted only a short time, as it was interrupted by the departure of the missionaries. According to the official explanation, the reason for closing the mission was the health of the missionaries.[51]

Following the example of the Presbyterians and Methodists who had organized congregations among the Southerners settled in Santa Bárbara, the Baptists also organized two churches: one in Santa Bárbara and another in a location called Station, a stop on the new railroad. The permanent missionary work of the Baptist Church was secured by the insistent appeals made by the church in Santa Bárbara and the individual action of A.T. Hawthorne, a Confederate general who devoted great energy to encouraging the opening of the Baptist mission in Brazil.[52]

In a letter addressed to the Board of Foreign Missions in 1873, the Baptist Church in Santa Bárbara declared, "We hope a large Baptist community in this country will be added to the great Baptist family of the world, teaching, preaching and practicing the faith once delivered to the saints."[53] In response to this plea, William Buck Bagby and his wife, Anne Luther Bagby, and Zachary Clay Taylor and his wife, Kate Grawfort Taylor, were sent to Brazil in March 1881 and in February 1882, respectively. In August 1882, the Bagby and Taylor couples moved to Bahia, making that province the central point for their missionary work.[54] They were joined by the former priest Antonio Teixeira de Albuquerque, who had joined the Baptist church in Santa Bárbara. According to the missionary Bagby, this location was selected for the following reasons:

> First, for its large population, the inhabitants being around 200,000. We find the mass of the population there immediately within reach. Second, the region surrounding the city is heavily populated. Third, it is linked by sea to other important points, by bays and rivers to large cities and towns and by two railroads to many places in the interior. Fourth, we will have in Bahia an empty field, whereas in Rio de Janeiro there are seven or eight missionaries of other evangelical denominations. In Bahia, there are only two and they are

Presbyterians from the North of the United States. There are no native laborers in the Province of Bahia, if we are not mistaken, while in the Provinces of Rio de Janeiro and São Paulo there are a good number of native missionaries and native workers. . . . Thus the need in Bahia and the surrounding region is greater than in the southern provinces.[55]

These considerations, which determined the choice of location, clearly show the concerns of these missionaries: they were focused completely on religious proselytism and the formation of local churches. In that way, in keeping with this simple objective, on 15 October 1882, two months after they had established themselves in Bahia, they organized the first National Baptist Church in Brazil, founded with the objective of "preaching the Gospel to the Brazilian people." [56]

WOLVES UNITED WILL NEVER BE DIVIDED

> In Brazil, where the Catholic religion is the religion of the state, there is no money for churches, nor a national clergy, nor well-functioning seminaries and there is barely any religious instruction. In the USA, on the other hand, all the regular free churches prosper.[57]

The introduction of missionary Protestantism in Brazil was weak and fragmented, quite far removed from the triumphalist ideas transmitted in the missionaries' reports or by some studies produced by Protestant historians. What caused and encouraged the presence of this triumphalism was the fact that Protestantism had achieved some partial and localized successes.[58]

Catholicism came to represent for Protestantism an adversary to be fought.[59] This adversary was everywhere and was firmly established in all segments of Brazilian society. For the Protestants, the same conflict of the sixteenth century was being reproduced in Brazil. The powerful old adversary of the Reformation would have to be vanquished for a second time. This victory would be possible only through alliances and coalitions, through a theological unity to be established among the diverse denominations. In a letter from Junius Newman published on 3 May 1873, his inclination towards a union of Protestants in Brazil is recorded. As he saw it, the Methodists ought to unite with the Presbyterians because the Gospel is a "necessity for the inhabitants of South America just as it is for the negroes of Africa, or for any other dark race." [60]

Thus, during this first stage of the establishment of Protestantism in Brazil, no denominational emphasis was given that might cause weaknesses. There was a heightened effort on the part of the denominational missionaries to strive for theological and doctrinal unity, without which the difficulties would be considerably greater. With this there occurred a theological and liturgical simplification because it would be counterproductive to present to Roman Catholics the theological differences among the various denominations. Rivalries would break out which would assuredly lead to increased distrust. This is what José Carlos Rodrigues claimed in his newspaper O Novo Mundo: "When an honest Roman Catholic wants to show that his religion is the only true one, he always appeals to two cardinal facts: the unity and catholicity of the Roman Church and, by contrast, the multiplicity of the Protestant sects." [61]

The different denominational missions were shaped by North American models of Protestantism, and they transplanted these to Brazil. The strategic routes followed there were practically the same as in the United States. Each denomination, on being implanted in Brazil, was obedient to its own previous formal characteristics and models of ecclesiastical governance—the Presbyterians with democratic representation and autonomy of their councils, the Congregationalists and Baptists with their direct democracy and autonomy of local congregations, and the Methodists with their episcopal governance. Faced with these models of the church, with their parochial and compulsory systems, the alternative was to follow the path of voluntary association. In theological terms, then, the emphasis was on finding unity. [62]

One important indication of theological unity within Brazilian Protestantism was the use of a common book of hymns. The hymnal, *Salmos e Hinos*, was published by Robert and Sara Kalley in Rio de Janeiro in 1861. [63] The theology found in this hymnal emphasizes the love of God for all sinners; the grace of forgiveness by accepting, through faith, the atoning sacrifice of Christ; a life visibly regenerated in social morality; and the expectation of eternal life in heaven. Basically two elements came to be emphasized: the theology of the *Spiritual Church* that justified and sought to conserve the social *status quo*, and certain traces of pietism with its characteristic emotionalism.

The theological and doctrinal boundaries that characterized the various denominations were pushed into the background, as part of the strategy aimed at the insertion of Protestantism into Brazil. In this way, there was among the Protestants a close collaboration in search of a unity that would make possible the removal of impediments and facilitate implantation. [64]

Another method employed to secure collaboration among the various Protestant denominations was the demarcation of geographic territory to be covered. In 1884 in Piracicaba, São Paulo, the Methodists convened the First Annual Missionary Conference, with the theme "The division of territory among the various evangelical churches, desirous of cooperating in the best way possible with the Christian denominations, showing them true kindness and love." Later, in 1900, the Synod of the Presbyterian Church regulated the way of covering territory, determining that no city with fewer than 25,000 inhabitants would be claimed by more than one denomination.

Naturally, such methods were aimed at preventing probable conflicts, like the incident between Kalley and Simonton, when the former, believing that the Presbyterian missionary was invading his territory and luring away his converts, created a tense controversy. While not properly part of a strategy of implantation, but much more a function of other factors, the common characteristics of Arminian and pietistic theology colored the Protestant denomination missions established in Brazil. [65]

The basic structure of Protestantism is underpinned by the doctrines of sin and salvation. The world is presented as being originally good and then later disordered and corrupted by sin. This preaching reinforces in the individual the notion that he is collaborator with God and ought to hope for the arrival of a new world, ageless, placed outside of time. The unity of Protestant theology was present in this Manichean vision of the world. The present world is characterized as evil, and man struggles and suffers in it as a pilgrim, until reaching a happy land. Success depends entirely on one's way of life. As a result of this construction of reality, it is up to Protestant theology to provide the adherent with rules for living that guide him in an effective and safe manner. The so-called Spiritual Nature is highlighted, in the sense that one is in this world and has to live here while awaiting the irruption of a better world.[66]

Protestantism began to determine its behavior on the basis of certain rules, and this new way of life tended towards characterizing the Protestant as someone who did not conform to the contemporary order of things. This nonconformity in practice turned out to be a conservative element, to the degree that it simply allows Protestants to reject the normal conventions of social life, to show their disinterest and, by withdrawing, to continue their interest in the advent of another world outside of time.

Missionary Protestantism appeared in Brazil as a representative of liberalism and modernity. At first it was considered radical, dangerous to traditional Brazilian society, because it upheld the liberal values of the nineteenth century. These new values included: a belief in progress, separation of church and state, political democracy, universal education, and freedom of conscience.[67] Nevertheless, what transpired was that Protestantism became incapable of keeping up with the transformations occurring within Brazilian society. Its ethic, which was severe and restrictive in all aspects of life, contributed a characteristic that was profoundly distinctive and identifiable with the group and the individual within the society at large. What happened was that a subsystem was created that was more or less differentiated from the prevailing system. This system was fundamentally conservative in nature and inhibited almost entirely the participation of Protestants in Brazilian society. It can be explained in part by a pietistic emphasis, which is not much given to theological reflection, and by the pre-millennial apocalypticism, which opposes the construction of any form of social utopia.

From the beginning of its implantation in Brazil, missionary Protestantism showed itself to be a counter-culture, its ethic providing its adherents with a strong element of cohesion, organization and social identification.

On the other hand, Protestantism attached excessive importance to this component of counter-culture, which turned out to be negative and inhibited its own development, requiring of its adherents a conduct that was radically different from the standards of behavior accepted by Brazilian society. This resulted in the great majority of potential sympathizers being offended and driven away, and the greater part of society at large reacted negatively.[68]

[However], the Protestant religious message proclaimed in Brazil through missionary preaching, which was linked closely to liberalism, led some politicians and intellectuals such as Rui Barbosa, André Rebouças, Tavares Bastos and Abreu e Lima to show some sympathy for Protestantism. But their interest and that of others was aimed not at the religious question *per se*, but rather at the intellectual, political and ideological perspectives represented by Protestantism that were in vogue at that time.[69]

In Brazil, the tone of Protestant missionary preaching was aimed basically at the problem of religious freedom and against the intransigence shown by the Catholic Church. The theological unity of Protestantism in Brazil was established, to a great extent, by way of confronting the Catholic Church.

The pattern of Protestant preaching in Brazil always had three elements: revival, polemics and morals. The objective of revival was to convert the individual; polemics, to convince him of the truth of Protestantism; morals, to make clear and inculcate the distinctive standards of conduct of the new religion. As a function of this, there was an emphasis placed on the freedom of the individual regarding his personal salvation, that is, he was able to accept it or reject it. This individual responsibility appears to have completely dominated Protestant missionary preaching in Brazil.

Another distinctive feature provided by Protestant preaching, which became common among the various denominational groups, regards the affirmation that all men are equal in the sight of God because of the universality of sin. That doctrine was stripped of its social content of protest, and for the Protestantism established in Brazil this prevented a more radical insertion into social problems, especially that of blacks. This was because the concern was not for changing the social order, but rather the acceptance of the *status quo* and submission to it, highlighting that social differences would be of no consequence at the time of the final judgment and that the definitive equality being presented would come in the hereafter.

The commentary by Boanerges Ribeiro regarding the activity of the American missionary Simonton illumines this Protestant behavior very well.

> Simonton is an enthusiastic republican but he is not in Brazil to subvert the monarchy, he is viscerally anti-slavery and he makes no secret of this, but he is not going to commit himself to the abolitionist campaign in Brazil. He envisages the insertion into the Brazilian religious scene of a new denomination made up of people who have a personal experience of God having forgiven their sins because they accepted Christ.[70]

While in Itú, in the interior of São Paulo province, Simonton recorded in his journal, dated 14 February 1861, that he had received correspondence from the United States concerning the outbreak of the North-South conflict. This occurred when South Carolina decided to secede from the Union. He says that predicting the course of events is a very difficult task, but he believes that God, in some way, "is opening the way to remove the oppression of slavery, even though from a human point of view the result to be expected appears to be quite the opposite." He also says, "I feel convinced that benevolent designs are hidden in some way beneath these providential shadows." [71]

The goal of the Protestant missions was the conquest of the Brazilian mind. This led to the employment not only of preaching and the distribution of Bibles and pamphlets, but also the creation of a system of schools at the primary, secondary and even university level as instruments of evangelizing propaganda.

NOTES

1. Luíz Gonçalves dos Santos, *Desagravos do Clero e do Povo Católico Fluminense; ou Refutação das Mentiras e Calúnias do Impostor que se entitula Missionário do Rio de Janeiro, e Enviado pela Sociedade Metodista Episcopal de New York para Civilizar e Converter ao Cristianismo os Fluminenses* (Rio de Janeiro: Imprensa Americana de I.P. da Costa, 1837), xxv.

2. *Imprensa Evangélica* (5 July 1884): 1-2. Founded by Ashbel Green Simonton in 1864, this newspaper had its first issue printed at Tipografia Universal de Laemmert, with 450 copies. Starting with the second issue, the printing was done by Tipografia Perseverança, since the Laemmert brothers had been threatened and so withdrew. In 1879, because of "special circumstances," the newspaper was transferred to São Paulo. *Imprensa Evangélica* was published for 28 years, playing a fundamental role in the principal and most difficult phase of the implantation of Protestantism in Brazil.

3. See H. Watjen, *O Domínio Colonial Hollandez no Brasil: um capítulo da história colonial do século XVII* (São Paulo: Companhia Editora Nacional, 1938), 349-350. In his work *História Documental do Protestantismo no Brasil* (São Paulo: ASTE, 1984), 316, note 173, Professor Reily makes brief references to the subject, citing even the Proceedings of the "Third Classical Assembly of Brazil, held on 3 January 1638, in Pernambuco," published in the *Revista do Instituto Geographico Brasileiro* (Rio de Janeiro: Imprensa Nacional, 1915), 1:723.

4. More complete information about the dispute can be found in two works by Padre "Perereca," (Luís Gonçalves dos Santos): *O Celibato Clerical e Religioso Defendido dos Golpes da Impiedade e da Libertinagem dos Correspondentes da Astréia, com um Apêndice em Separado do Sr. Padre Feijó* (Rio de Janeiro: n.p.,1827) and *A Voz da Verdade da Santa Igreja Católica, Confundindo a Voz da Mentira do Amante da Humanidade para Sedativo da Efervecência Casamenteira dos Modernos Celibatários* (Rio de Janeiro: n.p.,1829); and in the response given by Father Diogo Antônio Feijó: *Resposta às Parvoices, Absurdos, Impiedades e Contradições do Sr. Padre Luís Gonçalves dos Santos na Sua Obra Intitulada "Defesa do Celibato Clerical Contra o Voto em Separado pelo Padre Diogo Antonio Feijó"* (Rio de Janeiro: n.p.,1827). ["Ultramontanism," is the attitude within the Roman Catholic Church that argues for centralization of authority in the papal Curia, as opposed to national or diocesan independence. "Jansenism" is derived from the Flemish Catholic theologian Cornelius Jansen (1585-1638), whose interpretation of writings of Augustine of Hippo brought him into conflict with the pope. The term came to be applied loosely to clergy denying the infallibility of the Church with regard to dogma. Trs.]

5. See Luíz Gonçalves dos Santos, *Desagravos do Clero,* and *O Católico e o Medodista; ou Refutação das Doutrinas Heréticaque os Intitulados Missionários do Rio de Janeiro, Metodistas de New York tem vulgarizado nessa Corte do Brasil por meio de Huns Impressos Chamados Tracts, com o Fim de Fazer Proselitos para a sua Seita, &c.* (Rio de Janeiro: Imprensa Americana de I.P. da Costa & Co., 1838).

6. William Paul Tilbury, an English Catholic cleric who emigrated to Brazil adopted the name Guilherme Paulo, and took on responsibility for reading all publications in English from the Protestant missionaries. He had the help of James Andrews, another

Englishman and former Protestant supposedly converted to Catholicism. On finding news, information or references to Brazil, Tilbury published them in the Rio de Janeiro newspapers. This practice encouraged Father Perereca in his labors and provoked a violent reaction among the other Ultramontanists. See D.G. Vieira, *O Protestantismo, a Maçonaria e a Questão Religiosa no Brasil* (Brasília: Editora Universidade de Brasília, 1980), 34-35.

7. Santos, *O Católico e o Metodista*, xxv. Father Perereca used the expression "closed garden" frequently. In his work *Memórias para Servir à História do Reino do Brasil* (Belo Horizonte and São Paulo: Itatiaia/Edusp, 1981), 1:369, when speaking of the arrival of foreigners in the country, he states, "No longer is Brazil a closed garden, forbidden to the rest of mankind, no longer is it an ignored and forgotten country; already foreigners are now being welcomed who prefer to live here under the protection of the most benign prince on Earth."

8. Daniel Parish Kidder, *Sketches of Residence and Travels in Brazil, Embracing Historical and Geographical Notices of the Empire and its Several Provinces* (Philadelphia: Sorin & Ball, 1845), 1:312-313.

9. M.A. Rizzo, *Simonton, inspirações de uma existência: Diário do rev. Ashbel Green Simonton* (São Paulo: Rizzo, 1962), 52.

10. Ibid., 77.

11. Richard Francis Burton, *Explorations of the Highlands of the Brazil* (London: Tinsley Brothers, 1869), 1:227.

12. T. Davatz, *Memórias de um Colono no Brasil: 1850* (Belo Horizonte and São Paulo: Itatiaia/Edusp, 1980), 76. Davatz explains how he, a school master, was presented the opportunity of performing pastoral duties: "It is known about the Protestants that a settler in Ibicaba long ago delivered religious sermons over a lengthy period. Nevertheless, no such thing existed when we arrived in 1855. On the occasion of the celebration of Pentecost in 1856, a settler was granted permission to read sermons on Sundays and festivals, as well as to deliver prayers at burials. The settler in question carried out his duties with zeal and faithfulness until late September 1856, when I received the charge to take his place, so that, in addition to the job of school teacher, I had to serve also as pastor to both the living and the dead, excluding, naturally, the administering of the sacraments." (Davatz, *Memórias de um Colono no Brasil*, 137.)

13. Henry Koster, *Travels in Brazil*, 2nd. ed. (London: Longman, Hurst, Rees, Orme, and Brown, 1817), 2:239-240.

14. Thomas Ewbank, *Life in Brazil, or a Journal of a Visit to the Land of the Cocoa and the Palm* (New York: Harper & Brothers, 1856), 238-239.

15. Daniel Parish Kidder and James Cooley Fletcher, *Brazil and the Brazilians, Portrayed in Historical and Descriptive Sketches* (Philadelphia: Childs & Peterson, 1857), 134.

16. Santos, *O Católico e o Metodista*, 173.

17. Letter written by Junius Newman, dated 13 February 1873, and published in the *Nashville Christian Advocate* (3 May1873): 8.

18. Avé-Lallemont observed, "Until Brazil breaks the Catholic religion's chains on the State, the entire State will remain a territory of the Church, a captaincy of Rome." See R. Avé-Lallemant, *Viagem pelo Norte do Brasil no anno de 1859* (Rio de Janeiro: Instituto Nacional do Livro, 1961), 2:245. Avé-Lallemont observed, "Until Brazil breaks the Catholic religion's chains on the State, the entire State will remain a territory of the Church, a captaincy of Rome."

19. José Carlos Rodrigues, "O futuro e a América," *O Novo Mundo* (23 March 1871): 83. *O Novo Mundo*, founded and directed by José Carlos Rodrigues in October 1870 and edited in New York in the Portuguese language, was, judging by the testimony of contemporary publications, a fine, well-informed newspaper during its nine years of existence. Charles Anderson Gauld points out that *O Novo Mundo* achieved a circulation of eight thousand copies, extraordinary for that time. (Charles Anderson Gauld, "José Carlos Rodrigues, o patriarca da imprensa carioca," *Revista da História* 4 (October-December 1953): 429.)

20. F. Biard, *Deux années au Brésil* (Paris: Libraire de L. Hachette et Co., 1862), 208.

21. The exact number of southerners who emigrated to Brazil is unknown. Conflicting estimates vary between two and twenty thousand immigrants. See S.T.D.G. Silva, "A religião dos pioneiros americanos no Brasil, na região de Santa Bárbara d'Oeste, Estado de São Paulo," (mimeographed copy, 1997).

22. J.G. Rocha, *Lembranças do Passado* (Rio de Janeiro: Centro Brasileiro de Publicadade, 1941-1956) relates in detail the ministerial activities carried out by Robert R. Kalley and the development of the Igreja Evangêlica Fluminense (Evangelical Church of Rio de Janeiro).

23. M. Testa, *O Apóstolo da Madeira (dr. Robert Reid Kalley)* (Lisbon: Igreja Evangélica Presbiteriana de Portugal, 1963) recounts in detail the activities of Kalley on this Portuguese island.

24. Vieira, *O Protestantismo, a Maçonaria e a Questão Religiosa no Brasil*, 114. [Kalley gives an account of his Madeira experiences in *An Account of the Recent Persecutions in Madeira: In a Letter to a Friend* (London: John F. Shaw, 1844). Trs.]

25. E.G. Léonard, *O Protestantismo Brasileiro* (São Paulo: ASTE, 1963), 49-50.

26. W.A. Wedemann, *A History of Protestant Missions to Brazil: 1850-1914* (Ann Arbor: Xerox University Microfilms, 1988), 104.

27. Rocha, *Lembranças do Passado*, 1:61.

28. Kalley's extremely prudent behavior did not receive the approval of the Presbyterians Simonton and Blackford. Rocha justifies the behavior of the Scottish missionary, arguing that he "did not want to repeat on the South American continent his experience of great publicity and its consequences, interrupting his labors and vexing his co-workers, so he avoided making known what he intended to create on Brazilian soil, thus escaping the attention of the Anti-Christian spies, who were greatly aided by exaggerated news stories published in foreign newspapers. Indeed! With his experience, he knew perfectly well that all Protestant propaganda is watched carefully and all the news sections of evangelical newspapers are scrutinized minutely by those who prefer that ignorance of the truth prevail over the saving light that is found in Jesus Christ!" (Rocha, *Lembranças do Passado*, 2:34-35.)

29. Ibid., 1:75.

30. Vieira, *O Protestantismo, a Maçonaria e a Questão Religiosa no Brasil*, 120.

31. Reily, *História Documental do Protestantismo no Brasil*, 96-100.

32. In addition to Rio de Janeiro, Fountain Pitts was in the cities of Buenos Aires and Montevideo. In a letter to the Methodist Missionary Society, he observed that Brazil was a field "ripe unto the harvest" and that the population welcomed him in a kind and affectionate manner (letter, 2 September 1835, from Pitts to the Corresponding Secretary of the Missionary Society of the Methodist Episcopal Church. Reprinted in *Christian Advocate and Journal* (4 December 1835): 58). It is interesting to note that Pitts stayed in

Brazil for only a short time. One of his sons, a medical doctor, left Tennessee and immigrated to Brazil along with other southerners, settling in Santarém. The Rev. Tucker, who in 1888 organized a series of meetings in Santarém, relates that seven successive evenings of preaching occurred in the residence of Dr. Pitts, son of the late Rev. Fountain Pitts. (N.A. Guilhon, *Confederados em Santarém: saga Americana na Amazônia* (Rio de Janeiro/Brasília: Presença/INL, 1987), 104.)

33. Fountain E. Pitts, "A Call for Missionaries," *Christian Advocate and Journal* 10 (4 December 1835): 58.

34. Letter, 1 September 1836, from Spaulding to the Corresponding Secretary of the Missionary Society of the Methodist Episcopal Church. According to Spaulding's report, "We have been enabled to organize a Sunday school denominated the 'South American Missionary Sunday school.'. . . It is divided into eight classes—four male and four female teachers. . . . We meet half past four o'clock every Sabbath. We have two classes of blacks. One speaks English, and the other Portuguese. They appear at present much interested, and anxious to learn." Reprinted in *Christian Advocate and Journal* (2 December 1836): 58.

35. Daniel P. Kidder wrote *Sketches of Residence and Travels in Brazil* and several other works, as well as collaborating with the James C. Fletcher in writing *Brazil and the Brazilians* (Philadelphia: Childs & Peterson, 1857). During his travels in Bahia, he relates that the province had become an important center for the slave trade and that "this traffic in negroes, which has profit as its prime motive, provokes feelings of revulsion." He commented with irony on the ideas seeking to justify the traffic in human goods, "[The slaves'] condition [in Brazil] was in no way so pitiable as that of thousands of poor negroes in Africa, who had been captured in the wars of different tribes against one another, and who might be tortured or sacrificed if they were not redeemed. What a worthy enterprise, then, to send vessels to *ransom* those poor pagan natives, and bring them where they can be Christianized by baptism, and at the same time lend a helping hand to those who had been so kind as to purchase them out of heathen bondage." (Kidder, *Sketches of Residence and Travels in Brazil,* 2:44-45.)

36. *Twenty-first Annual Report* (Missionary Society of the M.E. Church, 1840), 15. The text reveals that the South American mission met many obstacles. In Rio de Janeiro in particular, it suffered formidable opposition from the religion established by the Empire.

37. Santos, *O Católico e o Metodista,* xxiv. Father Perereca expressed his disagreement with the Methodist attempts to break Catholic unity. "Faced with such clear, certain, and convincing proofs that the Church of Jesus Christ is one, holy, catholic and apostolic, into which Brazilians had the good fortune of being born, how is it possible that in the Court of the Empire of the Land of the True Cross, right under the nose of its emperor and of all the ecclesiastical and secular authorities, there are present laymen who are married, with children, called Missionaries of Rio de Janeiro, sent from New York by others just like themselves, Calvinist Protestants, to preach Jesus Christ to the people of the Province of Rio de Janeiro?" Further on, he argued that the Methodists ought to evangelize those who had not yet been evangelized. "Since they, particularly the Methodists, are such ardent missionaries, why do they not employ their holy zeal in catechizing the pagan Indians and preaching Jesus Christ to them in the middle of the jungle, following the example of the Catholic missionaries?" (Ibid., 172.)

38. Reily, *História Documental do Protestantismo no Brasil,* 84.

39. Ibid., 86-87.

40. Ibid., 87.

41. Guilhon, *Confederados em Santarém*, 101. [The original English source for this and other quotations from *The Copiahan* could not be located. The quotations from the newspaper are retranslations made from Guilhon's Portuguese translation. Trs.]

42. Ibid., 104.

43. Ibid., 143. James W. Koger observed that the locality was populated mainly by English-speaking people. (J.W. Koger, "Brazil Mission," *Annual Report - Board of Missions* (February 1884): 93-94.)

44. Guilhon, *Confederados em Santarém*, 143.

45. "Brazil," *The Gospel in All Lands*, 1882, 30-31.

46. There are two biographies of José Manoel da Conceição: Boanerges Ribeiro, *O Padre Protestante* (São Paulo: Casa Editora Presbiteriana, 1950) and Vincente Themudo Lessa, *Biografia do Ex-Padre José Manoel da Conceição* (São Paulo: Gráfica Cruzeiro do Sul, 1955).

47. According to the report dated 10 July 1866 from George Chamberlain. (Reily, *História Documental do Protestantismo no Brasil*, 112.)

48. "Brazil," 30-31.

49. In connection with the Civil War in the United States, Simonton recorded in his diary in 1861, "If at least the stain of slavery can be removed, this nightmare rooted out of the nation's body, even if it is a distant day, it will be a great victory." (B. Ribeiro, *Protestantismo no Brasil Monárquico* (São Paulo: Pioneira, 1981), 287-288.)

50. A.G. Mendonça, *O Celeste Porvir: a inserção do protestantismo no Brasil* (São Paulo: Paulinas, 1984), 27; Ribeiro, *Protestantismo no Brasil Monárquico*, 144.

51. A.R. Crabtree, *Baptists in Brazil* (Rio de Janeiro: The Baptist Publishing House of Brazil, 1953), 35. Over and above this, there is evidence that the main factor forcing the interruption of the mission was the imprisonment of Bowen. See J. dos R. Pereira, *Breve História dos Batistas* (Rio de Janeiro: Casa Publicadora Batista, 1972), 93.

52. It is probable that General Alexander Travis Hawthorne had come with a group organized by the Rev. Ballard Smith Dunn. See B.A. Oliveira, *Centelha em Restolho Seco* (Rio de Janeiro: published by author, 1985), 142.

53. H.A. Tupper, *The Foreign Missions of the Southern Baptist Convention* (Philadelphia: American Baptist Publication Society, 1880), 11. Letter is dated 11 January 1873.

54. In a letter addressed to the Board of Foreign Missions in December 1862, the Confederate general states, "I am surprised I never thought before of the city and Province of Bahia as the most appropriate place to locate our central mission. The more I reflect on it, the more I am convinced that there is no place in Brazil which offers more inducement than Bahia for the location of a permanent mission." (Oliveira, *Centelha em Restolho Seco*, 148.)

55. A.R. Crabtree, *História dos Batistas no Brasil: até o ano de 1906,* 1st ed. (Rio de Janeiro: Casa Publicadora Batista, 1937), 53.

56. Reily, *História Documental do Protestantismo no Brasil*, 130.

57. José Carlos Rodrigues, "Egreja official e egreja livre," *O Novo Mundo* (23 September 1873): 194.

58. Wedemann, *A History of Protestant Missions to Brazil*, 151. José Carlos Rodrigues states that the advance of Protestantism began to cause concern: "We also read recently a newspaper from São Paulo complaining bitterly about the large number of proselytes the Protestant mission has gained in that province." (José Carlos Rodrigues, "Idéias de religião," *O Novo Mundo* (23 October 1873): 3.)

59. Defending Protestantism, Rodrigues explains, "The unity and catholicity of the Catholic Church are true only in the sense that the same also applies to the Methodist, Presbyterian, Anglican, Greek and other churches. Regarding bodies visible and invisible, each has its own unity and all have the same right to catholicity as the Church of Rome." (José Carlos Rodrigues, "A multiplicidade de seitas," *O Novo Mundo* (23 March 1874): 98.) The theological and doctrinal differences among the diverse Protestant denominations contributed notably to heightening the polemics and aided the arguments of the Catholic apologists. One of the most famous controversies was between the Presbyterian pastor Eduardo Carlos Pereira and Father Leonel Franca. Franca used the theological differences and the existence of innumerable denominations or "sects" in denouncing the weakness of Protestantism. "The first symptom of instability in a religious society is its fragmentation into sects. An historical diagnosis of Protestantism shows the appearance of this from the first days of its existence." (Pe. L. Franca, *A Igreja, a Reforma e a Civilização* (Rio de Janeiro: Livraria Agir Editora, 1958), 237.)

60. The *Nashville Christian Advocate* published some extracts from a report by the missionary J.E. Newman (3 May 1873): 11.

61. Rodrigues, "A multiplicidade de seitas," *O Novo Mundo* (23 March 1874): 98.

62. When the Presbyterian Church in Brazil received its first two members at the beginning of 1862, a question arose: ought a person coming from the Catholic Church be re-baptized? After much deliberation and consultation with the Missionary Board in New York, the Reverend Ashbel Green Simonton resolved to take into consideration the arguments made by Dr. Kalley that it would not be prudent for there to be different procedures on this topic among the Protestants. (Ribeiro, *Protestantismo no Brasil Monárquico*, 25.)

63. Mendonça provides a useful analysis of the theology present in the hymnal *Salmos e Hinos*. (A.G. Mendonça, "Incorporación del protestantismo y la cuestión religiosa en Brasil en el siglo XIX: reflexiones e hipótesis," *Cristianismo y Sociedad* 92 (1987): 235-238.)

64. The greatest collaboration was between Presbyterians and Methodists. Kennedy relates as follows: "The Presbyterian Church, of generous heart, attended to the needs of the Methodists in this time of anxiety. Rev. F.J.C. Schneider, erudite minister of that sister church, came to Piracicaba to offer brotherly assistance to the Methodists. He carried out three tasks in that city: he helped missionaries in their study of Portuguese, he lectured at the Colégio Piracicabano, and he preached the gospel two or three times a week. One day the Rev. Dr. Chamberlain, another minister of the gospel, visited us and preached an excellent sermon to a select audience in the chapel." (J.L. Kennedy, *Cincoenta Annos de Methodismo no Brasil* (São Paulo: Imprensa Metodista, 1928), 26.)

65. [Arminianism derives from the teaching of Jacobus Arminius (1560-1609), Dutch reformed theologian. Arminius argued against the deterministic logic of Calvinism and claimed that the sovereignty of God was compatible with man's free will. Pietism originated with the teachings of Philip Jacob Spener (1635-1705). Spener attempted to introduce devotional and evangelical elements (experiential religion) into German Lutheranism. Pietism was one of the influences that shaped John Wesley's Methodism. (See *Dictionary of the Christian Church*, ed. F.L. Cross (London: Oxford University Press, 1958), 87-88 and 1071.) Trs.]

66. According to Grahan, "The missionaries spoke a lot more about the delights of paradise and the destiny of each soul after death, ignoring completely any notion of reform." (R. Grahan, *Grã-Bretanha e o Início da Modernização no Brasil* (São Paulo: Brasiliense, 1973), 306.)

67. Rui Barbosa showed sympathy with Protestantism on several occasions. He wrote, "Where Protestantism exists, there is industrial prosperity, strong and luxuriant like a tropical forest." (Grahan, *Grã-Bretanha e o Início da Modernização no Brasil*, 294.) André Rebouças noted in his journal the time he visited some Protestant school or chapel, emphasizing his favorable impression. (A. Rebouças, *Diário e Notas Autobiográficas* (Rio de Janeiro: José Olympio, 1938), 22-27.)

68. R.G.A. Frase, *A Sociological Analysis of the Development of Brazilian Protestantism: A Study in Social Change* (Ann Arbor: Xerox Microfilms, 1988), 339-340.

69. Sud Mennucci shows in a certain sense the interest of politicians in Protestantism. A letter from Luiz Gama to his son says, "Be a Christian and a philosopher, believe only in the authority of reason, and never ally yourself with any religious sect. God reveals Himself only in the reasoning of men, He does not exist in any church in the world. There are two books which I recommend to you for reading: The Holy Bible and the *Life of Jesus* by Ernest Renan." (S. Mennucci, *O Precursor do Abolicionismo no Brasil: Luiz Gama* (Rio de Janeiro: Cia. Editora Nacional, 1938), 145.)

70. Ribeiro, *Protestantismo no Brasil Monárquico*, 27.

71. Simonton's position is very clear on this matter. Making use of the information received about the conflict occurring in the United States, which had as a backdrop the question of black slavery, he affirmed expecting very soon the "beginning of the end" of slavery in Brazil. He declared, "If such a stain can be removed, taking away the oppression that weighs on this country, even though the day may remain distant in which this end will come to be completely attained, this would still amount to a great event. There would be a period of trials, of humiliation for the national pride, of confession of sins and of calls for God's help." (Rizzo, *Simonton, inspirações de uma existencia*, 79.)

CHAPTER II

"CONTRARY TO WHAT MANY THINK, BRAZIL IS NOT AN UNCIVILIZED AND BARBAROUS COUNTRY": MISSIONARY STRATEGY

WE HAVE NOT YET TRIED TO ORGANIZE A SCHOOL: EDUCATION

> The Reverend Harvey has a school here and teaches English. Thirty to forty youth attend and it is making progress.[1]

Education occupied a prominent place in the strategy of implanting Protestantism in Brazil. Brought by the Protestants, it received an enthusiastic welcome among the liberal minds of Brazilian society, who adhered to an ideology of progress and were concerned about finding an educational model that would replace the Jesuit scholastic system. For this group, the traditional educational system was expected to make room for a practical education centered on science and technology.[2]

James Cooley Fletcher was the first Protestant missionary to recognize the necessity or importance of education in the process of implanting Protestantism in Brazil. His work was aimed at stimulating the use of the North American model of education, promoting the translation of American books, correspondence between the emperor and the leading minds of New England, and communication among Brazilian and American thinkers.

The North American missionaries brought their interest in education with them and invariably played the double role of teachers and evangelists. In addition to these missionaries, Protestantism counted on the contribution of a sizable contingent of people specialized in education, especially women.

The relative success of the education offered by the North American Protestants contributed considerably to the implantation of Protestantism in Brazil. One may agree entirely with the claims of Antônio Gouvêa Mendonça, who said that while the "elite of Brazil, largely liberal, had no interest in the Protestant religion, they were interested in the education the missionaries offered."[3] It can also be acknowledged and affirmed that this interest in education had favorable repercussions and aided in the religion's permanent establishment in as much as the missionaries were welcomed as representatives of the desired liberalism and progress.

The educational and religious systems were inextricably linked, making it almost impossible to separate them. Therefore, it would not be possible to adopt a Protestant system of education without taking on, at its core, the religious system it advocated. The same Mendonça adds that "there is clear evidence that the missionaries addressed themselves to the ruling classes capable of modifying the social landscape of the country." These classes showed themselves to possess a religious impermeability and they resisted the Protestant religious message. Against this backdrop, "Due to the ideological structure of the nineteenth century, rather than to missionary strategy," the North American Protestant missions "directed education toward the elite and religious evangelization toward the poor masses."[4]

Even when confronted with great resistance, the efforts of education and evangelization were always components of a well articulated plan. For William Bagby, a Baptist missionary who functioned as a "teacher-preacher," the religious objectives would be achieved only by developing a "good and wise plan" that should include a program of education. According to him,

> Such schools will prepare the way for the advance of the churches. . . . Schools established on these principles will triumph over every enemy and will win the good will even of our adversaries. Send missionaries who will establish evangelical schools, and the irresistible power of the Gospel will go forward in South America and the land of the Cross will shine with the resplendent light of Christ's Kingdom. [5]

Many missionaries had the impression that society and religion in Brazil presented an open and promising field for a new religious alternative. And this new form of religion, or the process of converting Catholics to Protestantism, demanded building a solid base of support. Within the established plan, the face of Brazilian society would have to be changed using education as a base of support and also as an important component of missionary strategy. On proposing to the Presbytery in 1867 "The appropriate means for implanting the Gospel of Jesus Christ in Brazil," the Rev. Ashbel G. Simonton showed his concern for the long-term establishment of Protestantism. For him, the safest means would be through the "establishment of schools." [6]

Protestantism constituted a certain "way of life" and accepting it signified assuming changes in cultural patterns. The Protestant schools, intentional vehicles for this cultural transplant, arose in several parts of Brazil, almost always in provincial capitals and the more important cities, consistent with the vision of the missionary strategy. The introduction of Protestant education into Brazilian society coincided with the first missionary preaching and the organization of the first churches. This great interest shown by the Protestants toward education was due, in large part, to the real stumbling block to their aspirations presented by the lack of instruction.

Learning the Protestant doctrine would be difficult without reading the Bible, books, journals and newspapers.[7] In an article in the *Imprensa Evangélica* newspaper, the Reverend Eduardo Carlos Pereira affirms that

It is necessary for the sun of Christianity to come with its rays of liberty and brotherhood to feed the spirit and quicken the mind. It is necessary for the light of the evangelical truths to come to enlighten the poor. . . . May the revolution come as an effective means for the salvation of our country. Not a revolution by the sword,. . . but indeed by the word, a peaceful revolution, noble and enlightened in its ideas. [8]

Protestantism, considered the "religion of the book," finds its center in the reading of the Bible. Since the early days of the Protestant presence in Brazil, the Bible was considered the book of the Protestants. This was always used as a means of highlighting the superiority of Protestantism over Catholicism. The newspaper *Methodista Cathólico,* commenting on a journey by the emperor to the Province of São Paulo and finding Protestant Bibles in public institutions, says, "Everywhere the people are becoming judges of the law and, in the complete absence of the Roman Bible, they are convinced that there is no Bible other than the Protestant Bible." [9] To illustrate the link of Protestantism with the Bible, it is sufficient to read the text of José Carlos Rodrigues in *O Novo Mundo*:

The Bible must be in every home, in every heart; it must be kept, read, studied and loved by everyone. It is simultaneously the miniature of the history of the past and also of the future; the poem of divine mercy, the drama of human life, our journey on earth; the constitution of the universe, as we understand it; the code of eternal laws of morality; the medicine of the soul and even, because of this, the medicine of the body; the most sublime memorial of the divine art of the restoration of mankind, . . . but when would we be able to describe everything that is the Bible? [10]

Rodrigues' interest in the Bible was genuine and this can be confirmed not only on the basis of his initiative in translating the New Testament into Portuguese, but also by the fact of his having written a book about Jesus and by the support he gave to Protestants in the production and distribution of biblical pamphlets.[11]

The segment of society which offered the greatest opportunity for the task of conversion accomplished by Protestantism was the poor masses, so illiteracy was seen as a serious stumbling block. Since reading the Bible and religious hymns were important characteristics of Protestant worship, it is possible to conclude that the advance of the mission and the strategy of implantation depended fundamentally on the literacy of the adherents who were being admitted and of their children, who potentially would also embrace Protestantism.

Seeking to respond to this basic necessity, the Protestant missionaries set up a bible school[12] beside each church. The objective of these schools was to offer the minimum of instruction to allow the students to read the Bible. On many occasions, the missionaries went so far as to employ lay people in reading the Bible to illiterate proselytes, highlighting the importance of this activity. These "readers of the Bible" were used to compensate for the shortage of trained pastors. In part, they answered the inquiry made by Pereira, "In view of the expanse of Brazil and the circumstances in which the Evangelical Church finds itself, how are there to be found ministers in sufficient numbers, so that there will be someone everywhere to share the bread of eternal life?" [13]

The bible school linked to the church aimed at the education of the children and adults in Protestant principles and was directly related to the concern of introducing and guaranteeing the permanence and progress of Protestantism. The educational program as carried to its conclusion by the Protestants extended beyond the bible schools, which had as their direct objective the propagation of religious faith. This was made concrete in their regular schools, where the educational objective addressed the establishment of a Christian civilization based on the North American model. Indirectly, it had in mind the task of evangelization, linking a profoundly all-encompassing ideology to changing the direction of a society still in search of its way.

In this manner, the propaganda of the new religious emphasis was always intrinsically linked to the liberal educational practices of North America. The missionaries themselves always showed their conviction of the superiority of the Protestant religion, education, and culture that they were spreading. This is what Pereira sought to show in his article "O Romanismo e o Progresso" [Romanism and Progress], in which he asks, "Why is it that the Protestant countries generally have the advantage over Roman Catholic countries in instruction, morality, industry, commerce, wealth, and social life?" [14]

The Protestants discerned within Brazilian society a yearning for education. This is reflected in the *Imprensa Evangélica* newspaper: "On all sides the cry goes up "Educate! Educate!" [15] In an 1881 article entitled "Os Ingênuos," [16] the *Imprensa Evangélica* stated that the United States invested a lot in education and that it was necessary for Brazil to follow the same path, especially to take care of the *ingênuos*. However, what drove the writer to defend the inclusion of *ingênuos* in the public educational process was the fear that without education they would end up in prison. "Their education is our own defense. Their ignorance and depravity are mortal dangers." [17]

The Protestant missions' discernment and great concern, as revealed by investing in the area of education, was based primarily on the notion that the implantation of the Protestant religion in Brazil faced a problem of an ideological nature. From the beginning of the implantation there was a deep link between the theology of Protestant missions and North American ideology, namely that the regular schools established by the Protestants sought to reproduce an education shaped by norms that emphasized individualism, liberalism and pragmatism. It was believed that these factors would be able to overcome problems of an ideological nature.

It was acknowledged, particularly by the Protestants, that with respect to influence and acceptance by Brazilian society, the whole advantage lay with Catholicism since Catholicism had been implanted alongside colonization, with the religious characteristics of the Counter-Reformation. José Carlos Rodrigues acknowledged that the predominance of this brand of Catholicism, deeply ingrained in the lives of the Brazilian people, would be challenged in the event that evangelical Protestant education had the opportunity to prove its obvious superiority.

The editor of the *O Novo Mundo* newspaper clearly expressed a conviction that probably would be entirely accepted by the Protestant missionaries. According to the editor, Protestantism represented a superior culture that ought, necessarily, be shared with other peoples, because it was the expression of the Kingdom of God. Catholicism was a decadent religion that would provide "an opening for more solid beliefs" and the Lord's hand would be guiding and educating in the way that must be followed, and preparing for a higher degree of civilization." [18] It was claimed that the corroboration of this superiority lay in the fact that the United States had freed its slaves and placed a great value on education. The editor concluded that there was no possibility of slavery and education living side by side: "Anywhere that the so-called servile element prospers, thousands of men are prohibited from developing their hearts and minds."[19]

OUR HOLY RELIGION OUGHT TO BE DEFENDED AND AVENGED: CONTROVERSY

> *Any religion that does not promote good morals is the devil's. The Christian religion combats vice in all its forms and does not consent to partnership with sin.*[20]

Protestantism met much resistance and many difficulties in its work of implantation in Brazil. There was a pronounced oppositional attitude by the Catholic Church through newspapers, books, pamphlets and even physical persecution. In addition to this overt behavior, there was within Brazilian society an attitude of suspicion and alienation because of the temperament and characteristics adopted by Protestantism. By and large, Protestant religiosity did not mix with the spirit of the Brazilian people.[21] This is consistent with the conclusion reached by Thomas Ewbank:

> The more I see of this people, the more distant appears the success of any Protestant missions among them. Festivals are obstacles that can not easily be got rid of. The masses are too fond of them, and the national pulse beats in unison with them; moreover, there are powerful classes interested in maintaining them. Sundays, too, are universal seasons of recreation. Ladies laugh outright at the seriousness and alleged long faces of English families passing to church as to a funeral. . . . Protestants, it is said, degenerate here. The British chapel never received a native convert, while monks have drawn members from it. The Episcopal Methodists have had a mission here for some years, and have abandoned it.[22]

The declaration made by the *Imprensa Evangélica*, affirming that Protestantism and Catholicism are two systems "in open opposition to each other and in fact at war with each other," [23] reveals in large part the nature of the relationship between the Catholic Church and the Protestant evangelical churches in the nineteenth century. The Presbyterian newspaper compared the two models, seeking to highlight the existing antagonism.

Protestantism separates the state from the church; Catholicism wishes them to be joined. Protestantism builds institutions around the will of the people; Catholicism proposes building them according to the wishes of the Pope. Protestantism upholds religious freedom; Catholicism demands that each person hand over his conscience to the safekeeping of an ecclesiastical superior. Protestantism develops the faculties of understanding so as to stimulate the spirit of independence and personal strength; Catholicism subdues this spirit by its doctrine of passive obedience and submission. Protestantism has already placed the world on the course of progress and prosperity; Catholicism wants to bind it and send it back through antiquated and tortuous routes down which, unfortunately, it has already taken so many nations to ruin and desolation.[24]

For Brazilian Protestantism, Catholicism had from the beginning represented an adversary to be tackled. The controversy that developed as a consequence of this situation contributed enormously in stamping definitive characteristics on Brazilian Protestantism. Richard Francis Burton, author of the two-volume *Explorations of the Highlands of the* [sic] *Brazil*, highlights the way in which Brazilian Catholics perceived the Protestants. "The people from [Minas Gerais], like those from [São Paulo], have a certain horror of anyone non-Catholic. The Protestant is seen as an alien being. The whole of society's structure was derived from Catholicism and the Protestant was shut out." The author continues by pointing out that the tendency to persecute the Protestants was not strong, "although I have read the speech of a provincial deputy, who proposed to put to death a priest who became a convert or pervert to "Protestantism." [25] Burton was referring to José Manuel da Conceição, a Catholic priest who converted to Protestantism and became the first Brazilian Protestant pastor in the service of the Presbyterian Church.

The Methodist missionary Daniel Kidder sought to show that these arguments and conflicts arose because of the brute force of the Catholic Church and that the Protestants felt obliged to defend themselves against these accusations.[26] In his two-volume *Sketches and Residence and Travels in Brazil*, Kidder recounts that in the mission settlement directed by him and Justin Spaulding there was always a crowd of people seeking copies of the Bible. As soon as word got out about a new supply, many people appeared, "of all ages and conditions of life—from the gray-headed man to the prattling child, from the gentleman in high life to the poor slave." Many messengers appeared bringing word from parents or masters who wanted to take away a number of copies. One of these requests was signed by an Imperial minister who wanted Bibles for a school.[27]

Kidder sees all this activity as provoking much jealousy among some Catholic clergy. At the same time there appeared a newspaper, *O Católico*, aimed at combating the missionaries and the work they were carrying out. For Kidder, this opposition was actually always positive in that it "almost always had the effect to awaken greater inquiry after the Bible, and many were the individuals who, in coming to procure the Scriptures, said their attention was first called to the subject by the unreasonable and fanatical attempts of certain priests to hinder their circulation." [28]

The controversy was ever present and on many occasions was used as a strategic instrument to spread the Protestant message. Among the missionaries the message evolved in a climate of prudence, perhaps for political motives and also because of previous negative experiences. At the same time, it took on an open and aggressive form for the Brazilian pastors. The anti-Catholic sentiment was equally common among the missionaries and the native-born pastors.

The North American missionaries who worked in Brazil in the spreading and implantation of their churches came from a society in which Protestantism was the dominant religion and where broad religious liberty was the norm. This meant that even when confronting many problems and opponents, they always found great support on the part of their denomination of origin. The native pastors, in contrast, had been discriminated against with great vigor because of their apostasy from the Catholic faith and their proclamation of Protestantism. In this way, they encouraged an anti-Catholic posture that was always more argumentative and obstinate than that of the missionaries themselves. An example is Ashbel Simonton, who worked in Brazil as a Presbyterian missionary from 1859 to 1867. He always showed care in his relations with the Catholic Church, and in his activities there is no note of an obstinately argumentative spirit, but rather a proselytizing intent aimed at transmitting and consolidating in the faithful the principles of the new faith.

For Simonton, the official Catholic religion transmitted a false security since it was not based on a knowledge of the fundamentals of the faith, but on customs and the automatic rite of baptism. These customs and an ignorance of the Bible were what led to the superficiality of the religion as practiced. So, he concluded, the best religion was not that of the majority, but rather that which had the elements of access to true salvation within the reach of all. Penitence by voluntary corporal punishment frightened those who were weak, and the costly funeral arrangements became accessible only to the rich. The fear of a cruel and vengeful God left people terrified when thinking of the future life, pushing them into superstitions and manipulation by men who used religion as a means of livelihood and business.

In the sermon "A morte e o futuro estado dos justos" [Death and the future state of the justified], published in 1868 by *Imprensa Evangélica*, Simonton clearly spelled out the notions he had of Catholicism.

> Catholicism is a sad system. We don't know of anything more painful in the midst of the blindness of the human spirit. This blindness came from the abandonment and ignorance of the Bible on the part of the theologians and is reflected in the faithful who know nothing of the existence of God, of their souls, of immortality and the life hereafter. The liturgical practices, rites, ceremonies, pomp, and intermediaries (saints) identify the Catholic Church as a pagan religion that depends greatly on mythology. It is not Christian because it strays from the Gospel. Also, it is the religion of the rich because they are the only ones who can afford the cost of the ceremonies needed to save their souls. The Catholic worship is inferior and diminished in that it asks for intercession

by friends in the court of heaven. Further, Catholicism is contradictory because the better a person is the more ceremonies have to be celebrated for his benefit, which shows his greater difficulty in passing to the "better place," when the opposite is what should be true. This religion is Christian in name only, far from its origins, mythological, better serving the rich, inconsistent, supported by a superficial ceremonialism, and responsible in large measure for the irreligiosity reigning in society. These are the characteristics of the Catholic Church, due to the opportunities it offers its followers - and this is the religion of the majority.[29]

Justus Nelson, a missionary of the Methodist Church who worked in Belém do Pará, joined the polemical battle in newspaper articles regarding questions related directly to the Catholic Church. We can say that his objectives were to demonstrate the Protestant zeal for Biblical truths, in opposition to Catholic custom, in addition to providing new openings for Protestant propaganda. Following the same approach as the other missionaries, the main points in his argument were purgatory, the Virgin Mary, indulgencies, the Mass and the priesthood.

In the article "A redenção da Amazônia" [The Redemption of the Amazon], published in the *A República* newspaper in Belém do Pará, Nelson expounded on a social question, namely prostitution, which, according to him, "is the principal problem."[30] The attack he made departed essentially from a religious argument perspective and aimed clearly at denouncing the participation of the Catholic Church in maintaining the situation.[31] In the argument involving the Feast Day of Nazareth, Nelson stated that, in addition to Brazilians, he found many North American immigrants participating in the festivities. He claimed, "With great sorrow, I met among the crowds several pleasant and generous young men known to me who arrived in Brazil perfectly honest and here took their first steps toward vice." He concludes the article by listing the names of several people who should take on this responsibility.

His Excellency the Reverend D. Antonio has ecclesiastical authority to finish once and for all the support the church gives to this atrocious business. Let the reverend senator canon and the reverend general deputy canon cast out the abominable lotteries that they presently promote, and wash from their consecrated hands these dark blots, on a crusade against this evil that is devastating their nation. They will have much to give account before God of on this matter.[32]

It is important to note that the debate ignited by Nelson's position earned him a trial and the risk of deportation. The 17 November 1886 issue of the same newspaper, *A República*, reproduced an article published in *O Liberal*, which with irony calls into question the possibility of deportation. The article reads:

The Reverend Justus H. Nelson has committed a deplorable error; he forgot that the political situation of the province, under the influence and command of the canon senator and the canon deputy, is one of gambling, and that of the most pernicious type - lotteries. He denounced gambling during the Feast of

Nazareth! Woe to the mouth that said such things! "A foreigner is going to preach morality to us?" exclaims the *Diário do Gram Pará*! . . . If he doesn't like it here he can take himself elsewhere. His article is a lampoon. Are you listening, Mr. Nelson? The good people who presently rule Pará elevate gambling to the level of an institution, against which, dear sir, as a foreigner you cannot speak. They say they want immigrants. . . to replace the slave laborers and to gamble, not to become citizens. Please understand this. The Constitution, making use of its privileges as a lady, speaks more frankly: send him as a gift to the chief of police and ask him to exercise his right to deport him. This punishment is the only (written) penalty that can appropriately punish the foreigner who crushes under foot all the laws and natural rights of gambling, both public and constitutional. Mr. Nelson, you are not able to deliver admonishment; in this land this is one of the new privileges of the chief of police! Why is it that Mr. Nelson distributes free Bibles instead of roulette wheels. . . or lottery tickets? Change course. A foreigner such as, for example, the gentleman commendator [Antônio] Homem de Loureiro [Sequeira], can have a political newspaper or direct insults with impunity at Brazilians that he cannot form partnerships with or buy; he is able to donate money to elections, etc. He is a benefactor. But it is unacceptable to preach morality and protest against gambling, which also impoverishes the foreigners, Catholics as much as Protestants; whoever does this deserves to be deported, a wholesome means of attracting immigrants who will play roulette wheels and lotteries. Let's change the tone. We are quite certain that making faces at Mr. Nelson will not kill him. The two conservative newspapers are truly ridiculous. Continue, thrash the vice, even though it is patronized by all the canon senators and deputies; transform the quill into the whip until it expels the vice from civilization, and count on us to listen with you to the admonitions of the police, or to suffer ostracism with you since there are no judges in Berlin.[33]

Nelson acknowleged that a change in this state of affairs was possible. "Right and purity must prevail one day," [34] and, according to him, this would happen naturally through Protestantism. The same type of argument was used by the Methodist missionary James W. Koger: "It falls to the Christian evangelicals to liberate the unfortunate victims and restore the true light." [35]

The role of liberator and inaugurator of a new era, the destiny of Protestantism, was to serve as a constant basis to fuel the hotly contested arguments with Catholicism.[36] It was not only the missionaries who advanced arguments like this. Tavares Bastos, in *Cartas do Solitário* [Letters from the Hermit], argued that the ideal model of religious organization was that of the United States, where all denominations were permitted but none received support from the state. Positions like this contributed to Bastos being denounced on numerous occasions as a Protestant. However, such a fate could not be confirmed since the accusations were based solely on the fact of his having defended Robert Kalley when the customs authorities confiscated evangelical pamphlets, and also on his liberal ideas about religion.[37]

It became quite common to attribute to Protestantism innumerable virtues that, in contrast to the values supposedly defended by Catholicism, were aimed at emphasizing the possibilities of their development in Brazil.[38] The article "Os dous systemas" [The Two Systems], published in *Imprensa Evangélica*, serves to highlight this antagonism.[39]

Countless arguments promoted by the missionaries and Protestant pastors challenged the qualifications of the Catholic clergy. Without any proselytizing intent, Louis Agassiz, a Harvard professor and a naturalized citizen of the United States, described the wedding ceremony of a black couple, pointing out the priest's crudeness and poor manners.

> I thought what a strange confusion there must be in these poor creatures' minds, if they thought about it at all. They are told that the relation between man and wife is a sin, unless confirmed by the sacred rite of marriage; they come to hear a bad man gabble over them words which they cannot understand, mingled with taunts and abuse which they understand only too well.[40]

The writer later remarks, "There are several obstacles to [the country's] progress. . . . Among the influences unfavorable to progress is the character of the clergy." [41]

The work undertaken by the Protestant missionaries aroused displeasure on the part of the Catholic Church. These reactions stirred up endless arguments. In spite of the advice for care and discretion given by Robert Kalley to the newly-arrived Ashbel Simonton, we are able to see, based on the exhaustive reports contained in the work *Lembranças do Passado* [Recollections of the Past] by João Gomes do Rocha, that Kalley himself had to confront serious disputes during his missionary work in Brazil. This was in spite of his always writing under a variety of pseudonyms as a way of avoiding direct attacks on him or his followers.

As for the pastors native to Brazil, the argument was much more bitter. Eduardo Carlos Pereira, ordained a Presbyterian pastor in 1881, carried out markedly anti-Catholic activities, argumentative and lacking any of the discretion and care exhibited by the missionaries. Much more than a strategy aimed at Catholic adherents, the argument he developed sought to show that Catholicism had strayed far from Christianity. We are able to summarize his position using several points extracted from his book *O Problema Religioso na América Latina* [The Religious Problem in Latin America]. [42]

According to Pereira, the Catholic Church had disfigured Christianity and become pagan by structuring itself in keeping with the following elements: an attachment to tradition, the formulation of a new trinity embracing Jesus, Mary and Joseph, saints and meritorious works, indulgencies, priestly absolution, purgatory, Masses, worship of the Virgin Mary, monopoly of the clergy, a magical use of the sacraments (*ex opere operato*) and the Pope as the embodiment of the visible Church.[43] In light of these aberrations, the Catholic Church had failed completely in its civilizing mission.[44] Comparing Catholic countries with Protestant ones, he concluded that Roman Catholicism was the great evil of Latin America, responsible for its moral and material backwardness.[45]

José Manoel da Conceição, former Catholic priest and the first Protestant pastor from Brazil, did not carry out proselytizing activities.[46] Nevertheless, he performed a fundamental task in spreading the Protestant faith, while also continuing arguments with the Catholic Church. He received greater attention than the foreign missionaries on account of his having been a priest who then became an adherent to Protestantism. A letter by Antônio Pedro de Cerqueira Leite reads, "The name of Father José Manoel is spread throughout the universe, you can't go anywhere without hearing his name." [47]

The receiving of Conceição into Protestantism caused some apprehension among the Presbyterian missionaries. Naturally, they recognized that with the help of the ex-priest the possibilities for the growth of Protestantism would improve significantly. What they feared and wanted to avoid was provoking the Catholic Church. With this in mind, the missionary A.L. Blackford recommended to the New York Board, "Don't announce anything about him!" The missionary argued that the profession of faith by the ex-priest ought to be done in Rio de Janeiro and not in São Paulo.

> We are all in agreement that perhaps it would be better for the time being if he came to live in Rio and took his first steps here; since this is the first case in the country of a priest converting to Protestantism, we don't know what consequences will follow from the manner in which this will be addressed.[48]

In his labors as a Protestant pastor, José Manoel do Conceição proclaimed with care the new faith he had embraced but he also argued with the Catholic Church. His argumentation did not deviate from the tenets adopted by the missionaries, but he was firm and incisive.

Based on the debates entered into and the argumentation used by the foreign missionaries and the Protestant Brazilian pastors, Brazilian Catholicism looked like pre-Reformation Christianity, aggravated by the typical practices of popular Catholicism: the use and adoration of images, holy water, rosaries, relics, superstitious blessings, the sign of the cross. . . . In summary, the arguments were based on religious and doctrinal questions and the target was always the Catholic Church.[49]

Even when the subject was not linked directly to the religious question, the opportunity was not lost to highlight this conflict. For example, in an item published in the *A República* newspaper, we find

> A news item regarding an incident involving an Englishman named Stephen Henderson, a poor man and the father of a large family. He was crossing a ford in a river and sustained an injury. Joaquim Mamede da Costa and Miguel Severino do Monte, who were passing in a train, organized a collection to pay for the hospital expenses. The text highlights that there were only a few people who did not contribute, among them some fathers from the Providencia.[50]

HE PREACHED TO AN EAGER MULTITUDE THAT FILLED THE ROOM: PROSELYTIZATION

> *Every man is a slave when, instead of believing in Christ in*
> *order to be saved, he is obedient to God's commands, follows*
> *the rituals and ceremonies of the Church, and keeps holy days*
> *and holy weeks.*[51]

Proselytization, an attempt developed by the Protestants to convert Catholics, became a constant practice and a permanent strategy. Naturally this position taken by Protestantism from the beginning of its implantation in Brazil contributed considerably to the creation of direct conflict with Catholicism, since it involved replacing principles of faith and religious practices that were deeply rooted in Brazilian society.

All the missionaries and Brazilian pastors carried out proselytizing practices, convincing Catholics to abandon the Catholic Church and embrace Protestantism. For them, Protestantism represented a true alternative religion and Protestant preaching was reduced almost entirely to confronting the Catholic doctrines and practices with their Protestant counterparts, always stressing the invitation to abandon the way of error and enter into possession of the truth.

This religious fervor, which brought to this *mission* a sense of "otherness" that was almost Hebraic, was accompanied by an undisguised proselytic Americanism represented powerfully by the North American missionaries. A Protestant religiosity bearing the marks of North American society was being proclaimed to the Brazilians.

Directly or indirectly, the polemic entered into by Protestantism and Catholicism nearly always contained some proselytizing aspect. The Methodist missionary Daniel Kidder, one of several who carried out identical activities, states, "The enterprise of circulating Bibles and evangelical tracts was not overlooked during my residence there. All providential openings for doing good were gladly embraced, and arrangements were made to establish the scriptures on sale, with tracts for gratuitous distribution." [52]

At the end of a long conversation with Father Feijó,[53] the Methodist missionary asked the former regent what he and the other priests thought about their distribution of Bibles among the populace. Very pleased with the encouraging response, Kidder reports that he could hardly sleep that night, so gripped was he by the evidence of the goodness and providence of God, who had guided his footsteps in the direction of the person who would be most able to help in the fulfillment of his mission.[54] Following the example of other missionaries, Dr. Kalley also engaged in an immense proselytizing activity and was involved in a boisterous debate.[55] Despite this and other argumentative encounters, Kalley was accused on innumerable occasions of maintaining a position that was considered overly cautious.[56]

The missionary activity developed by the ex-priest José Manoel da Conceição was not focused on proselytization. Justifiably, Boanerges Ribeiro claims that the Reverend Conceição "did not organize churches, nor is he known to have received anyone at all into the Presbyterian communion." [57] Ribeiro claimed that Conceição did not want the establishment of a "Protestant Church transplanted from another race and culture, a different tradition and temperament; rather, he sought a deep reforming movement linked to Biblical enlightenment that would make possible the creation of a Brazilian Christianity." [58]

In general terms, Protestant behavior during the time of its implantation in Brazil was directed toward a practice of proselytization, since almost the whole of Brazilian society was symbiotically tied to the Catholic Church. The difficulties met were many and the converts few, considering the amount of labor expended. Consequently, the proselytizing activity carried out by Protestantism failed to produce any impact or great repercussion. [59]

As an example, we can point to the struggle of a certain Methodist pastor who traveled in one region conducting weddings and visits and delivering sermons. He describes the work carried out during a week in April 1887. On the 16th he went as far as Palmeiras and in the evening he preached in S. João da Lagoinha; after the service he conducted the wedding of Antônio José Barbosa and Maria Rosa da Conceição; he preached at Palmeiras in the evening of the following day; on the 18th he traveled to the plantation of Captain Modesto de Campos and preached to a congregation of more than fifty, including many slaves from the plantation; on the 21st he went to the plantation of Eduardo de Campos, staying there for two days, preaching twice to a large group. [60] This was the strategy adopted by Protestantism in order to penetrate Brazilian society. A broad proselytizing activity was carried out, conducting worship services in homes and any other available space, inviting the Catholics to participate.

Protestantism was confronted by many difficulties in the labor of implantation. Of these, two can be highlighted: the small number of people engaged in the work, and the careful policing undertaken by factions within Catholicism. [61]

NOTES

1. Letter dated August 1868 from Joe McGee, an immigrant living in Santarém, to the editor of *Brazilian Reflector*, an American journal edited in the south of Brazil, disputing the news that the colony was in decline. (See Guilhon, *Confederados em Santarém*, 103.)

2. An example of this enthusiastic welcome is the defense of the Colégio Piracicabano, a Methodist school established in September 1881 in the city of Piracicaba, delivered by Rangel Pestana in the São Paulo Provincial Assembly. The city's inspector of educational institutions decided to close the Protestant school, alleging its failure to conform to two rules by having mixed gender classes and also having no teacher to teach the religion of the state. In his address, Rangel Pestana argued that the "reactionary inspector was, in the name of the state religion, compromising a useful institution with a

well-deserved reputation for its services in the spreading of education." (See "Fechamento do Colégio Piracicabano," *Methodista Catholico* (15 March 1887): 1.)

3. Mendonça, "Incorporación del protestantismo y la cuestión religiosa en Brasil," 42.

4. Ibid.

5. A.R. Crabtree, *História dos Batistas no Brasil: até o ano de 1906*. 2nd ed. (Rio de Janeiro: Casa Publicadora Batista, 1962), 69-70.

6. Ribeiro, *Protestantismo no Brasil Monárquico*, 184.

7. The concern over education was one of the priorities of missionary work. The nature and depth of the changes that the missionaries desired to introduce in society demanded literate converts. It was indispensable that a Protestant at least be able to read the Bible and certain religious literature. Vincente Themudo Lessa supplies much information about publications sponsored by Protestantism in Brazil. (V.T. Lessa, *Annaes da Primeira Egreja Presbyteriana de São Paulo (1863-1903): subsídios para a história do protestantismo* (São Paulo: Edição da Primeira Egreja Presbyteriana Independente de São Paulo, 1938), 229-236.)

8. E.C. Pereira, *Imprensa Evangélica* (17 October 1879): 329-330.

9. "Viagem imperial," *O Methodista Catholico* (1 December 1886): 3.

10. J.C. Rodrigues, "Uma tarefa gloriosa," *Imprensa Evangélica* (23 April 1872): 115.

11. H.C. Tucker, *Dr. José Carlos Rodrigues (1844-1923)-a brief sketch of his life* (New York: American Bible Society, n.d.), 24-36.

12. [Bible school is the translation of *escola paroquial*, which literally means "parish school," but the context makes clear that "bible school" is a more accurate rendition. The word *colégio* will be translated as "regular school," meaning a school meeting Monday to Friday with a wide list of subjects taught. Trs.]

13. J.C.Pereira, "Os meios próprios para plantar o reino de Jesus Christo no Brasil," *Imprensa Evangélica* (25 January 1881): 7. It is important to note that this document was read by the missionary Ashbel Simonton before the Presbytery of Rio de Janeiro, 16 July 1867.

14. E.C. Pereira, "O romanismo e o progresso."

15. "Que lugar deve ocupar a escola no trabalho de um evangelista?" *Imprensa Evangélica* (19 December 1878): 401. It is important to note that this reasoning was quite widely disseminated in Protestant circles. Stewart deplored the fact that Brazil had not been settled by Protestants: "With the wealth and power and increasing prosperity of the United States before us as the fruits, at the end of two hundred years, of the colonization of a few feeble bands of Protestants. . . there is no presumption in the belief that, had a people of similar faith, similar morals, similar habits of industry and enterprise, gained an abiding footing in so congenial a climate and on so exuberant a soil, long ago, the still unexplored and impenetrable wildernesses of the interior would have bloomed and blossomed in civilization as the rose, and Brazil from the sea coast to the Andes become one of the gardens of the world." (C.S. Stewart, *Brazil and La Plata: the personal record of a cruise* (New York, G.P. Putnam & Co., 1856), 85-86.)

16. [The word *"ingênuo"* has been left untranslated throughout this text since it defies accurate replacement with a single word. It is used to identify a child of slaves born after the promulgation of the Law of the Free Womb and who was, by this legislation, born free, but had an obligation to provide service to the mother's master for 21 years. The term *ingênuos* was used to distinguish these children from *libertos*, that is

slaves freed by, say, manumission or "self-purchase." This law, passed in 1871, is also referred to as the Rio Branco Act since it was introduced by the administration of the Viscount Rio Branco. Trs.]

17. "Os ingênuos," *Imprensa Evangélica* (4 April 1881): 115.

18. J.C. Rodrigues, "Idéias de religião," *O Novo Mundo* (23 October 1873): 3.

19. Ibid.

20. J. Nelson, "A festa de Nazareth e o jogo," *A Republica.* (11 November 1886): 3.

21. Speaking of the characteristics of the Brazilian male, Sérgio Buarque de Hollanda cites the Methodist missionary Daniel P. Kidder and speaks about the aversion of Brazilians to ritualism. See S.B. Hollanda, *Raízes do Brasil,* (Rio de Janeiro: José Olympio, 1977), 112. Koster asserts the following: "It should be recollected that we are living among a people who are deeply riveted to their own forms and ceremonies of worship, whose devotedness to their church establishment surpasses every other feeling." (Koster, *Travels in Brazil,* 2:224-225.)

22. Ewbank, *Life in Brazil,* 238.

23. "Os dous systemas," *Imprensa Evangélica,* (1 September 1877): 132.

24. Ibid.

25. Burton, *Explorations of the Highlands of the Brazil,* 1:406.

26. Kidder, *Sketches of Residence and Travels in Brazil,* 1:143.

27. Ibid., 1:138. [Samples of letters can be found in appendix D to Kidder, *Sketches of Residence and Travels in Brazil,* vol.1. Trs.]

28. Ibid., 1:140.

29. A.G. Simonton, "A morte e o futuro estado dos justos," *Imprensa Evangélica,* 1868.

30 J. Nelson, "A redenção da Amazônia," *A República* (23 January 1887): 3.

31. Ibid.

32. In an article published in the same newspaper, the Methodist missionary attacked the Feast of Nazareth and gambling. "It must be confessed that gambling is the main support of the Feast of Nazareth. This is asserted by the festival-goers themselves. It is called a religious festival. . . . Every good man admits that gambling is an evil—a plague on morality; and nowhere in the world is it less poorly suited than to the festivity of Nazareth. The pulpit of the church of Nazareth ought to be the first to promote the abolition of gambling. Yet, how much does it do to this end? It receives several milréis for its share in this massive exploitation of the superstitions and vices that are the focus of the festival, and then it remains silent. Any religion that does not promote morality is from the devil. The Christian religion combats vice in all its forms and does not consent to being associated with sin." (J. Nelson, "A festa de Nazareth e o jogo," *A República* (11 November 1886):3.) It is important to point out that this article was reprinted in *Methodista Cathólico* (22 December 1886): 3-4.

33. "Deportação," *A República* (17 November 1886): 3. [The final phrase is a play on the expression "*Ainda há juizes em Berlim*" [There are still judges in Berlin]. The phrase is the concluding comment in the eighteenth century account of a mill owner who refuses to accept that Frederick II of Prussia had the right to destroy his mill in order to improve the view from the palace. The mill owner placed his trust in the legal process. The article in *O Liberal* indicates that such trust would be misplaced in Brazil. Trs.]

34. Nelson, "A Redenção da Amazônia," 3.

35. Koger, "The country and people of Brazil," *The Gospel in All Lands* (20 July 1882): 27.

36. E.C. Pereira, "O romanismo e o progresso," *Imprensa Evangélica* (21 November 1885): 170.

37. T. Bastos, *Cartas do Solitário* (São Paulo: Cia. Editora Nacional, 1938), 116.

38. Ribeiro, *Protestantismo no Brasil Monárquico*, 20. The author comments on the meeting of Simonton with Kalley. See also Vieira, *O Protestantismo, a Maçonaria e a Questão Religiosa no Brasil*, 113-133.

39. "Os dous systemas," *Imprensa Evangélica*, (1 September 1877): 132

40. J.L.R. Agassiz and E.C.Agassiz, *A Journey in Brazil* (Boston: Tichnor and Fields, 1868), 180.

41. Ibid., 496.

42. E.C. Pereira, *O Problema Religioso da América Latina: estudo dogmático-histórico* (São Paulo: Empresa Editora Brasileira, 1920).

43. Ibid., 400-405.

44. Ibid., 400.

45. E.C. Pereira, *Imprensa Evangélica*, (17 October 1879): 329-330.

46. Earlier we showed that Brazilian pastors developed proselytizing activities. In the specific case of ex-priest José Manoel da Conceição we are able to say that this activity was not developed in a conventional form, that is, his concern was not for gathering new members into his Protestant denomination, but rather to bring them to a knowledge of Jesus Christ in the Protestant form that he had adopted.

47. Ribeiro, *Protestantism no Brasil Monárquico*, 117.

48. Ibid., 109.

49. An item from the *Catecismo Evangélico* is evidence of the bitterness of the debate. "What is meant by the term 'Protestant'?" Answer: "Whoever protests against the false doctrines and practices of the Apostate Church of Rome." See "Catecismo Evangélico," *O Presbiteriano* (March 1908): 3.

50. Nelson, "A Redenção da Amazônia," 3.

51. "Sois escravos ou livres?" *Imprensa Evangélica* (20 June 1878): 194.

52. Kidder, *Sketches of Residence and Travels in Brazil*, 1:321.

53. [Diogo Antônio Feijó, 1784-1843, was ordained to the Roman Catholic priesthood in 1809 but is better known for his political career. The General Assembly elected him Sole Regent in October 1835 during the minority of Dom Pedro II. He resigned from the office in September 1837. Trs.]

54. Ibid., 2:314-317.

55. Bastos, *Cartas do Solitário,* 111-117.

56. "Neither the Reverend Simonton nor his colleague the Reverend Blackford were able to appreciate the reasoning on which Dr. Kalley based his methods and conduct employed in the evangelization of Brazil. . . . The principal reason for this *modus operandi* was the experience he acquired during the significant work of evangelization which he started on the island of Madeira—so pleasant and full of hope at the outset and which, nevertheless, was almost rooted out (thanks to an imprudent publication). He had no wish to experience again great publicity, and its consequences, interrupting his labors and vexing his co-workers. . . . Indeed! With his experience he knew perfectly well that all Protestant propaganda is watched carefully and all the news sections of evangelical newspapers are scrutinized minutely by those who prefer that ignorance of the truth

prevail over the saving light that is found in Jesus Christ." Rocha, *Lembranças do Passado*, 2:34-35.

57. Ribeiro, *Protestantismo no Brasil Monárquico*, 129.

58. Ibid., 206.

59. In the opinion of Professor Mendonça, "This contact was weak and fragmented and Brazil was a long way from being Protestant." (Mendonça, *O Celeste Porvir*, 141.) On the other hand, Vieira speaks of "the threat of a Protestant invasion," providing minute detail. (Vieira, *Protestantism and the Religious Question in Brazil* (Ann Arbor, Michigan: University Microfilms, 1977), 531-651.) The newspaper *O Novo Mundo*, for its part, reprinted the concern expressed in a São Paulo newspaper "complaining bitterly about the large number of proselytes that their Protestant missions had won in the province." (J.C. Rodrigues, "Idéias de religião," *O Novo Mundo* (23 October 1873): 3.)

60. "Noticiário," *Methodista Catholico* (1 April 1887): 4.

61. Rodrigues drew up a balance sheet on the fiftieth anniversary of Brazilian independence, showing that little progress was made in the moral/religious area during this time. "Today, the Gospel is not read or understood any more than it was in 1822. We believe it accurate to say that the Holy Scriptures have never been printed in Brazil, and we, who have had martyrs of all kinds, for whom the bards weave new laurels every year, we have never had a Brazilian layman dedicate himself exclusively to the sacred and glorious work of spreading the good news of salvation through Jesus Christ. The religious teaching given to our youth is a calamitous fraud committed against the best and holiest impulses of their hearts. Not only is it scanty; it is also based more on human traditions, superstitions regarding hell and purgatory and thousands of lesser gods, than it is on faith in the great work of Jesus Christ, and that which he taught to the sons of men. . . . In Brazil, there is much slavery beyond that of the Africans and their descendants." (J.C. Rodrigues, "Meio século," *O Novo Mundo* (23 August 1872): 186.)

CHAPTER III

"SLAVERY IS LIKE A THORN THAT PENETRATES THE FLESH AND CAUSES EXCRUCIATING PAIN BUT WHICH WE DO NOT WANT TO PULL OUT, FOR FEAR THAT THE OPERATION WILL FURTHER INCREASE THE PAIN": THE INSTITUTIONAL PROTESTANT MESSAGE AND SLAVERY

COMPARE THE BLACK IN AFRICA, IN HIS CANNIBALISM AND APPALLING CONDITION, TO OUR SLAVE: AMERICAN PROTESTANTISM AND SLAVERY

> *For two years they have been successfully preaching the faith and winning proselytes for Methodism, corrupting the children and slaves of Catholics. These misguided parents and masters entrusted them with teaching and indoctrinating their children and slaves without themselves knowing what they were learning in the Bible and Sunday schools.*[1]

In order to understand the content of the institutional message of the Protestantism implanted in Brazil, especially by the North American Methodist, Presbyterian and Baptist missionaries, it is essential to explain the position of these churches toward slavery in their native land. It is not possible to speak of American Protestantism as if it were homogeneous. "North" and "South" were more than simple geographic designations. There were deep economic, political, social and cultural differences between these two regions.

By the middle of the nineteenth century, the institution of black slavery in the United States had existed for three centuries and was already deeply rooted. The big change occurred when, by the initiative of John Rolfe, the cultivation of tobacco began. Since tobacco required a greater amount of manual labor, the importance of labor from Africa started in 1619. This was the beginning of the slave-based society that came to characterize Virginia and other southern states.

The religious zeal of Puritanism lost its force in the midst of these new conditions of relative prosperity. The Puritan principle of the value of work lost its validity with the increase in slavery. The Anglican Church continued being the church of the majority in the colonies, not because it adhered to an Anglicanism with Puritan tendencies as in the early years, but rather because it offered an easy-going aristocratic Anglicanism adapted to the emerging slave-owning society.

The Anglicans carried out little missionary work among the slaves. One of the reasons was the existence of deep-rooted principles that forbade having a slave as a brother in faith. Therefore, there were those who said that anyone who had been baptized could not continue to be subjugated in slavery. This in turn meant that the plantation owners had an interest in avoiding the conversion of their slaves.

In 1667, in light of the debate that was taking place, a law was promulgated [in Virginia] that stated that baptism did not change a slave's condition of servitude. This fact confirms the way in which the religious establishment adapted itself to the prevailing socio-economic-political interests. Notwithstanding that this law took care of the slave labor issue, little was done to educate or convert the slaves because many thought that to keep them in ignorance was one of the best means of being assured of their services and docility.

At the beginning of the nineteenth century, new social and economic forces of dizzying proportions developed in the United States. This development can be traced principally to the following:

1) growth in population, especially as a result of immigration;
2) rapid expansion of the frontier;
3) founding of new cities and the formation of a network of permanent domestic trade;
4) development of a transportation system;
5) organization of finance firms to support industrial development and the creation of inventions that were applied in various sectors of industry;
6) forming and accumulation of great fortunes arising from the development of railroads and unbridled land speculation;
7) discovery of new sources of wealth such as gold and oil; and
8) creation of a new social stratum - the urban social class.

The development of social and economic forces did not occur in the same way in all parts of the country. Thus, it is of fundamental importance to know something of the characteristics of each of these two large regions, since we know that in Brazil the dominant influence on the missions was southern Protestantism. The economy in the South of the United States was predominantly rural, whereas the North was engaged in a process of rapid industrial development. This regionalization into two large areas developed along political and economic lines.

In truth, there was no chain of mountains, no great river, no physical obstruction, nor any natural frontier separating the South from the North. Thus, the South was never a unique or monolithic region, easy to distinguish and describe. It was always a random collection of geographically distinct sub-regions.[2] What has been sought are common factors among the southern states that can be identified as generating a distinct identity. Beyond the rural-agricultural and city-industrial characterization present in the South and North respectively, the most accepted means of differentiation focuses on the absence or presence of black slaves.[3]

Up to a certain date, probably prior to 1830, a good proportion of southerners considered slavery a necessary evil.[4] As the years advanced and the northerners' abolitionist propaganda exerted pressure, there began to be frequent attempts to secure the means of justifying slavery. We can say that from this time to the outbreak of the Civil War, a good proportion of the intelligentsia of the South was committed to the task of defending the practice of slavery. There came a time when the maintenance of slavery was important not only for underpinning the economic structure, but was also indispensable for the survival of the entire socio-cultural ideological apparatus that had grown up around slavery.[5]

It can be said that throughout the conflict, what prevailed was the defense of the interests of the large slave owners, the instigators and inspirers of the idealizations and justifications that brought the rest of society into the search for explaining the practice of slavery and into the campaign defending what were considered the rights of the South. Pseudo-scientific arguments were advanced to prove that black slaves belonged to an inferior race particularly adapted to agricultural work. The Bible and the Federal Constitution were constantly cited as sanctioning the practice of slavery. The argument most frequently made was that slave owners were guided by profoundly paternalistic principles and, as a result, the slaves experienced better conditions than if they had remained in Africa.

As a secondary development, this ideology justifying slavery took on its own formulation expressed in moral and religious terms. According to the southerners, the abolitionists were no better than whited sepulchers, filthy within, pious hypocrites interested only in destroying the political influence of the South in order to impose their own oppression and thus degrade the South, which was independent, cultured and enlightened. For southerners concerned with morality, accusing others of sin was unsuited to those who worshiped the god of riches and who tolerated paid slavery that was worse than black slavery. For the northerners, on the other hand, the southerners were sinners and deserved the punishments of hell. The more extreme and radical called for intervention from a severe and just God to destroy the Sodom and Gomorrah of the South.

Historically, the abolition campaign had its beginnings in 1835, with the formation of numerous organizations in an anti-slavery torrent that had enormous impetus and influence and had mobilized all the humanitarian ideas of the enlightenment, transcendentalism, and Christian theology, of free thinkers, workers' unions, and social utopians, and of political and literary romanticism.[6]

In the South, a climate was evolving that encompassed the racial supremacy of the white man and the irremediable inferiority of the colored races. In Puritan theocracy there was the conception of whites as an elect people. There were also

Calvinist sentiments among the successive waves of immigrants, as well as the sectarian character of all Protestant thought, which set up barriers between groups or denominations. In addition, there was the aggressive character ascribed to federalism and localism, neutralizing the egalitarian effect of the politics of the national state, plus the extreme isolation of rural communities, which allowed the persistence of superstitions, myths and prejudices, around which converged passions and personal interests. Finally, there was the spread of science-based trends of vague generalizations that were easily popularized among people who were semiliterate. By virtue of these unique historical circumstances, it was possible for the racial doctrine advocated in the South to find fertile ground.

Therefore a strong animosity arose between the two groups, North and South. On both sides there were the same moral imperatives, the same religious enthusiasm. Thus, the southerners claimed that slavery was a Christian institution recognized by the Scriptures in both the Old and New Testaments. Hence, the South, rather than sinful, was conducting itself as a benevolent and God-fearing society that took on the mission of teaching Christ's Gospel to the pagans, offering them the means of salvation.

Inevitably, there were far-reaching consequences for the life of the nation. The southerners elaborated intellectual defenses of slavery, developing the theory by which slavery was a positive good. So much so that they rejected the theory of John Locke, who affirmed that natural law repudiated slavery; likewise the nation's Declaration of Independence, which stipulated, "Freedom is the inalienable right of all men." They adhered instead to the Aristotelian philosophy that extolled the fact of some being born to dominate and others to be dominated.

The Protestant presence in the United States had always been very strong from the beginning of colonization. While the nascent aristocracy continued loyal mainly to Anglicanism, the lower stratum of society was inclined toward dissenting movements.

Since the purpose of this work is not to describe the specific thinking on the theme of black slavery in each Protestant church of the United States, what can be done is to choose one of the churches and provide a summary of its position on the topic. The Methodist Church is the most appropriate choice since, in the period between the end of the eighteenth century and the first half of the nineteenth, this was the movement that succeeded in achieving the most progress through recruitment of an extraordinary number of adherents.

Shortly before 24 May 1738, the date of the religious experience of the Englishman John Wesley and the birth of the Methodist movement, Wesley had already expressed his opposition to slavery several times. In his diary on 23 April 1737 during a stay in North America, he records a friendly conversation he had with a young slave. Upon recognizing her deep interest in the biblical teachings he delivered, Wesley noted in his diary, "The attention with which this poor creature listened to instruction is inexpressible." [7]

A similar experience occurred the following week. John Wesley observed that a young slave bore on his body deep signs of the oppression of slavery. The plantation owner, Mr. Bellinger, had sent a young slave to accompany Wesley to Purrysburg, South Carolina. On seeing him, Wesley recognized that there was before him only half a person because so little remained of the individual. Deeply troubled, Wesley lamented the poor lives that "were vilely cast away, through oppression, through divers plagues and troubles!" [8]

In his contact with this slave, the founder of the Methodist movement perceived his great interest in learning the Gospel lessons, just as had happened with the young slave woman. As a result of these meetings, Wesley began thinking of a plan for evangelization aimed at reaching black slaves. He concluded that one of the most effective means of teaching Christianity would be to seek out some conscientious plantation owners who were willing to cooperate and inquire if they owned slaves who knew the English language. After this first stage, the next task would be "to go to [these slaves], from plantation to plantation, staying as long as appeared necessary." He indicates that he had been with three or four plantation owners in the Carolinas who had shown a willingness to participate in his project.[9]

These first encounters are significant since they reveal the position of John Wesley and Methodism on this question. Beyond an interest in the task of catechism and an effort toward admitting black slaves into the bosom of the Methodist movement, John Wesley also strongly opposed the trade in African slaves, forming the Society for the Suppression of the Slave Trade. He agreed completely with the position adopted in 1772 by Lord Mansfield, who stated, "that as soon as ever a slave set his foot upon English territory he came free." [10]

Wesley's convictions were fundamental in shaping the anti-slavery mentality of North American Methodism. The first Methodist conferences in the United States continued to reflect this commitment. At the Baltimore Conference held in 1780, which was attended by seventeen Methodist pastors, a declaration was composed as follows, "slavery is contrary to the laws of God, man, and nature - hurtful to society; contrary to the dictates of conscience and pure religion, and doing that which we would not others should do to us and ours."[11]

At the same conference a rule was approved that prohibited possession of slaves by members of the Methodist Church. Where slaves were owned, they had to be freed and not sold. Those who did not comply with this decision were to be expelled: "Try those in Virginia another year, and suspend the preachers in the states of Maryland, Delaware, Pennsylvania, and New Jersey."[12] At the Christmas Conference held in 1784 the subject was discussed again, and as a result a decision was taken to "extirpate this abomination from among us." This time a period of one year was given for either compliance with the decision or leaving the Methodist Church.[13] However, this new discussion of the topic showed that the issue was not as easily resolved as the Baltimore Conference had wanted.

The positions of John Wesley and others adopted at several conferences confirm that from the beginning of its implantation in the United States the Methodist Church showed itself deeply against the regime of black slavery, demanding obedience from its leaders and other members. Beyond this, it undertook great efforts geared toward conducting missions among the slaves, receiving them as regular members in their communities.

In the South toward the end of the eighteenth century, signs of discord in relation to slavery were more frequent. In 1795 in South Carolina a group of twenty-three Methodist preachers signed a document recognizing the "intrinsic impropriety and evil of slavery and its harmful consequences for society." The tenor of this document was that preachers ought to free their slaves if they could do so legally, and if this was not possible, "pay them for their work and seek their liberty." [14]

The Great Awakening was a movement of spiritual revival that saw the conversion of thousands—slave and non-slave—and signified a phase of great expansion for Methodism.[15] Many blacks, both slaves and non-slaves, became pastors and achieved work of great influence among their fellow blacks. There was the case of Harry Hoosier, or Harry "Black," who gained his freedom at a young age. After his conversion following a sermon by Francis Asbury, he came to accompany this Methodist bishop on many of his missionary journeys. Contemporaries described Hoosier as an eloquent preacher and Thomas Coke came to consider him "one of the best preachers in the world." [16]

Innumerable black pastors played distinguished roles in the history of the Methodist Church. Among these can be mentioned Richard Allen, who worked in Pennsylvania and New Jersey; Henry Evans, who organized the Methodist Church in Fayetteville, North Carolina; John Stewart, missionary among the Wyandot Indians in Ohio; and Jarena Lee, a passionate preacher of the Gospel.[17] The number of blacks in the Methodist Church grew at a dizzying rate. In 1786, the first year for which statistics identify the race of its members, among the total of 18,791 Methodists there were 1,890 blacks, which is more than 10%. By 1790, this number had grown to 11,682 and, in 1797 there were 12,215, representing almost a quarter of the total membership.[18]

The rapid growth of Methodism in the southern states brought with it a resistance to the ideas defended by John Wesley and his first leaders. The strong anti-slavery position adopted in the first phase of the establishment of Methodism in the United States soon lost ground to attitudes of a different nature, aimed at being conciliatory and accommodating toward economic and social realities. Less than a year after the declarations made at the Christmas Conference, another meeting in Baltimore suspended them. Thomas Coke attributed this to the great opposition and resistance encountered in certain regions. Another declaration issued in 1800 recommended that Methodist pastors be more cautious when tackling the issue. A letter sent to the General Conference of 1800 provoked the slave owners of the South and substantiated the reports that many itinerant pastors were emissaries and promoters of insurrections and rebellions. The letter said,

> We have long lamented the great national evil of negro slavery which has existed for so many years, and does exist in many of these United States...The whole spirit of the New Testament militates in the strongest manner against the practice of slavery, and the influence of the Gospel wherever it has long prevailed (except in many of these United States) has utterly abolished that most

criminal part of slavery, the possessing and using the bodies of many by the arbitrary will, and with almost uncontrollable power.[19]

Beginning at the outset of the nineteenth century, the official positions of the Methodist Episcopal Church recommended prudence. Bishop Francis Asbury recognized that missionary access to slaves had become more difficult as a consequence of the historical commitment of Methodists concerning abolition, concluding that this position caused the loss of a great number of members. Lamenting this situation, he showed that the Methodists were losing the opportunity to exercise influence with the slaves and stressed that the Methodist emphasis on emancipation was closing doors for missionary progress, in that there was a symbiotic relationship between society and the slavery model.[20]

Asbury, Coke and other leaders of Methodism discussed the question. At risk was the continuation of missionary work with the slaves. If there was an interruption, Asbury recognized that the harm to blacks would be much greater. In order for the plantation owners to once again allow the Methodist missions among the slaves, it would be necessary to change the catechism. The emphasis would need to be placed on the conversion and salvation of the slaves, rather than on their emancipation and equality in relation to whites.

From the beginning of the nineteenth century onward, movements causing discord and the repudiation of slavery became less frequent in the South. Missions among the slaves were developed with the single concern of carrying out the work of *evangelization*, without any aspiration toward emancipation. If on one hand this gradual adaptation by the Methodist Church to the new reality veered in a conservative direction, on the other hand the Methodist tradition itself and adherence to its principal antislavery rules presented extreme difficulties in their administration. Thus, there was a relative accommodation and tolerance, but not specifically an explicit or formal endorsement of slavery.

Contributing to the strengthening of this disposition to tolerance and coexistence we have the example of William Capers, a Methodist preacher in South Carolina who in 1815 decided to carry out an experiment with his slaves. Owner of a small farm with a few slaves, Capers was responsible for the pastoral care of a certain parish, or circuit, as it is called by the Methodists. Needing to be away for several months, he left the administration of his property to the slaves. According to the agreement, they would enjoy total freedom during this time, being able to do whatever they wanted. Upon returning after several months, Capers found the fences and the crops destroyed, the animals gone (eaten by the slaves) and the slaves hungry. From this experience, Capers concluded that slavery was the best alternative for them, since the blacks were a race of children, and that emancipation would bring them misfortune and misery.[21]

This was how the Methodist Church found a response to this conflict. Involvement with slavery came to be limited to caring for the spiritual well-being of slaves. The Methodist General Conference of 1824 strengthened this direction and announced that the work of pastors ought to be focused on making the owners responsible for the role they should play among their slaves, making sure that they prayed, read the Bible, and participated in religious services.[22]

A significant increase in this missionary work occurred in 1828, when Charles Baring, an important plantation owner in Combahee River, South Carolina, invited the Methodist pastors George W. Moore and Samuel W. Capers to preach to his slaves.[23] The results were considered very positive, and after this numerous plantation owners requested that the Methodist Church send missionaries to their plantations.[24]

In 1847, twenty-five Methodist pastors were working in seventeen missions organized by the South Carolina Conference. The plantation owners built the churches requested by the missionaries and contributed toward the payment of salaries and other mission expenses. An article published in the *Christian Advocate and Journal* described this positive cooperation between missionaries and plantation owners. In general, the Methodist missionaries experienced free access to the workers on the plantations and the work developed by them was praised by the plantation owners, since they were collaborating in the creation of a harmonious and productive climate.[25]

We find in the words of William Capers, now a Methodist bishop, a summary that illustrates quite well the task of most of the Methodist preachers in the southern United States. "Our missionaries inculcate the duties of servants to their masters, as we find these duties stated in the Scriptures. We hold that a Christian slave must be submissive, faithful, and obedient." [26]

Ignoring some small differences, it can be said that the behavior of the remaining Protestant churches in the southern states was very similar to that of the Methodist Church. Initially the evangelization of the slaves was marked by a concern for emancipation. It was recognized that there was an incompatibility between the Gospel and slavery. Later, as the southern economy evolved and came to depend more and more on the slave regime, and "slavery had become a cherished domestic institution interwoven with the very framework of society,"[27] a concern for the preservation of the economic model became the priority, giving rise to more restrictive laws and rules aimed at impeding the access of blacks to the evangelical faith.

With vigorous revival movements happening in the South, church membership increased dramatically. Many slave owners came to play a role in the churches and gradually assumed control.[28] The discussion on emancipation disappeared, to be replaced by a theology of spirituality that emphasized the "liberation of the soul." The northern abolitionists' accusation regarding this "mutilation of the Gospel" achieved nothing. Little by little this strategy, which consisted of winning over the trust of the landowners with the sincere objective of rendering spiritual aid to the slaves, moved beyond being only a strategy to become a means of social control. The slaves were taught docility and submission, emphasizing that the road to emancipation would have to remain in the hands of divine providence. Beyond the concern and zeal for the "souls" of the slaves, the expansion and growth of the Church was an important motive that drove Methodist efforts and de-emphasized any other scruples.[29]

This historical path laid out by Methodism in the southern states was strengthened by the doctrine of a Spiritual Church. Defended principally by J.H. Thornwell, this doctrine came to be widespread throughout the South. Its basic premise established that the fundamental principle of Holy Scripture is, "Give to Caesar what is Caesar's, and give to God what is God's." (Mark 12:17) Thus, political and social questions pertained to Caesar and spiritual questions such as conversion and behavior became part of the Church's concern. Thornwell claimed, "The Scriptures not only fail to condemn slavery, they as distinctly sanction it as any other social condition of man." [30] The strength of this doctrine lay in its supposedly biblical basis, such that to condemn slavery as a sin was the same as rejecting the Scriptures. On the basis of this principle it was proven that the anti-slavery opposition was incredulous, heretical and in opposition to the Bible.

The intensification of the conflict and the growing differentiation between North and South resulted in the breakup of the Protestant denominations and eventually of the nation itself. Among the Presbyterians, the division occurred in 1837. Out of the division arose the New School, which can be described as the evangelical front of the North, and the Old School, representing the more conservative wing of the South. The thesis defended by the Old School was not to discuss slavery, since, consistent with the doctrine of the Spiritual Church, this was a political question and therefore escaped the jurisdiction of the Church. The New School of the Presbyterian Church broke off in 1857, the Old School in 1861.[31] The two southern wings united in 1864 under the title of Presbyterian Church in the United States, and the two northern parts united between 1869 and 1870 with the name of the Presbyterian Church in the United States of America.

The Baptists divided in 1845. The essential and characteristic element of Baptist ecclesiology was the complete autonomy of the local congregation. However, with the creation of the Missionary Society, the Baptists evolved in the direction of a denomination. The domestic and foreign branches focused on missionary work had to discuss the problem of slavery. In the 1840s they began to oppose sending owners of slaves as missionaries, and in 1844-45 both organizations rejected slave-owning candidates. On the basis of this decision, the Baptists in the South met on 8 May 1845 in Augusta, Georgia and organized the Southern Baptist Convention or the Southern Baptist Church.[32]

Among the Methodists, the division occurred in the same period. In 1843, the Methodist Wesleyan Church of America was organized to include only non-slave-owning members and in 1845 there arose the Methodist Episcopal Church, South.[33]

On the other hand, the revival movement, which strengthened in 1858, introduced a large group of blacks into the Protestant churches. At this time before the Civil War, blacks participated in the same churches as whites, although they were segregated. This occurred in the North as well as in the South and is explained in part by the reluctance to allow slaves to create independent institutions, with all that this implied, and by the patriarchal responsibility carried out by the master among them. After the Civil War, the great majority of blacks who had converted to Protestantism organized their own churches.

A HOME WAS FOUND FOR THE SOUTHERNERS, A REFUGE FROM MISFORTUNE, A HOME NOT SADDENED BY SCENES OF GRIEF OR DEATH: IMMIGRATION INITIATIVES

> *As to the suitability of emigrating to Brazil, I believe it will depend entirely on the judgment of each person and on personal circumstances. If you have decided to emigrate, it would be difficult to find a better place to go to than Brazil. But if you are well and happy here and can bear the calamities of domination and are willing to adjust (as some people certainly are), perhaps it would be best to stay where you are. At the least, I think you would not like Brazil.[34]*

In the second half of the nineteenth century, there occurred in Brazil important changes of a social, political, economic, cultural and religious nature. The elements that brought about these changes have been discussed in Brazilian historiography and by foreign researchers of this subject. The differences in interpretation can be found mainly in questions of moving from servile manual labor to a wage system and of the restructuring of society in accordance with the new system.

Brazil's participation in the international economic sphere was limited to market production, using slavery and plantations. Of vital importance for the process of accumulating capital was the expansion and organization of consumer markets.

Pressure regarding abolition was intensified by Britain from the moment the Industrial Revolution began to take shape within its empire. The new demands of industrial capitalism, in terms of social and economic transformations, were imbedded in this liberal ideology's discourse. The viability of this system was linked directly to the formation of consumer markets for manufactured products and the supply of raw materials in bulk. Faced with this new scenario, slavery was condemned. For the theorists of liberalism, slavery came to be considered inhuman, and for those involved in the new economic order, it became an evil shackle.

Consistent with this new economic state of affairs, Britain invested with greater force in an attempt at socio-economically remodeling Brazil. Relating to the slavery question, the promulgation of the Aberdeen Law[35] officially blocked foreign trade in blacks, causing its substitution by an intensified domestic trade in slaves, which displaced servile manual labor from areas considered in decline to others undergoing open expansion.

The champions of the servile labor system, who had concentrated a large portion of their capital in slaves, reacted as "loyal" defenders of the system. Richard Francis Burton asserts that the large plantation owners, "some of them owners of three to four thousand slaves, were horrified when faced with the possibility of any sudden and premature means of depopulating their vast coffee, sugar, tobacco and cotton plantations." [36] For many of them the cost of servile labor was well below that of paid labor. The firm belief lingered that the modification of the system and the adjustment to a new international economic order could come about in a slow and gradual manner, without major traumatic solutions. Daniel P. Kidder himself, in the short time he was in Brazil, came to recognize this peculiarity of Brazilian society.

> Almost every step in Brazilian progress has been prepared by a previous grad-
> ual advance: she did not leap at once into self-government. She was raised from
> a colonial state by the residence of the Court from Lisbon, and enjoyed for
> years the position of a constituent portion of the Kingdom of Portugal. The pre-
> sent peaceful state of the Empire under D. Pedro II was preceded by the decade
> in which the capabilities of the people for self-government were developed
> under the Regency. The effectual breaking up of the African slave-trade is but
> the precursor of a more important step.[37]

A question that arose with great frequency each time the subject of an end to slave labor was addressed, was who would take their place. It is Kidder himself who reiterates this question, "If it be asked 'Who will be the laborers in Brazil when slavery is no more?' the reply is that [even though the noose of slavery be parted, the man and a better man yet exists;][38] the supply will come from Germany, Portugal, the Azores and Madeira, and other countries." Farther on, he includes immigrants from the South of the United States.[39] The editor of *O Novo Mundo* pondered the same topic, identifying the need in Brazil to overcome the prejudice with regard to work.

> Before we arrange for immigrants to come from afar, let us move our own peo-
> ple towards rural work, for they do nothing in the cities. Let us convince this
> multitude of candidates for public jobs that they degrade their own nature and
> nation upon exchanging the freedom of the owner, dependent only on himself
> and God, for servility and the torments of a life with no future, rendered sterile
> by the iron hand of Authority and by mean prejudices of a society corrupted by
> slave labor. Let us make men out of them, and let us make their wives wise,
> turning their eyes away from the costly garments that their husbands cannot af-
> ford, to the sublime spectacle of an industrious couple, making their living from
> the soil by the sweat of their brow and thus fulfilling the designs of the Most
> High.[40]

The scarcity of slave manual labor, the expansion of production and the inevitable need in the medium term to substitute for this manual labor, made possible, in the second half of the nineteenth century, the emergence of scattered experiments with paid immigrant labor.[41] In the 1840's, an attempt was made to establish non-slave labor with immigrants from Portugal, Switzerland, and Germany. The attempt was by Senator Nicolau de Campos Vergueiro on his plantation in Ibicaba, in the Province of São Paulo. Between 1852 and 1855, this system was used on approximately thirty plantations, but it resulted in failure for a number of reasons.

The biggest problem was not the lack of economic viability of the new process, but rather the inability to relate to a rural proletariat on a purely contractual basis. Major problems, disputes and desertions arose as the workers became aware of the rule of submission to which they were subjected. In addition, increased inflation and the leveling-off of the price for exported coffee added to the debts that workers owed to plantation owners. This created a climate of revolt by the immigrants and the governments of their countries of origin. The lack of success in these experiments brought about a period of economic stagnation and a delay in immigration to Brazil.

The failure of the experiment did not alarm most of the plantation owners since they were able to benefit from the slave system through the trade of blacks between provinces. Experiments were carried out with differing wages paid to workers, but the truth is that the plantation owners were able to delay the intensive use of immigrant workers not only because they could count on a supply of slaves through domestic trading, but also because they considered this system less onerous and more lucrative.

Pressured by a series of domestic politico-economic occurrences, the immigration movement was revitalized in the 1870s. The 1871 Law of the Free Womb declared the freedom of the children born of slaves in Imperial Brazil, addressed the situation of the *ingênuos* after their birth, regulated the compensation for the slave owners, and determined how the law would be implemented. Attention then returned to the question of immigration.

The disdain for the native-born laborer, the indigenous Indian, and the free black was absolute, and they were all socially marginalized. For Tavares Bastos, freeing up immigration was the solution to the country's fundamental problem. The decried incompatibility of these native workers with the realities of the new market place characterized their inferiority. From this perspective, such social groups were rejected, disqualified or stifled: the black was disorganized and dangerous, the Indian was barbaric and violent, and the *sertanejo*[42] was lazy. Only the immigrant was seen as suitable for the new economic situation, sufficiently valued regarding specific bourgeois virtues: he was honest, industrious, literate and law-abiding.

At the end of the 1860s, with a considerable reduction in the number of European immigrants, the Imperial government turned to immigrants from North America and Poland. According to the sponsors of this new contract labor, these new immigrants would bring substantial improvements in agriculture, would offer important contributions in new planting techniques and, in the case of the Americans from the South, would impart to the Brazilian farmers their knowledge of the cultivation of cotton. José Carlos Rodrigues, editor of *O Novo Mundo* and an enthusiastic supporter of immigration to Brazil by Americans from the South, emphasized the contribution of this migration as being of fundamental importance to Brazilian agriculture. His enthusiasm was based on what he called the "Farmer's Creed."

> American farmers, out of long experience shaped by unremitting vigilance, were able to develop what can be called the Farmer's Creed. It is very popular in that country and it should be in Brazil too, so that the laws of farming become well known. It says: "We believe that the soil, like its steward, enjoys eating and so should be well manured. We believe in large harvests, and that they make the soil and the owner richer than they were. We believe that all

agriculture should be overseen by a good farmer. We believe that the primary fertilizer of any soil is an industrious, enterprising and intelligent spirit, and without it, lime, guano, and manure are of little value. We believe in good fences, good places of abode, good orchards, and enough children to harvest the fruit. We believe in a clean kitchen with a neat wife; we believe in a good pantry and in a clean conscience." We hope that soon Brazilians will unite to these articles of faith, as first and foremost, the following: We believe in free labor and only in free labor.[43]

Coming from a different perspective, one can consider that the proposed immigration to Brazil by Americans from the South had another motivation. Unlike the motivation flaunted by the Brazilian liberals, there were socially conservative elements, especially from the South of the United States, who viewed with optimism the Imperial Brazilian government's backing of immigration and large-scale ownership of slaves.

There was almost universal support for the arrival of North American immigrants. However, it is important to note that a variety of questions were raised indicating negative aspects of this immigration. Quintino Bocayuva, in a letter from the United States published in the newspaper *Diário do Gram Pará* on 1 April 1867, questioned this type of immigrant when he said that, "the man from the South, a ruined landowner who saves from the shipwreck the remains of his fortune, used to servile labor and, like us, having all the bad habits acquired in this type of industry, is never going to turn the soil and scatter the seed himself."

Bocayuva pointed out that the goal of these immigrants was to find in Brazil the same model to which they were accustomed before the Civil War. He was convinced that nearly all "hoped and wanted to find slaves to rent." For Bocayuva, Brazil's future depended on the emancipation of slaves.[44] Without abolition, these immigrants would continue to replicate the same model as Brazilian plantation owners.[45]

The immigration of North Americans to Brazil, especially southerners, was encouraged by the writings of travelers and the stories of Protestant pastors. The book *Sketches of Travels and Residence in Brazil*, written in 1845 by the Methodist missionary Daniel P. Kidder, became very popular in the southern United States. In another book, *Hunting a Home in Brazil*, James M. Gaston, a doctor from South Carolina, awakened great interest among southerners by telling of his travels in Brazil in 1865. In 1866, the Rev. Ballard S. Dunn, who also had the goal of attracting immigrants, wrote *Brazil, The Home for Southerners*. The Rev. Richard T. Henington, a Methodist, wrote innumerable enthusiastic letters that were published in his home newspaper, *The Copiahan*, of Crystal Springs, Mississippi. In one of these he goes so far as to recommend that his readers make due allowance for his information, since every time he hears news of the oppression prevailing in the South after the war, his enthusiasm increases in support of emigration to Brazil. In his letter of 14 March 1867, Henington claims:

The future promises nothing for us but poverty and humiliation for a long time to come. What can be expected from a conqueror who is oppressive and tyrannical in his crazed greediness? And are we to remain calm and satisfied when there is neither hope in the present nor assurance in the future for our lives, liberty, or property? . . . It is natural that we turn our backs on them and seek refuge and safety in another place, but where, ah, where? Some went to Mexico, but in vain. However, finally a door was opened. In many southern hearts hope gleamed and they rejoiced with this assurance: at last, a "home was found for the southerners," a refuge from misfortune, a home not saddened by scenes of grief or death.[46]

Certain newspapers from the South of the United States called this movement for emigration "Brazil fever." Norma Guilhon describes how all of the "Old South" became excited at the thought of emigrating to Brazil.[47] In contrast to Henington's ardent enthusiasm, several other voices were raised pointing out serious disadvantages awaiting the immigrant.   The Methodist J. J. Ransom commented in 1879:

I advise nobody to leave the United States to come to Brazil. The climate, the laws, the religion, the people, the language, every and each thing that affects your daily life, is so widely different from what you know, that you are almost sure to be discontented. Your children will lack the opportunities of education, and will be exposed to the most frightful perils on account of the corrupt life of all classes of society. . . . Nearly all the Americans in this country are poor, and I do not expect you to get rich by coming.[48]

Ransom's opinions, discouraging North American immigration to Brazil and saying that only adventurers and those living in misery should risk such a change, produced deep annoyance among the Baptists settled in the Santa Bárbara region.[49]

The southerners were encouraged by the prevailing system of large-scale slave ownership in Brazil. This is the conclusion of Henington when he affirms that "many immigrants came to Brazil thinking only about the possibility of using slave labor. For many this was the most powerful attraction in their desire to emigrate, impelled to come by their desire to recreate here, in some form, the lifestyle that existed 'in the immense rural community that was the antebellum South.'" This desire was increased by much propaganda in the newspapers that promised that in Brazil the North Americans "would not suffer the horrors of Reconstruction" and that in that country there were "points of view similar to those of the South." [50]

An argument that was quite encouraging was the possibility of reproducing and perpetuating the southern society demolished by the Civil War. As an example, one can point to a passage in a letter dated 18 May 1867 from Henington, with travel reports transcribed in Ballard Dunn's book *Brazil, The Home for Southerners*. "What really catches one's attention are the black slaves, just as it was in our country before the war. What existed there can also be found here. . . Today I attended a service in the English Church and heard a good sermon." Later, Henington mentions the land's fertility and returns to the topic of slaves, relating that "in his colony a slave can be obtained for eight hundred dollars."[51]

The reality was not quite as "rosy" as the Methodist missionary describes it. In fact, he himself suggested to his readers that they sufficiently scrutinize his assertions, ignoring the conclusions shaped by his personal enthusiasm. In the same book, he also speaks of the failed efforts of those who went to Brazil, achieved nothing and returned to the United States.[52]

The same conclusion was reached by James B. Bond, United States consul in Pará. After receiving innumerable complaints from immigrants regarding the Brazilian government's failure to honor its contract, he concluded that the real reason for these immigrants' failures was due entirely to their belief that it would be possible to reproduce in Brazil the same model of the antebellum South. According to him, the emigrant from the South who wanted to succeed in Brazil would have to leave his preconceived notions behind. "If he abandons his home only because he is indignant at the assertion of equal rights on the part of those who until recently were judged to have no rights at all, he will find here that the free black, or at least the black man born free, has all the privileges of a white citizen, and greater privileges than the white man if a foreigner." [53]

Societies were organized by those who were interested in emigration, with the objective of subsidizing a trip by representatives who would seek to verify the fertility of the land, the climate and the facilities offered by the Imperial Brazilian government. The Rev. Ballard Dunn, rector of St. Philip's Evangelical Church of New Orleans, was one of those representatives, coming to Brazil in 1865 shortly after the end of the Civil War. He traveled through the south of the country and decided to settle in Alto Jequiá, in the Province of São Paulo. Returning to the United States, he placed an announcement in newspapers, and wrote the book *Brazil, The Home for Southerners*, which was designed to entice southerners to come to Brazil. He also chartered a ship and brought immigrants at various times when he was in the United States.[54]

Geographically, North American immigration to Brazil took two different routes: to the north, to Pará, and to the south, especially to Rio de Janeiro and São Paulo. Henington explains that Rio de Janeiro became the meeting point for the Confederates, who remained there until they had decided which destination to head for or who wanted to purchase slaves. The exceptions were those who had traveled already knowing that they would settle in the north of Brazil.[55]

It is beyond question that this North American immigration had a distinctly religious hue. Joined with the questions of a political and economic nature were the messianic character of "Manifest Destiny" and the fulfillment of God's plans through the establishment of a new civilizing process. In an enthusiastic defense of the United States, José Carlos Rodrigues, editor of *O Novo Mundo*, reveals something of this messianic self-righteousness.

> The truth is that the grandeur as well as the beauty of the American government rests precisely on the fact that it does not join under the same institutions only a single nation, but rather all the nations on Earth. It is the embryo of the society of the future, the most perfect approximation to the reign of Christianity, which among men sees only the man, with the same hopes and with the same heritage. . . . It is not difficult to foresee that the future destined for America is to become the theatre of work for the men of the Old World. Just as Europe has been

the seedbed for mankind and ideas, America is destined to be the field where all this might be transplanted in order to blossom under that common sun of the "reign of the saints of the Most High" that Daniel saw so far off. (Daniel 7:21-26). Just as in former times when the Jews served to keep the Law of the Eternal until the arrival of the time when it would be spread among the nations, likewise now America is reserved to be the depositary of the Law of Christianity in its application to the governance of peoples, and to represent the image of the one people that all peoples of the future will become. This ideal is elevated, noble and powerful. It has the ability to dominate our entire political life, without ever being brought into doubt by myriad points of view, because it is sufficiently broad to encompass all order of ideas of those who have hope. It is truly as broad as it is infinite, like all thought that comes from Jesus Christ; an ideal able to attain all possible sacrifices from us, and to inspire our lives' entire path like a brilliant light that at the same time will be our happiness and our salvation. In art, good taste is developed through good models. Let us also educate ourselves with this ideal that the great master of humanity himself declared concerning the human family. Let us thus form a national character. Whatever our opinions about incidents relating to the course of things in this country, let us declare with one voice the great goal toward which we are headed. Let us cultivate this spirit, and let us have faith in the Gospel. Only thus will we gradually transform our national image in accordance with the light of the highest civilization; we will be able to arrive there soundly.[56]

The first groups of North Americans arrived in Brazil between 1866 and 1869. They settled in the region of Santarém (in the Province of Pará), in the valley of the Rio Doce (Province of Espírito Santo), in the valley of the Ribeira and in the municipality of Santa Bárbara (Province of São Paulo). In addition to these locations, there was some small interest in the city of Rio de Janeiro and in other regions in the Provinces of Pernambuco, Bahia, Minas Gerais and Paraná. In Pará, the experiment failed for a number of reasons, among them the complete lack of structures for preserving North American cultural elements, including the non-existence of Protestant churches that could reproduce cultural and religious aspects, in addition to the absence of family groupings compatible with the desired cultural model that could aid in the perpetuation of values.

In the south of Brazil a different geographical trajectory created conditions that were more favorable to shaping the singularity of North American immigration (climate, organized economic context, etc.). By 1870, in the colony of Santa Bárbara, the majority of the southern states were represented, even if reality did not correspond to the idealized image. In the initial decades following their establishment in Santa Bárbara, they showed a marked preference for agricultural activity. Small farmers, they kept their interests focused on agriculture, producing a variety of products on a small scale for their own consumption.

Among these immigrants, the great majority initially had been small landowners, preachers, small business owners, or military officers. A small number had been large landowners dedicated to one-crop farming and slavery who had lost everything in the War of Secession, or still owned their land but did not have sufficient capital for carrying on production under the new labor situation.

The idea of large landownership with one-crop farming, and consequently slavery, was present in the minds of the vast majority of the immigrant southerners

One can imagine the influence on candidates for immigration by texts like that of Richard Henington. In a letter published in August 1867 in the newspaper *The Copiahan*, his arguments were extremely seductive, reinforcing ideas present in the minds of that population. Henington claimed that it would be difficult for anyone to find a better place to emigrate.

> For the true Confederate, there are many advantages in Brazil: there four of the most important qualities of a country are joined in a most fortunate way—excellent land, wonderful water, a good climate and good government, in addition to other important factors. The slave system to which we are accustomed is strong, there are no high taxes and no military dictatorship. There are no equal rights for blacks enforced at the point of a sword; no usurpation of power; no violation of constitutional rights; no laws of eminent domain whereby one man can forcefully strip another of his property; no confiscation or oppression. Justice is meted out equally to all, and there is liberty, the major foundation of government. There we will find character and feelings more in accord with our own and, above all, that same tolerance and generosity found in southern gentlemen. Of merit is the manner in which men are judged: Brazilians value highly the character of people from the South and are ready to give them a warm welcome.[57]

Henington said the following about the amount of money required by a southerner to organize his new life in Brazil.

> I think that a man with a family of reasonable size is able easily to start his life with four or five hundred dollars and, after three or four years working about two hours each day, he will be able to acquire the same as if he worked here the entire day. For me it would be much better to work there, where I can get twenty-five *alqueires*[58] of corn per acre, than here, where I can get only twenty. Here, if I don't work myself, I have to deplete my limited capital and pay another person; but there the perspective is different—there are thousands of descendants of Indians and poor people who can be hired at a reasonable price and who will work a lot harder than the blacks here. Furthermore, if you have sufficient money, you can buy as many blacks as you want for work.[59]

THE TIME HAS COME WHEN BRAZIL OUGHT TO CAST OFF SLAVERY PERMANENTLY: ABOLITIONIST INITIATIVES

> *The law of Christianity, which we profess to follow, says that the black man is our brother; certainly we can delay our obedience to this law until we study it and convince ourselves of its truth. But when all is said and done, it is still the same divine law, holy and immutable; it is an essential relationship between us and blacks.*[60]

The boundless kindness, most mild temperament and pacific character of Brazilians—the generosity of slave masters.

Father Perereca, a radical Ultramontane priest, highlighted a portion of the report prepared by the Methodist Justin Spaulding, a missionary based in Rio de Janeiro. The priest observed that, "beyond the ravaging of souls," Methodism held "brazenly. . . secret plans regarding our slaves." The missionary's text said:

> What will be the final result of slavery, and when it will end in this country, is impossible to say. . . . All we can do is to be in the diligent and exceedingly discreet use of the means, watch the signs of the times, and enter every opening door of Providence, however small, is do them good. It will occur to everyone, the least acquainted with the nature of this subject, how much wisdom, even wisdom from above, one needs to conduct this part of the missionary work. Any inconsiderate and violent measures might fix and rivet upon [the slaves] the chains of bondage but the stronger and the longer. [61]

In the first half of the nineteenth century, the denunciation made by Father Perereca against these "hidden motives" found an echo within Brazilian society. To strengthen his argument, he explained that the scheme was identical to that achieved by the Anabaptists in Jamaica and Virginia, where much blood of whites and blacks had been shed in the early 1830s.[62] According to Father Perereca, the authorities needed to pay attention because the Methodists were followers of a doctrine affirming that the only subjugation should be to Jesus Christ and that no other authority, political or religious.

The Methodist mission led by Spaulding lasted only five years, being disbanded in 1841. Father Perereca's fears were not borne out. There was no opportunity for any abolitionist initiatives, much less one driven by a Protestant denomination. The protagonists in the struggle for abolition would not be the Methodists, nor Robert Kalley with his Congregational Church, and even less the Presbyterians with the pioneer Ashbel Simonton openly opposing the system of subjugation of slaves and lamenting profoundly the fact of finding himself "in the midst of the horrors of slavery." [63] The course of emancipation would follow its own unique path, with very little participation by the Protestants.

Another Methodist, the immigrant Richard Henington, who settled in Pará in the 1860s, alluded to this idiosyncrasy that was a part of the abolition process.

In Brazil slavery exists just as it existed here in the United States and it is not true that abolition has already been decreed there. The emperor does not have that power, and the legislature is not inclined to carry it through. A bill was introduced in the legislature to free slaves within twenty years, but it will be a while until blacks are freed. Yet, let us suppose that such an event will occur—I am certain that circumstances will prevent what happened here. Brazilians are not simple-minded and their government is better than people think.[64]

Even recognizing his interest in attracting immigrants to Brazil, the Methodist missionary's words about the progress of the process are quite accurate. In the second half of the century there was general consensus on the need to bring about abolition. The fuse was lacking to ignite the courageous and radical beginning to the process. While no such detonator appeared, the official movement crept along slowly, seeking to accommodate the innumerable interests concerned with black slavery.

For many, the conflict that occurred in the United States could repeat itself in Brazil. However, the true nature of Brazilian society, marked by an apparent consensus on the necessity of bringing about abolition, defused any possibility of conflict. How could there be a war of the same proportions as in the United States if there were not two opposing factions in Brazil?

Henington complained frequently about the presence of "Yankees" in Brazil, "poisoning people's minds with the idea of abolition, saying that blacks ought to be freed." This missionary had immigrated to Brazil and had encouraged the arrival of many others, with the idea of replicating in Brazil the model found in the southern United States, and he despaired at the Yankee presence and wondered in vain, "Where shall I hide from them?"[65]

At the beginning of the 1870s it was widely recognized as a necessary and unavoidable fact that slavery would become extinct, even officially. Making this happen depended exclusively on choosing the best way and the right opportunity. According to the traveler Richard Francis Burton, freeing the slaves was nearly a national consensus and he said that it would be difficult to find an educated person in Brazil who did not desire the abolition of slavery. "Everyone wants abolition."[66]

Burton documented and accepted as correct this argument that acknowledged abolition as if it were only a day away. Everyone everywhere said that it was only a matter of time. Slave emancipation was knocking at the door. Measures had already been taken to start the process and make it irreversible, and for its completion there remained only the resolution of a few details. This conclusion was essentially unanimous. The question is that the details were complex and, despite a political willingness to carry out this measure, there was concern about finding some way to sort things out. Thus, the intention was abolition, but first there was a need to find another economically viable model of labor to replace slavery, in addition to creating a mechanism that would provide indemnification to slave owners for any economic loss on investments made in the purchase of black slaves.

Tavares Bastos, accused of being Protestant because he had affirmed that the religious organization of the United States was ideal for Brazil, and also because of his friendship with Kalley and James Fletcher, also maintained that slavery was a doomed institution and that its end was irrevocable. Agreeing with the official imperial government position about everything being simply a question of time, he proposed shortening this time through a careful and prudent examination of the system. He concluded that the problem most "embroiling our society" was to discover how to achieve abolition of slavery without revolution and without going down the same path already trodden by the United States.[67] He admitted that on philosophical principles he defended immediate emancipation, but for practical reasons, and keeping in mind the concrete circumstances present in the nation, he was in favor of a systemic and rational solution avoiding negative financial consequences.[68]

In the 1880s, the Ultramontane newspaper *O Apóstolo* repeated the argument confirming this call for emancipation. "In Brazil the idea of emancipation is like a rock dropped into a void. Woe to anyone who attempts to stop it for he will be crushed. It is the idea of the century, it is the yearning of the nation." [69] The 7 June 1884 edition of the Presbyterian newspaper *Imprensa Evangélica* reproduced paragraphs from an editorial in the newspaper *A Gazeta de Notícias,* insisting on the idea that emancipation was the consensus of Brazilian society.

> The slavery question today is reduced to two terms: slavery as an institution and slavery as an element of public wealth. Slavery as an institution has no one to defend it. There is the press that is most openly against abolitionist propaganda; there are all the farmers' organizations proclaiming it in their manifestos; there are those deputies in the parliament who have found greatest fault with the government; and there are the slave owners themselves talking more loudly than all others, spontaneously freeing any property for which the law provides them a guarantee of indemnification.[70]

The idea of abolition as an extremely necessary gesture was widely shared and even some foreign newspapers affirmed this call for emancipation. *The New York Times* reported that, "Every public man in Brazil recognized the fact that something should be done to destroy the institution. Everyone agreed that human bondage should not go further." [71] While on vacation in the United States, Ashbel Simonton, the first Presbyterian missionary in Brazil, commented on the crisis in his country and affirmed its willingness to abolish slavery.

> I confess that the problem of our political destiny presents too many complexities for us to try to solve it. I see clearly, and can imagine vividly, the danger of both interfering with slavery and leaving things the way they are. I see neither peace nor tranquility while slavery continues. It cries out for justice. Sooner or later judgment will come. From the beginning I have never doubted what God, like us as a nation, says regarding the controversy of slavery. There has to be a way of promoting abolition.[72]

Regarding the conflict that occurred in the United States, Simonton several times revealed his position in favor of the abolition of slavery. As to the possibility of a movement of similar scope in Brazil, he was more skeptical and reiterated the opinion that, "the day is still far off when this goal will come to be achieved fully," fostering the possible hope for the "beginning of the end" of slavery.[73]

Even the emperor himself had shown his support for emancipation on innumerable occasions. He was in favor of such a measure but failed to implement it. According to his own and others' claims, the structure of the society was organized with its base in the system of slavery, and abolition would immediately produce a chaotic situation throughout the country. The emperor defended a slow and gradual solution and he acknowledged the validity of the fear expressed by the Viscount of Itaborahy: "Today, all the nation's work is being carried out by slave hands; free these slaves and they will immediately abandon labor and wind up dying in misery, inebriated by a liberty that they do not know how to enjoy. Meanwhile, the old master, the true producer in this farming nation, will also be reduced to poverty for lack of workers." [74]

A message came from the French Council for Emancipation, signed by the Duke of Broglie, its honorary president, and by fourteen others, including two Protestant pastors—Borsier and Edouard de Preseensé, claiming that the abolition of the slave trade was an incomplete measure and that total emancipation was necessary. Since "Brazil never viewed slavery as a divine institution," the emperor replied, "the emancipation of slaves, a necessary consequence of the abolition of the slave trade, is simply a question of form and opportunity." The text points out, therefore, that the moment had not yet arrived and he informed them that, "when the painful circumstances in which the nation finds itself permit, the Brazilian government will consider as an objective of primary importance the achievement of that which the spirit of Christianity has long demanded of the civilized world." [75]

The emperor's cultivation of his image as an abolitionist was contested by large segments of Brazilian society. In 1887, the *A República* newspaper of Belém, Pará, questioned the emperor's abolitionist fervor and maintained that his real intention was to weaken and divide the movement. The accusation was made that the emperor's objective in passing himself off as an abolitionist and pretending to go in the same direction as those who endanger their lives in "grandiloquent contest to liberate the nation from this shame that makes us a sad exception in America, is to weaken the course of public opinion, divert it, or even stop it."

This newspaper also defended the necessity of establishing criteria in order to determine who were the true abolitionists. One could not be an abolitionist and at the same time defend the economic interests of those who exploited slave labor. "If it is possible to align oneself with the group of patriots who assumed the defense of slaves, while remaining faithful to those who live by exploitation of blacks and the arduous labor of slaves who are daily drenched in sweat in order to produce profits for your feasts, then his majesty the emperor is an abolitionist." [76]

The emperor's adherence to the movement was information well spread through the media of the time. Even the foreign press praised the sovereign's open and modern mindset. *The Independent*, a North American newspaper, compared the societal behavior of the two countries, Brazil and the United

States, on the question of the abolition of slavery and enumerated many points that worked to Brazil's advantage; "There are circumstances in Brazilian life and manners which make the agitation of the question of complete emancipation a very different matter from what it has been in [the United States]". It was noted that in the United States it was only possible to approach the question in a gentle and careful fashion, whereas "in Brazil, the Emperor is the principal Abolitionist, and there is no restriction, legal or prescriptive, on the fullest discussion of the subject." [77]

The Nation newspaper followed the same line of argumentation and claimed that the periodical *O Novo Mundo*, which recently had been created by José Carlos Rodrigues, could collaborate in the implementation of the emperor's ideas. The Nation argued that *O Novo Mundo* was a much-respected and well-run enterprise and that, "We will rejoice greatly in the fact that it can contribute to moving forward as the Empire's most urgent need the emperor's most recent project, which is to bring slavery to an end." [78] On the occasion of the promulgation of the Law of the Free Womb, the position taken by the *Tribune* pointed out the conservative aspect of the legislation, since the House had eliminated an important item in the bill approved by the Senate, namely the emancipation of slaves owned by religious orders. The newspaper maintained that the law that was passed was deceitful, "a kind of illusory compromise struck with iniquity," since it postponed to the following generation a concession that should be granted immediately.

Nevertheless, despite this trickery, the legislation represented a victory because throughout the empire it imprinted on slavery the stamp of official disapproval. It had been decided that from that point on the buying and selling of human beings had become an evil that was only to be tolerated provisionally, because it was a deeply-rooted practice that could not be abolished abruptly. "In this way public sentiment is encouraged to oppose this evil, and furthermore it only stimulates the voluntary emancipation that has already been common in Brazil for many years." [79]

According to the commentaries recorded in the media of the time, everyone wanted emancipation of the slaves and was ready to cooperate. This expectation is reflected in a pastoral letter from Bishop Pedro Maria de Lacerda of the Diocese of São Sebastião in Rio de Janeiro. He announced the law of 28 September 1871 concerning the freeing of the children of slaves and called on all faithful Catholics to carry it out. The prelate said that all rejoiced on this "day of compassion and of just liberty," but despite all the positive expectations,

> Brazil feels its muscles quiver and its limbs weaken; because it is going to experience a deep and radical transformation. New and unknown horizons open all around; a future never before experienced will unfold before our eyes, which at present are terrified; new relationships will arise in the bosoms of our families, and customs never before practiced will need to be adopted. But all this is serious and risky, as has wisely been observed, chiefly because other customs have flourished for so many centuries and have deeply become deeply rooted over the course of more than three hundred years. [80]

The Protestant José Carlos Rodrigues commented on this interesting letter from the bishop, and he agreed with the extraordinary change that would occur in Brazilian society following the end of slavery, but he did not agree with the excessive fear and the constant procrastination. For him, following the Civil War, Brazil condemned slavery and began to count the days to its end. The influence of public opinion was such that the head of state solemnly pledged the nation to do away with the institution. Nevertheless, he pointed out that, with the outbreak of the war with Paraguay, the slavery question had been deferred, left for later. With the war concluded, the topic returned once more to the agenda, "but the executive branch did not show itself equal to the challenge and had to be repudiated by the nation. Others equally prudent were called, but they were no less timorous and also cowered in the face of this task." [81]

Rodrigues defended the need for immediate energetic and revolutionary action, not allowing governmental authorities to claim that they were unable to assume responsibility for proposing the necessary reforms because the "issue is very inflammatory." He ridiculed such behavior. "The fact is that the social body has need of an operation to stay alive, and the operation being somewhat difficult, the doctor who was called in to perform it stepped back in fear of assuming responsibility for the act." [82] In order for the "idea of the century" to take on concrete form, all that was needed was to determine the type of indemnification that would be offered to slave owners. There was not the slightest concern with discussing the role of the ex-slave in the new society. What mattered was guiding the course of the abolition movement, seeking to reconcile it with the interests of the slave owners. Thus, the emancipation process remained stalled, because there was no consensus regarding indemnification. The primary objective was to avoid any damage or financial loss to the slave owners.

That much-discussed indemnification was accepted by the editor of *O Novo Mundo* as being legitimate. For him, the fact that slave ownership had been legitimized by the state gave the owners certain rights that could not suddenly be stripped away. This was his conclusion. The slave was the property of his owner and the state did not have the right to usurp this good, this property. "When we want to open up a road or a canal, society appropriates property from the citizens who own the land or buildings necessary to carry out the project, no matter how dear these are to their owners." [83] The solution, according to the future editor of the *Jornal do Comércio*, was to raise society's awareness so that they would demand that slave owners make the sacrifice of selling their slaves at market price to the state. This was the sacrifice that Rodrigues asked of the slave masters. Society needed to take on its role and duty of demanding from the slave owners some type of arrangement.

> For the good of the public cause as members of a Christian country, we need your property to redress the effrontery to our fellow-citizens, in order to open up for our land a road that will take it straight to the place that the Lord has destined for it, in order to excavate the only channel through which He pours out his greatest blessings on the nations. [84]

In an article, "Contra a escravidão" [Against Slavery] published on 18 February 1887, the newspaper *A República*, addresses the question of the indemnification demanded by slave owners and defended by José Carlos Rodrigues.

> Indemnification? If someone deserves this, it is certainly not those who for so long have lived getting rich at the expense of the poorest of captives; if someone deserves this, it is certainly not those who for so long have held blacks in harsh and cruel subjugation. Those who clamor for indemnification are the victims of this exploitation. Those who request indemnification rightly, most rightly, are the slaves. The law ought to protect them against those who rob them of even more than property and their life; they rob them of their dignity. The roles are being reversed here. The law displays flagrant contradictions. The torturers are the victims, while the innocent are the criminals.[85]

The *Imprensa Evangélica* reproduced a letter from Christiano Benedicto Ottani sent to the Centro Abolicionista da Escola Polytecnica. Opposing the indemnification initiative, Ottoni states:

> It is my opinion that financial indemnification is doomed and ought to be completely eliminated. In the nation's current financial state, it seems clear that it will be impossible to collect taxes for an emancipation fund at the level required for the desired purpose. Furthermore, fourteen years' experience dividing such a subsidy among all the Empire's municipalities, with fees charged by hundreds of local officials subject to strong influences by interested parties, has demonstrated that this system has served and will continue to serve only to nourish abuses, immorality and indecent speculation.[86]

The move toward abolition proved to be very sluggish because the core concern was the accommodation of innumerable political and economic interests. Emancipation of the slaves was not the focus, even though the system was inhuman and there was a need to restore the dignity of more than a million and a half people. Positions like that taken by the abolitionist newspaper *A Voz do Escravo* claimed that the central question was the freeing of the slaves, pure and simple. "The freedom of education, of worship, of commerce, all this is nothing when faced with the freedom of a million and a half of our fellow citizens." [87] For this southern Brazilian periodical, the quibble was over the conciliatory emphasis within the abolition process. The prediction of economic chaos, the destruction of long-established labor relations and other problems that could arise from decreeing an end of slavery—these were nothing in the face of the central issue, which was freeing such a large number of people.

The abolition of slavery is a question of 'sooner or later' – the politics of gradualism.

The theory of slow and gradual politics is old: it is found in the presentation delivered by José Bonifácio to the Constituent Assembly of 1823. Condemning slavery, which for him was admissible only as long as Brazil was subject to Portugal and "its ancient despotism," he explained that the method of eliminating the danger would be a gradual abolition. "It is time . . . for us to be done with this barbaric and butchering trade; it is also time for us to eliminate gradually the remaining vestiges of slavery among us." [88]

Brazil's intuitive intelligence, which can resolve problems without conflict or war, was central to Bonifácio's presentation, dominated by a naive optimism regarding slavery and addressing it from this perspective. Such intuitive intelligence, which can be linked with Sérgio Buarque de Holanda's "cordial man," explains the opinion expressed innumerable times from the beginning of the nineteenth century through the 1880s, that slavery in Brazil would be condemned in the end. [89]

The successive laws that gradually imposed limits on slavery were the fruits of this "intuitive intelligence" and were seen as confirming the wisdom of a policy that sought to solve problems without resorting to wars and major conflicts. This was the vision of Frederico L.C. Burlamaqui, in his 1837 publication, that gradualism was the formula for uniting all of society in the cause for abolition. The "heroic measures" ought to be "applied slowly, with greatest circumspection and over a long period." [90] There were many other proposals of this nature, and we can highlight a few of them. The first was the law proposed by Ferreira França, proposing the emancipation of slaves whose masters died without heirs. Once free, these men and women would be obliged to become members of black or mulatto confraternities. [91]

Another proposal that deserves to be remembered is that of the Bahian deputy Antônio Pereira Rebouças. Developed in 1830, it foresaw in Brazil the application of legislation similar to that promulgated in Portugal regarding Moorish captives. The slave would attain his freedom when he could pay the total value of his purchase price plus twenty percent. [92] A second proposal by Ferreira França aiming at the gradual extinction of slavery projected its end in fifty years: in the first year one fiftieth would be freed, in the second year one forty-ninth, and so on. [93]

The great majority of proposals for gradual action—against trafficking or slavery itself—were instruments aimed at avoiding an immediate solution. The objective was to postpone the question for the future. While in 1850 the end of slave trafficking represented an important victory for those factions fighting for abolition, the defeated who clung most fiercely to slavery developed a most peculiar rationalization, seeking to delay the decision to end the institution. In as much as abolition was a 'sure thing,' an unavoidable event desired by almost the entire society, a large single segment of the Brazilian landowning class transformed this 'natural' inevitability by seeking to maintain slavery for as long as possible, in the form in which it existed in 1850. [94]

In contrast to the early emancipationists who saw the extinction of slavery as a distant possibility to be achieved in the long term, many abolitionists argued for the necessity of stipulating a specific date that would allow only for the resolution of matters relating to the process of replacing slave labor.

At the same time he was closely watching the unfolding of the Civil War in his own country, the Presbyterian missionary Ashbel Simonton also showed a certain familiarity with the way in which Brazilian society was dealing with the issue. For him, there was a "hope that did not appear too great to be cherished" for the "beginning of the end" of slavery, taking into account the innumerable laws already adopted that had the merit of progressively restricting the slavery model. Simonton spoke of the possibility of removing the blemish that oppressed the nation, but recognized how distant was "the day in which this end shall come to pass completely." This great event would occur only after the passage of a fixed period of time. Society needed to be prepared for this great happening, which would mean "a period of trials, of humiliation of the nation's pride, and of confession of sins and supplication for God's help." [95]

The end of the intercontinental traffic in slaves and several other measures allowed a glimpse of the possibility that abolition would be completed in the near future. Daniel Kidder and James Fletcher, representatives of the American Bible Society who lived in Brazil for several years, expressed a profound conviction that "slavery is doomed in Brazil." This optimistic attitude originated in the prevailing climate in Brazil, where, according to them, "everything is in favor of freedom." This led them to predict the abolition of slavery "before another half-century rolls around." The wide-sweeping benevolence of the Brazilian slave system, with "the facilities for the slave to emancipate himself," implicitly condemned the slave system. It was only a matter of time, as these Methodist representatives of the Bible Society prophesied. [96]

At the same time they were pointing to a set date, which obviously was not borne out, the two missionaries concluded that the arrival of the abolition of slavery could be a concrete and irreversible reality, as revealed through another important means for emancipation that had been adopted already, namely, the effective cessation of the trade in African slaves. They argued that such a measure represented the death sentence of the system, "the precursor to another more important step." Frederico L.C. Burlamaqui's gradualism thesis was accepted in several other aspects of Brazilian life. Thus, Kidder and Fletcher confirmed that, "Almost every step in Brazilian progress has been prepared by a previous gradual advance." By means of a brief historical reflection, they commented on the innumerable steps taken by the nation, which "did not leap at once into self-government," but "did take constant steps." Likewise, the effective cessation of the trade in African slaves was only a precursor step to something more important. [97]

Fletcher actually expected that the abolition of slavery in Brazil would occur within a short period of time. With this objective, he carried out important activity, becoming the main vehicle of American anti-slavery propaganda. He was dedicated to the distribution of Bibles as much as anti-slavery literature. According to Davi Gueiros Vieira, "Among the many anti-slavery books that

Fletcher distributed, there was one that had a major impact in Brazil. This was the work by George Livermore about blacks and the American Revolution." [98]

Fletcher's activity as a distributor of anti-slavery literature became widely known. At his suggestion and heeding the advice of Tavares Bastos and other politically liberal Brazilians, Professor Agassiz, on an expedition to Brazil, brought with him a shipment of books on this topic.[99] Thus, Fletcher made a major contribution to the anti-slavery movement in Brazil.

On a certain occasion the secretary of the Anti-Slavery Society in London wrote a letter to Deputy Tavares Bastos about the progress of the abolitionist movement in Brazil. In this letter, the secretary mentioned having discovered the name of this deputy from Alagoas in a letter from Fletcher published in several newspapers in the United States regarding the emancipation of slaves in Brazil. The tenor of the document reveals that this was the beginning of a productive correspondence between Tavares Bastos and the Society in London.[100] Many of Tavares Bastos' ideas concerning the abolition of slavery were adopted by José Carlos Rodrigues. Commenting on the book *A Província - estudo sobre a descentralização no Brazil* [The Province: A Study of Decentralization in Brazil], the editor of *O Novo Mundo* drafted a deeply religious text, filled with Protestant theology:

> What is it we want Brazil to become? What is it that we are all working toward, those of us who, guided by opinion, direct Brazil's destiny? What is the point towards which Brazil is being pushed by the spirit of modern ideas? It is democracy, . . . it was Jesus Christ who came to gather in the lost, the neglected, the slaves of society and of sin, and He elevated them to the status of His brothers and sisters and God's children; it was He who humiliated the ruling class who impose heavy burdens on the people; it was He who declared everyone equal before the Eternal Father, and proclaimed His will that no one, not even the least of them, should be lost; it was He who lifted up and sanctified even more the least of these, in accordance with their sacrifice and humiliation; it was He who established as the principal purpose for mankind the salvation of his soul, and the responsibility and the exercise of liberty that derives from it; it was He, then, who delivered mankind to God and also to himself, with absolute ownership over his soul, his life and his destiny. Jesus Christ was the true founder of democracy, of individual rights. He was not bothered with society: He went to its source, to its individual components. But that's not all. Jesus Christ revealed to humanity whence it had come, where it is and where it is headed. He declared that we started from the same root; that we are sunken and lost in sin, that we are capable of a relative perfection, that this should be our goal, and consequently that all of us, each and every one, should work toward attaining this high level for the common glory of the Creator, the Redeemer and the Freed.
>
> He also told us that after this journey on Earth, we will all return to the same hands that created us. Therefore, Jesus Christ eliminated all distinctions of class and caste, completely undermining their foundation: He taught that each man on his own is fallen, and that he is also capable of indeterminate progress. There are no longer men born to be slaves, nor others born to be free. The old class distinctions, which were taken to be intrinsic, are now attributed to the true cause, to mere circumstances, which can be modified indefinitely.[101]

An identical rationalization was expressed by the Viscount of Sinumbu, according to a dialogue recorded by Professor Agassiz. This scientist said that Sinumbu believed that emancipation would have to be achieved gradually in Brazil in a series of steps, the first of which had already been taken. A large number of slaves was freed annually by the goodwill of their masters; an even greater number was ransomed using their own money; the traffic in slaves had ceased quite a time ago; "the inevitable result of this must be the natural death of slavery." [102]

Louis and Elizabeth Agassiz visited the Pinheiros farm, which belonged to the Commendator José de Souza Breves. It was located close to the city of Rio de Janeiro and held more than two thousand slaves. The Agassizes reported on the situation of a little old woman more than one hundred years of age. She had already won her freedom, but "seemed to be very much attached to the family," and had never wished to abandon her situation. This fact led them to conclude that slavery in Brazil had a comforting aspect to it and that emancipation would be regulated by legislation. [103]

The tenor of the conversation between a North American and a Brazilian owner of slaves gave Louis Agassiz "the feeling that the end of slavery was inevitable." Asked by the North American if the slaves belonged to him or if they were hired, the Brazilian responded, "Own them—a hundred and more; but it will finish soon. It finished with you; and when it finish with you, it finish here, it finish everywhere." [104] These words, according to Agassiz, were said without any indication of complaint or sadness, but as an unavoidable fact. Later, he mentioned that this sense of inevitability was reinforced definitively by the blow struck to the institution of slavery in the United States, which was thus fatally wounded not only in Brazil, but "it finish everywhere."

This characteristic of slavery in Brazil, mixed with a certain camaraderie between master and slave, influenced the vision of innumerable Protestant missionaries. For them slavery always hung by a thread, with abolition about to happen. The 'generosity' of Brazilian society made them view everything as working in favor of abolition. And it was creeping along. Agassiz mentioned the 100-year old slave woman who had been freed many years before by her owners but refused to leave them.

The Agassizes noted that facts like this gave slavery in Brazil a comforting aspect and allowed for great hope. "Here, complete emancipation is considered a topic under discussion, to be regulated by law in order to be adopted. Giving a slave his freedom is not thought to be something extraordinary." [105] Commenting on the Law [of the Free Womb] of 1871, the bishop of Rio de Janeiro claimed that Brazil deserved accolades and applause for the "boundless kindness, the most mild of temperaments and the peaceful character of Brazilians," who had taught the United States a great lesson by avoiding in Brazil a repetition of the bloody war that had occurred in the U.S. [106]

Beginning in the 1870s, abolitionist propaganda in Brazil became much sharper, albeit limited to the narrow confines of the Brazilian elite. For many reasons, and also because they realized that the slave system was deeply rooted in Brazilian society, the abolitionists advanced slowly, fearful of the possibility of upsetting the dominant interests. In his article "A lavoura e o crédito" [Agriculture and Credit], José Carlos Rodrigues, right at the start of the publication of his newspaper, sought prudently to highlight his abolitionist positions, justifying this by saying that he did not intend to make wild claims. "We are neither agitators nor propagandists." He strove to affirm that his abolitionist proposals were coherent and came neither from a philosopher, nor a student, nor someone who had nothing to lose.

> A very erroneous idea regarding those who advocate the most rapid emancipation is the one that has generally existed and is still found wherever there is slavery. In general, the abolitionist is seen as one of two types: Either he is a philosopher, old, obstinate, devoid of possessions, out of touch with great matters of the day, and, with one foot in the grave, is horrified by what he perceives to be sin; or he is a youth overflowing with noble ideas, but without a single practical purpose, seeing a great deal in the heavens and nothing on Earth, fond of ranting in support of the slave, whom he supposes is broken and oppressed. For our part, we assert that we have no intention of speaking thoughtlessly on this matter.[107]

In another article, he declared that he defended the abolition of slavery and took into consideration the material interests of the affected parties. He maintained that the end of slave labor, such as happened in the South of the United States, would result in material improvement for the planters. "Moreover, when we ask that slavery in Brazil be ended as soon as possible, we are not carried along by a mere desire from propaganda on behalf of a beautiful word and against an ugly name; nor do we ignore the material interests of the parties involved." [108]

The Civil War in the United States was an important milestone in slavery. With an argument similar to that of Louis Agassiz on the conflict having struck a mortal blow to the institution of slavery both in the United States and in the other countries of the West, the editor of *O Novo Mundo* reveals that, "Now is the appointed hour." After an historical enumeration of the many countries that had abandoned the system, he declares, "Only Brazil is left! . . . The only country in South America that did not declare the emancipation of slaves in its declaration of independence." Brazil and the United States were the only two countries "in the entire New World that did not address this matter" and, with a "tremendous war," the United States erased its "black page." [109]

José Carlos Rodrigues pointed out that, following the war in the United States, with the condemnation of the institution, there was a solemn declaration from the Brazilian emperor pledging to end slavery. He enumerated, however, other historical factors that stymied the process. According to him, the Paraguayan War had delayed abolition and with the end of the war the Executive Branch had lacked the courage [to follow through on its pledge]. He concluded that the solution for the nation was to follow the example of others that had taken "quick, energetic, and revolutionary measures." [110]

Rodrigues appeared quite enthused by the 1871 decision expressed in the Law of the Free Womb. For him, such resolutions by the Legislative Assembly "exceeded all our expectations, and those of the entire world. There no longer exists that sluggish Brazil, indifferent to its own interests and always suspicious of progress. Brazil of October 1871 is a state that makes its citizens proud." Pointing out that in the first issue of the newspaper, in October 1870, he had judged that emancipation would come about only through "great sacrifice, an action taken because of a sacred motive," he praised the fact that twelve months later the nation "gave us the glory of offering us . . . the adoption of a plan for emancipation, gradual but sincere and efficacious. This, we repeat, is more than was expected by Brazil's greatest friends. . . . We should give thanks to the Most High." Rejoicing with happiness, José Carlos Rodrigues proclaimed with bold letters in the editorial of his newspaper, "Henceforth no one will be made a slave in Brazil." [111]

It is important to note that such enthusiasm was not shared by many press organizations, and even less so among innumerable Brazilian abolitionists. *O Novo Mundo* itself presented an article extracted from a North American newspaper showing deep disappointment with the law because an important part of it had been excised by the Senate, to wit, the paragraph that mandated the freeing of all slaves owned by religious orders. The newspaper affirmed that it had no doubts regarding the extinction of slavery within a short period of time, well before the date set by the legislation, and it pointed to positive examples such as the Benedictine Order, which, even without being obliged by the law, had freed all its slaves. [112]

The 24 December 1871 edition of José Carlos Rodrigues's newspaper carried an article "Libertação de escravos na Bahia" [The Freeing of Slaves in Bahia], underscoring several cases of the freeing of slaves, as well as the praise delivered by American periodicals for these actions carried out by the Benedictines in Brazil. "We report with satisfaction this generous act." [113] The *Jornal do Comércio*, the leading organization of the Brazilian press of that time, with strong links to the conservative wing of politics, passed over the Law of the Free Womb without mentioning it. In the section "Requested Publications," however, it included a long article, probably written by someone from the Benedictine Order, telling how the Order had prepared for the emancipation of the newborn children of slaves and expressing concern for the social predicament of the captives following this victory.

The text claimed that the humanitarian action by the monks had been paralyzed by pressures from the slave-owning segment of society, and that a more radical and decisive position—the Order's true intent—had not been taken only out of prudence and apprehension of "causing harm to private property, which was believed to be threatened by the advance of the idea of emancipation." [114] Defense of this gradual abolition process, which was closely tied to the legislative sphere, was justified by means of the characterization of the Brazilian reality, which was quite different from that found in North America. A good part of the texts published by José Carlos Rodrigues in *O Novo Mundo* sought to compare the situation in the South of the United States with that in Brazil.

"O trabalho dos emancipados" [The work of the emancipated] highlighted the opinion of people from the South of the United States several years after the

Civil War. And he suggested that those in Brazil who appeared so concerned and even terrorized by the prospect of the emancipation of blacks "would do well to listen to their brothers in the southern states, who, like them, a few years ago had slaves and judged them indispensable to their interests, not only materially but even morally." [115]

Thus, the journey on behalf of the abolition of slavery was clearly reformist, focused essentially on the legislative sphere. The newspaper *O Novo Mundo* itself showed that the abolition of slavery in Brazil would have the legal route as its only alternative. No proposal was considered that did not involve the legislative route. The newspaper pointed out the existence of a strong movement in support of "practical abolition," and that the people's will "was not being expressed in their legislative chambers," nor were they "understanding the will and needs of the country." Nevertheless, the central concern of the newspaper continued to be immediate abolition, provided it was consummated by official legislated means. [116]

After 1871 a radical change can easily be seen in the message of *O Novo Mundo*. With the Law of the Free Womb passed, José Carlos Rodrigues reduced dramatically his interest in the topic of emancipation. Henceforth the basic question was to point out the advances made by the South of the United States without recourse to slave labor. [117] The impression one gets is that the victory aimed for had been achieved, in the degree to which the newspaper acknowledged that the State itself had already decreed the terms of abolition in a slow and gradual manner. Many were speaking in terms of a limited time, so that this consensus in favor of a slow and steady abolition cooled the more pressing revolutionary impetus. [118]

Following a line quite different from that of the extremely optimistic Kidder and Fletcher, the Methodist missionary Junius Newman, who came to the interior of the Province of São Paulo accompanying immigrants from the South, revealed that Brazilian laws regarding the elimination of slavery would not be carried out within the proposed twenty-five year period. In 1875, when writing about the Methodist mission in Brazil, he spoke about this prediction of twenty-five years, concluding that this would not be long enough. "I think not sooner." [119]

It was Joaquim Nabuco, one of the most important abolitionist leaders, who presented a proposal for abolition that was entirely linked to the legal sphere. In his most important work, *O Abolicionismo*, [Abolitionism] Nabuco outlined the landscape of abolitionism and argued that this movement should position itself as a project for reconstructing national life, degraded to the core by the destructive action of the slavery system. He suggested that the route to be taken by this project should limit itself exclusively to the legal realm, since the only remaining option was the revolutionary approach, which was unacceptable to him.

In a letter written in 1880, Nabuco announced that he was going to introduce a piece of legislation establishing 1 January 1890 as the deadline for complete abolition of slavery in the empire. He himself recognized that setting such a long time limit represented a compromise, but he understood this to be the necessary route and the only means of overcoming difficulties that were already quite great. A fixed deadline like 1 January 1890 would give the plantation own-ers time to "prepare for the great evolution, and at the same time would awaken in the hearts of the slaves an inestimable hope, of infinite value, that their life would become less and less arduous, approaching liberty." [120]

Measures similar to those proposed by Joaquim Nabuco were defended by Senator Christiano Benedicto Ottoni in a letter sent to the Centro Abolicionista da Escola Politécnica and reprinted by the *Imprensa Evangélica*. He pointed to legislative measures that should be taken and the necessity of two of them:

> 1. To establish rules that for complete implementation do not require more than a maximum of time that anyone would dare to extend beyond ten years, with strong probabilities that such a time limit will never be reached. This condition will infuse the hearts of the wretched slaves with the balm of hope, and will be an element of peace, safety and social well-being.
> 2. Not to stipulate freeing everyone at once within a fixed time period, but to begin to emancipate immediately an adequate percentage of the slave popula-tion each year. [121]

The newspaper *Imprensa Evangélica,* undoubtedly influenced by the popu-lar, polite and controlled character of the abolition movement, modified its position and began to show some concern with the abolition of slavery starting in the 1880s, more precisely in 1884. According to this periodical, Joaquim Nabuco, following the example of John the Baptist, would be the "voice of a prophet, crying in the desert, and his work deserved to be read by all who loved their country and sought its progress." [122]

In the following year the Presbyterian newspaper felt more at ease, affirm-ing that God would punish the nation for its oppression of the slaves and disap-proving of the legislation presented by the Saraiva ministry for the emancipation of the slaves. It noted that the law did not merit the trust of those who desired freedom for the slaves, and that, "For the well being of the country, and also for the relief of a cruelly oppressed race whose only crime is being born into slav-ery, we sincerely wish that an effective law be adopted for their complete eman-cipation in as short a time as possible." [123]

In the meantime, following an approach similar to the abolitionists, who were calling for progressive abolition linked directly to the legislative sphere, the *Imprensa Evangélica*, at the times when it spoke out, assumed a much more propagandist role and did not maintain a firm and radical stance. Its proposals favored either gradual emancipation or else freedom with compulsory service to former slave owners for yet a few more years.

In the mid-1880s, the missionary James W. Koger repeats his extreme opti-mism in an official report sent to the Methodist Church in the United States when he refers to the process of slave emancipation in Brazil. He says that out of a population of more than twelve million, one part lives subjugated under the shackles of slavery; however, and this is the source of his optimism, "the shackles are being removed voluntarily by many of the owners with incredible speed in all parts of the Empire, accelerating the phasing in of the Law of the Free Womb of September 1871." [124] Another letter, this one written by the

Methodist missionary J.J. Ransom and read at the Missionary Conference of Tennessee in 1881, repeats the information conveyed by Koger. Ransom merely informs, without much enthusiasm, that, "It is possible that slavery will be abolished within twenty years—all children born starting from this date are born into freedom." [125]

The Methodist Thomas D. Smith, in an article in the *Advocate of Missions*, points out that almost all Brazilian society showed its willingness to abolish slavery. "One party favors gradual emancipation, the present law governing slavery; another urges immediate emancipation." [126]

Slaves are the talents entrusted by God to the whites—Slavery as a necessary evil

Writing about the emancipation of slaves, the editor of *O Novo Mundo* observed that one of the basic principles of Christianity is that "the black is our brother." For him, even if a delay occurred in obeying this principle, it was certain that everyone was going to discover, sooner or later, that this was a divine law, holy and immutable. Whoever most promptly recognized and obeyed this doctrine would most quickly receive the rewards "that the Father has set aside for those who follow His inspiration and His teaching." [127]

The Protestant José Carlos Rodrigues repeatedly defends his abolitionist calling in the pages of *O Novo Mundo*. He was convinced that the time had arrived for the nation "to rid itself of slavery forever." Nevertheless, at the same time he argued for the necessity of rapid emancipation, Rodrigues also upheld the idea that the institution of slavery represented a "necessary evil." This probably was based on a Calvinist fundamentalist exegesis on the ninth chapter of the Gospel of John describing the curing of the man blind from birth when, responding to a question from the disciples as to the reason this man was born blind, Jesus explained that this had occurred "so that God's work might be revealed in him, the blind man."(John 9:3, NRSV)

Thus, José Carlos Rodrigues also recognizes an expediency, a utility, in maintaining slavery. In other words, he points to slavery as a necessary evil. "If there was no slavery on the Earth, God's children would not be able to carry out, in His image, the sacred and glorious mission of freeing them, and the most elevated part of their being would not be able to be exercised." [128]

Ideas proliferated abundantly about slavery being a necessary evil, a minor evil, a benefit to blacks. They are present, for example, in Henry Koster's book *Travels in Brazil in the Years from 1809 to 1815,* which claims that Brazilian society had completely adapted to the slave system and had developed arguments to justify black slavery as being as much a positive condition as liberty. "In Brazil there are several excellent men who will entertain the idea that the Africans are saved from death by the slave-dealers, and that if they were not purchased by the Europeans their countrymen would murder them." [129]

Koster mentions the Catholic ecclesiastical membership among the many honest people who brandished this type of justification, pointing out that "one of the chief arguments with the priesthood is the advantages which the Africans receive from their entrance into the Catholic Church." He explains that if clerical concern was simply for the baptism and consequent catechism of blacks, "How much better it would be to teach them the Christian religion upon their native soil, without all the miseries to which they are subjected by their transportation!" Koster concludes that an important step toward the abolition of slavery would be the possibility of raising clerical consciousness to the realization that "by their voice they were sanctioning one of the most shocking systems under which the world ever laboured." [130]

Along the same line denounced by Koster is the thinking of Thomas Davatz, schoolmaster and Lutheran pastor, author of *Memórias de um Colono no Brasil* [Memories of a Colonist in Brazil]. He assessed the black slaves in Brazil as being, in general, men with a good appearance and physical build. Later, he repeated the well known biblical argument that justified black slavery as a divine curse, derived from the curse of Noah. (Genesis 9:20-27) "Were it not in their nature to be subjugated to whites, because of the curse of Noah on Canaan that keeps them subjugated, it would be easy given their considerable numbers for them to take vengeance on their traffickers and oppressors." [131]

Ideas like that of Davatz did not originate in Brazil. They came from elsewhere, particularly from the United States, and they had considerable impact. Take Reverend Dr. Thornwell, professor of theology at the Presbyterian Seminary in Charleston, South Carolina, who wrote, "Our slaves are our solemn trust and while we have a right to use and direct their labors, we are bound to feed, clothe and protect them. . . . They are moral beings, and it will be found that in the culture of their moral nature we reap the largest reward from their service." [132] The argument used most often by southern ideologues was that of the slaves showing themselves incapable of self-sufficiency, and it fell to their masters the Christian duty of providing this for them. Thus convinced that the religious doctrine of the abolitionists was heretical, they refuted their arguments and counterattacked with vigor, alleging that abolition would be a failure of Christian responsibility in relation to other human beings.

William Gilmore Simms, a writer of great prestige in the South of the United States, argued that slave owners had a moral duty not to free their slaves unless they were sure of their ability to survive. Appropriating the well-known Biblical parable of the talents, he said that the major question was, "How have we employed the talents which were given us—how have we discharged the duties of our guardianships?" According to the exegesis he made of the text, the slaves were the talents delivered to the whites, who would have the duty and the obligation of managing them. If the whites did not carry out their obligation, there would be appropriate punishment. [133]

Quite similar were the ideas of the Reverend John H. Witherspoon, aimed at clearing up doubts and helping to understand slavery as a necessary evil. In a letter written to his wife in May 1837, he says:

> I have been from my youth up, opposed to slavery as it exists in the South, on the score of expediency. Nothing has so prostrated our Southern country in point of domestic improvement as slavery. And yet I believe African Slavery, lawful and not unchristian, and that it is better for them, on the whole, than lib-

erty, without a due preparation for the reception of the blessing. Some may attribute this view to selfish motives but I have nothing to gain from it. I never willingly and heartily bought or sold a human being. I have done so, for the accommodation of the slave and my own domestic peace and comfort but never for gain, from the "love of filthy lucre." [134]

In a conversation with a veteran journalist of one of the most influential newspapers in the southern United States, José Carlos Rodrigues heard a defense of this concept of slavery as an extremely positive fact for blacks because of the possibility of them coming to know a new and developed world, freed from the barbarism in which they had lived:

> The plantation owners in the southern states were very fond of the institution and considered it divine. Compare the black in Africa, in his cannibalism and appalling condition, with our slave of yesteryear: Do we not have reason to be proud of our great work of opening up to these persons the doors of civilization and of Christianity? And would it not be better for us to continue this trade if we are able to show results such as this?[135]

Rodrigues does not agree with such arguments and responds that, "no one has the right to enslave blacks so as to improve their condition, just as no-one can capture an unhappy white person so as to make him happy in slavery." According to the editor of *O Novo Mundo*, while in the southern United States people loved the institution of slavery and presented innumerable justifications for distinguishing it, the situation in Brazil was quite different. Everyone argued that slavery was simply a sin inherited from the Portuguese, "but this acknowledgment did not seem to arouse the usual consequences." Everyone admitted slavery was like a sin and thought that this simple admission already served as expiation of their guilt: "We believe that we have therefore paid what we owe to justice." [136]

Louis and Elizabeth Agassiz, authors of *A Journey in Brazil*, approach the situation of blacks from another angle. Upon observing a group of blacks in Rio de Janeiro singing and dancing the fandango, they commented, "Looking at these half-naked figures and unintelligent faces, the question arose, so constantly suggested when we come in contact with this race, "What will they do with this great gift of freedom?" [137] They denounced slavery but regarded the blacks as "lacking in intelligence," lesser and dependent individuals.

The law of Christianity says that the black is our brother—
racial democracy

Slavery was always accepted more easily by the Catholic Church than by the Protestants. Based on the systems of class stratification of Antiquity and the Middle Ages, the Catholic Church interjected these systems into its theology and organization and was thus able to accept slavery as one of the consequences of human sin and to affirm that, notwithstanding this, slaves and owners were equal before God.

With this reformist concern, defended by the Protestant abolitionists, there developed a style of pedagogy that sought to highlight certain peculiarities of Brazilian society. There was an effort to show that harmonious racial relations were strong, free from prejudices, and quite different from the situation in the United States. As Fletcher and Kidder said, the obstacles placed in the way of the free black in the United States were insurmountable. The Anglo-Saxon race, they claimed, could be "moved to generous pity for the negro, but will not yield socially." In Brazil the opposite was the case; "If a man have freedom, money, and merit, no matter how black may be his skin, no place in society is refused him." [138]

For the North American traveler John Codman, the challenge associated with the integration of free blacks into Brazilian society was resolved more easily than in the United States. In Brazil, "There is black blood everywhere stirred in; compounded over and over again, like an apothecary's preparation. African blood runs freely through marble halls, as well as in the lowest gutter." [139] In 1846, the Reverend Walter Colton highlighted this contrast.

> It is for us Americans to preach up humanity, freedom, and equality, and then turn up our blessed noses if an African takes a seat at the same table on board a steamboat. Even in our churches he is obliged to look out some obscure nook, and dodge along towards heaven as if he had no business in the 'narrow way'. [140]

James B. Bond, the U.S. consul in Pará, urged Southern immigrants in Brazil to become better acquainted with Brazilian realities. He pointed out that those Southern immigrants who did not succeed in becoming accustomed to Brazil, for the most part failed because they did not adapt to Brazilian society's way of life. To those who immigrated because they did not agree with the rights given to blacks, he advised them to leave their prejudices behind. And, ironically, he raised the possibility that "they who fly from contact with the black man at home will, if they settle in this country, in all probability and at no distant day, behold the detested color shading the cheeks of their own descendants." [141]

Even recognizing the existence of conflicts between owners and slaves, it was pointed out as a viable possibility that whites and blacks could live in harmony once slavery was effectively abolished by an official act and blacks had become free laborers.

The emphasis given by Nabuco and Ottoni, proclaiming a progressive abolition, was an attempt at reconciling the interests of slave owners. For Nabuco, in spite of the conflict among social classes, national reconstruction could be achieved peacefully, since there was harmony between the races. Slavery, by general good fortune, had not embittered the slave's soul towards his owner, "nor did it arouse between the two races the two-way loathing which naturally exists between oppressor and oppressed. For this reason, the contact between the two races outside slavery was never bitter, and the man of color found every avenue open before him." [142]

This supposed racial harmony would have been possible because the situation prevailing in Brazil was the opposite of that in the United States. This comparison was made by Kidder and Fletcher with quite a bit of optimism and on the basis of judicial considerations. "The Brazilian Constitution recognizes, neither directly nor indirectly, color as a basis of civil rights; hence once free, the black man or the mulatto, if he possesses energy and talent, can rise to a social position from which his race in North America is debarred." [143] Kidder and Fletcher's argument was repeated by the North American newspaper *Independent* regarding the passage of the Law of the Free Womb in 1871.

> Color is no obstacle of rank in the state, the church or the army. Men of all hues are senators, noblemen, high dignitaries of the church, ministers of state, knights of the orders of the empire; and no-one thinks strange of it. In such a condition of society . . . it cannot be long before slavery will be obliged to remove itself out of the way of the development of the immense resources of that immense empire. Of course, it is but a question of time, and, as we believe, of no very long time. [144]

For these two missionaries, the Brazilian slavery system, even though it was deeply rooted in racial differences, had not brought about color prejudices because contact between the races had, from the beginning of colonization, produced a mixed population. They pointed out that there was no racial hatred in Brazil like that found in the United States. Upon their emancipation, blacks would be transformed into citizens, able to participate equally in the privileges that the slave system had kept open to all without distinction. Miscegenation, it was supposed, explained the absence of racial problems and revealed resolutely the possibility of the establishment of a racial paradise. Another Protestant, Thomas D. Smith, spoke of Brazil as "the paradise of miscegenation, and the fruit is a woeful deterioration, physically, mentally, and morally." [145]

Eugene Genovese observes that historians insist on supporting the mistaken theory that southern plantation owners maintained quite limited contact with their slaves and were hard on them. According to him, the reality was quite different. First, very few of them possessed a great number of slaves and, second, the majority of owners knew their workers by name and were able to distinguish their individual qualities. Finally, it was quite common for workers to recognize their owners as kind people. [146]

Kidder and Fletcher expressed surprise at the degree of interaction between owners and slaves in Brazil. "In the houses of the wealthy Fluminenses you make your way through a crowd of little wooly-heads, mostly guiltless of clothing, who are allowed the run of the house and the amusement of seeing visitors." Corroborating the difference in customs, Kidder commented:

> A friend of mine used frequently to dine in the house of a good old general of high rank, around whose table gamboled two little jetty blacks, who hung about their "pai" (as they called him) until they received their portions from his hands, and that, too, before he commenced his own dinner. Whenever the lady of the house drove out, these pets were put into the carriage, and were as much offended at being neglected as any spoiled only son. They were the children of the lady's nurse, to whom she had given freedom. Indeed, a faithful nurse is generally rewarded by manumission.[147]

Belief in the possibility of achieving a more peaceful emancipation in Brazil was defended by many segments of Brazilian society. The *Imprensa Evangélica* said that, "Brazil could give to the world this unique example of a nation that delivered social reform of this magnitude without ruining itself, and without disturbing the peace in which it has lived for many years." [148] A vision very similar to that of the *Imprensa Evangélica* was formulated by Bishop Pedro Maria de Lacerda, of Rio de Janeiro, encouraging the adoption of the law of 28 September 1871 that decreed the emancipation of the children of slaves.

> Brazil feels its muscles quiver and its limbs weaken, because it is going to ex-perience a deep and radical transformation. New and unknown horizons open all around; a future never before experienced will unfold before our eyes, which at present are terrified; new relationships will arise in the bosoms of our families, and customs never before practiced will need to be adopted. But all this is serious and risky, as has wisely been observed, chiefly because other customs have flourished for so many centuries and have become deeply rooted over the course of more than three hundred years. But with honor and praise there occurred in the great nation of South America that which in the great re-public in North America happened only after a war with gigantic and numerous hecatombs of human victims, drowned in the blood of their brothers. Thus, due to the unsurpassed kindness, the most gentle temperament and the peaceful character of the Brazilians, it is to be hoped that whatever starts will continue and progress, that fears will be only momentary timidity, which will be fol-lowed by complete and universal approval, and that some day we all will be amazed at ever having feared for a single moment any unrest and harm.[149]

José Carlos Rodrigues made note of what he called the "error of appraisal" made by many Brazilians who compared the condition of slaves in the United States and Brazil, deducing that in that country the slave was treated much more harshly. Protesting against these preconceived notions, he showed that the way slaves were treated in the United States was neither better nor worse than in Brazil. The origins of this prejudice were due to exaggerations in the North American press and to the influence of the book *Uncle Tom's Cabin*. It is a cer-tainty, he added, that because the southerners truly believed in the institution of slavery, they took greater care towards the slaves and exercised a more rigorous and intelligent discipline that demanded the exercise of the slaves' mental faculties. Slavery was based on religious beliefs and ideals, differing from the purely material motivation observed in Brazil. It was this profound conviction that allowed the South to fight to maintain the institution, caring even for multiplying the number of blacks through the organization of plantations specializing in their reproduction.[150]

The emphasis on the absence of racial prejudice, while at the same time noting the alarm regarding the conflict between classes, shows a concern that is fairly specific and even pedagogical. If on the one hand an attempt was being made to affirm that racial commingling would be verifiably brotherly and that a reconciliation between the classes would be possible upon the abolition of slavery, on the other hand abolition should occur within the limits of governmental action.

In Brazil, the absence of racial conflict encouraged a peaceful transformation, so the task of freedom that was to be implanted would be greatly facilitated. Therefore, all that remained was the social question—whether the system of slave labor could be solved in a simple and peaceful manner by way of abolition, complemented by the gradual transformation of former slaves into paid employees without great risks to the interests of slave owners. This was the position of Tavares Bastos, "Between the immediate emancipation of all (a financial impossibility) and the freeing of future generations, it seems to me that therein lies the dilemma. As a philosopher I prefer the first; Brazil's circumstances force me toward the second." [151]

Among the steps taken by Tavares Bastos towards encouraging phased emancipation was the proposal aimed at freeing the unborn beginning in January 1866. In that year, when he learned of the decision by the brothers of St. Benedict's monastery to free the children born of their slaves from that day hence, he pointed to this gesture as worthy of noble imitation. Later, he presented to Parliament a proposal "prohibiting henceforth the formation of societies, companies and corporations, be they civil or religious, while possessing slaves. And, as to those that were already functioning and owned slaves, he determined that the children born to their slaves after the date contained in the law would be considered free, with the remainder being freed after a period of twenty years." [152] Aiming to avoid any risk of circumventing the legislation, he stipulated that such organizations would be prohibited from selling their slaves.[153]

The innumerable articles published by José Carlos Rodrigues in *O Novo Mundo* point out only the positive aspects of post-Civil War North America. As an exception, in the issue of April 1871 he drew attention to some negative facts, among them that the United States was agitated by the question of Santo Domingo[154] and that of the Ku Klux Klan. He also said that high taxes and other oppressive factors had stimulated the emergence of a desire for revenge, giving rise to secret societies such as the Ku Klux Klan, which injured and killed left and right.[155]

The Yankees are poisoning the people's minds with the idea of abolition—black danger

Ashbel Green Simonton, North American missionary of the Presbyterian Church, was in Brazil when the Civil War started in the United States. Completely opposed to slavery, he watched the unfolding of events with great impatience. "Who can now predict what the course of events will be in the United States, no longer 'united'?" In spite of great fear and apprehension, he trusted that, "In some way that is impossible to imagine, God is opening the way to removing the oppression of slavery, though from the human perspective the expected result appears to be the opposite."[156] Despite dark and dramatic events, he believed that in the long run the result would be positive.

The frequent information about the intensification of the conflict and the lack of knowledge as to its resolution caused deep unrest also in Brazil. While on vacation in the United States, Simonton followed the conflict closely. "The problem of our political destiny appears too complex to attempt to puzzle it out." Whatever the resolution, both a change to the slave system and its continuation certainly represented great danger. The missionary could not foresee "peace or tranquility as long as the regime of slavery continues," because "it is a system that cries out for justice. Sooner or later judgment will come. I have never doubted, from the beginning, what God's quarrel with us, as a nation, has to say regarding slavery." [157]

In spite of being openly opposed to slavery, the pioneering Presbyterian asserted that, "The peace and the tranquility of the past have been destroyed and a terrifying question hovers over the nation." [158] With the conflict in the United States as a model and reference point, it became much more difficult for the Brazilians to get themselves embroiled in a movement that defended a radical change in the system. Since the basic motivation for the existence of the clash had been black slavery, many thought it possible that an identical conflict would spread to Brazil, and they even pointed to several signs indicative of this eventuality. In several articles, the editor of the newspaper *O Novo Mundo* sought to show this was impossible, especially because of the differences between the two countries.

The simple fact of highlighting that Brazilian society as a whole was in favor of abolition aimed at emphasizing the impossibility of a repetition of the North American conflict in Brazil. Rodrigues showed that, with regard to the very costly price paid by the United States, "the blood of a million men," there was not the least possibility of Brazil paying its obligation in the same coin. He added that the only price to be paid "for our sin and the sin of our ancestors is this crisis of change." In the meantime, Brazilian society continued to haggle and to refuse to pay the price demanded.[159]

Even without the possibility of there occurring in Brazil a conflict similar to that in the United States, it is certain that from the middle of the 1860s slavery came to be discussed with greater insistence. The topic was broached from widely different perspectives, coming even to speak much more about the danger represented by the slaves. The conflict in the United States had raised this question. The missionary Simonton explained that having destroyed the "peace and tranquility of the past," the conflict between North and South brought to the surface a "terrifying question:" "What ought to be done with the black race?" [160]

This issue had been discussed in Brazil since the first half of the nineteenth century. Frederico L.C. Burlamaqui, for example, acknowledges in 1837 the politics of gradual emancipation as an efficient way of uniting the entire society in favor of abolition with the important advantage of avoiding giving rise to an enemy race. He said that "heroic measures" should be "applied slowly, with great circumspection and at long intervals." At the same time that safe and effective steps would be taken toward the objective of complete emancipation, the politics of gradualism also had the virtue of preparing the attitudes of the slaves in a parsimonious fashion. Thinking about the Presbyterian Simonton, who was frightened and fearful due to the extent of the conflict in his own country, it is possible to believe that he would agree with this politics of gradualism in so far as it would not destroy the "peace and tranquility" in such a sudden and abrupt fashion.[161]

Many considered the possibility of discounting the black race, believing that with abolition it would no longer be possible to count on the cooperation of slave laborers. Along the same lines, others thought it would be very difficult to keep blacks working after the arrival of another regime. Ina von Binzer, in *Alegrias e Tristezas de uma Educadora Alemã no Brasil* [Joys and Sorrows of a German Educator in Brazil], showed that it was possible to predict what could be expected from freed blacks. For her, only a minimal portion that would not be very productive would remain in the fields, and it would not be possible to count on the black population for an agricultural workforce. "Nor should one think in any way about an impulse that indirectly might come to favor the country in the next ten years, either in agriculture or in industry." [162]

So, what was to be done with blacks? What was to be done to eliminate or even diminish the danger they represented? With abolition would there not be revolts seeking compensation for the oppression suffered during the centuries? These were the questions discussed in Brazil. Observing from afar the unfolding of the conflict in the United States, Simonton even came to consider the possibility of the government "creating a system of colonization or training," as a way of controlling the impulse of the former slaves, principally following the first moments of life under the new regime.[163] In the article "O trabalho dos emancipados" [The Work of the Emancipated], José Carlos Rodrigues pointed out that in any city in the South of the United States, no matter what hour of the day, one could find from ten to a hundred blacks, former slaves, sleeping in the streets. This fact was foreseeable and could not be otherwise. If many whites, with their better education and having always been free, were also vagrants and could be found on the streets, why should the blacks' first reaction be surprising?

Rodrigues further maintains that only a portion of the former slaves would behave in this manner. The freed slaves in the South could be divided into three groups: the first contained the more intelligent and entrepreneurial who saved with the goal of buying their own land; the second, and the largest of the three, was formed by those who worked and earned money but quickly spent all the wages they received; and finally, the third class, also numerous, was formed by "professed vagabonds" who wanted nothing to do with work and wandered about the cities. With articles like this, the author aimed at easing the minds of the Brazilians, telling them that there was nothing to fear and there was no possibility of waves of revenge by blacks. He added that if on the one hand there was no danger to be feared, on the other there were also very positive benefits: "The principal fact in this situation is that the former slave owners were very happy to find themselves free of the scourge of "this servile element" of society." [164]

It was commonly claimed that the black would be incapable of suddenly assuming his freedom without any preparation or seigniorial oversight. In the view of many, especially the owners, the slave who was free or liberated ought not be abandoned to his own fortunes, for if such were to occur, the slave would certainly not turn to the disciplined work that would be useful for the nation. This was the theory of Senator Inhambupe, for whom blacks, "unable to govern themselves," ought to be handed over to guardians or tutors for a time "to guide them towards what is necessary for their happiness." There was no serious and genuine concern for the "happiness" of blacks in the senator's proposal. His objective was to exclude blacks from all social interaction and send them back to Africa. Faced with the question of what to do with the slaves, as formulated later by the missionary Simonton, he had a reply on the tip of his tongue: "Abolition would result in a great benefit to the nation, since it would bring the opportunity of "unleashing from us this savage race, which corrupts our customs, the education of our children, the progress of industry, and all that is of value, and has even lost our pure language!" [165]

Alongside Simonton, there were many others who were afraid of the consequences of the Civil War in the United States. It was impossible to expect that there would be any defense of abolition of the slave regime in Brazil on the part of the Protestant missionaries, and even less by the southern immigrants who had arrived there. Thus, in the first years following the conflict, the arrival of these immigrants, the beginning of Protestant preaching, and the formation of the first churches meant a pause in whatever expectations there were on the topic. It was not possible that they would defend for Brazil the same outcome as in their country of origin. Even those from the North who were followers of the abolition movement, as was the case of some missionaries, had to cease for a time and not give voice to any proposals on this topic. They were obliged to wait for some years until an accommodation occurred in the United States. Only then were they able to get a clearer reading on the situation and discern the possibility of imitating the North American example.

The unfolding of events in the United States was followed closely by abolitionists and Protestants in Brazil. At the same time that an economic catastrophe was feared, the impossibility of black success in the new social reality was also foreseen. It was José Carlos Rodrigues who sought to bring to Brazil this new panorama of North American society. Innumerable articles in the newspaper *O*

Novo Mundo were written with such a goal in mind, evaluating the post-Civil War situation in the United States, pointing out the visible economic progress of the southern states, which before had been slave states.

In a simple note published during the newspaper's first year, Rodrigues not only reported the progress gained by the United States, but also pointed out that President Grant, in his year-end message to the U.S. Congress, claimed that it would be very useful to acquire the Dominican part of the Island of Santo Domingo (Hispaniola) with a view "toward immediately rendering slavery intolerable in Cuba, Puerto Rico, and also in Brazil." In his commentary on the president's remarks, Rodrigues emphasized that this declaration was quite a show, something never before seen, "a president seeking the incorporation of a territory because it will contribute to the extinction of slavery in other countries." [166]

In the article "Progresso da raça Africana nos Estados Unidos" [Progress of the African Race in the United States], published originally in the newspaper *Gazeta de Notícias* and reproduced in *O Abolicionista* on 27 August 1881, two years after the closing of the newspaper *O Novo Mundo*, Rodrigues asserted:

> When the Civil War erupted . . . it was believed that emancipation, if it was achieved, would not be of much benefit to the African race. General opinion was that the blacks were destined to disappear when faced by the stronger race. The women, abandoned to laziness and drunkenness, living without comforts in mud huts, would not be able to produce a race stronger than themselves that would guide them and free them from the evils of ignorance and the circumstance of belonging to a greatly inferior race. Such was the general opinion. [167]

Rodrigues said that sixteen years after the end of the war, there was sufficient experience and it was possible to evaluate what had happened to blacks. Two things had happened in that time. "Blacks are not only alive, they are living prosperously, and they work and help the nation become rich," and they demonstrated the ability to compete as equals "with any European in certain types of work." [168] One could not demand that former slaves be capable of carrying out with perfection every type of activity; however, this inability was not due to natural ineptitude, but to the lengthy period of enslavement to which they had been subjected.

After sixteen years there had already been an adjustment in the situation in the United States and it was possible to recommend to Brazil that it follow this example. "The advice I give is this: Put an end to slavery immediately," proclaimed the future editor of *Jornal do Comércio.*

> Slavery is like a thorn that penetrates the flesh and causes excruciating pain but which we do not want to pull out, for fear that the operation will further increase the pain. Here in the South there is not a single farmer who wishes the return of slavery, or who doesn't say that there are evils that work for the good, referring to the Civil War. But Brazilians must immediately attend to the moral and technical education of young blacks. They must help blacks in every way. They must to get used to seeing them as co-participants in God's promises through Jesus Christ. [169]

In the monthly meeting in his church held on 3 November 1865, Robert R. Kalley pointed out that slaves had been subjected to harsh punishments and ill treatment. Such oppression produced a dangerous cycle, with the consequent build-up of hatred and feelings of revenge. For the Congregational pastor, "The slave is not the son of his owner, he does not work because he loves his master nor because he wants to be noble: he works for him like a beast, without receiving recompense of any sort for his work; the slave works only because he fears the threats of blows and inhuman punishment at the hands of one who is a robber of another's freedom.[170]

In the first half of the nineteenth century, however, before the conflict in the United States, important uprisings had already been recorded that had provoked fear in the Brazilian population. The slave uprising in the imperial capital in January 1835 created a deep uneasiness. An article published in the 20 March 1835 issue of the *Aurora Fluminense* pointed out that the movement was the source of a profound sense of fear and had instilled terror. Sharing in this anxiety, the newspaper noted that the clues and documents that had been discovered confirmed that the insurrection had been plotted carefully and kept in complete secrecy. "Fortunately, such dark designs came to naught; but the dire and dangerous consequences that can result from other similar attempts require us, Sir, to open our eyes to the great urgency of taking serious and effective steps to prevent them." [171] Among the remedies taken, the newspaper writer claims to have requested from the central government authorization to expel from Brazilian territory all free Africans who were a danger to the nation's peace.

Thomas Davatz, school master and Lutheran pastor, author of *Memórias de um Colono no Brasil* [Memories of a Colonialist in Brazil] explained that the fact that an important slave uprising had not occurred was due to the "divine curse," "Noah's curse on Canaan that kept them in subjugation." For him, this justification became reasonable and believable in as much as it would be easy for the slaves, because of their large number, "to take revenge on their traffickers and oppressors." Even while making it clear that the greater "part of established social forces supported the institution of slavery" and that the slaves, "reduced to a condition of servility, could not rebel," Davatz drew attention to the latent possibility of conflict, since the "entire nation is weakened" by slavery.[172]

George Gardner, author of *Travels in the Interior of Brazil*, wrote his work at the end of the first half of the nineteenth century and also confirmed the fear of Brazilian society over the possibility of a widespread insurrection by slaves. "A general rise of the black population is much dreaded, which is not unreasonable, when the great proportion it bears to the white is taken into consideration." [173]

There was fear not only with respect to an organized and massive insurrection. The newspaper *Imprensa Evangélica* pointed out that just as the slaves never had any protection against cruel masters, thus was it also impossible for the state to offer guarantees for the lives of slave owners and their families, especially those established in the interior regions of the country. There were many risks in so far as "when within a man the wild beast is unleashed, he does not know what he is doing and draws the blood of everyone he meets, good and bad, guilty and innocent." [174]

Differing from the conception adopted by the Lutheran Thomas Davatz, of submission as the consequence of the divine curse, the editor of *O Novo Mundo* was of the opinion that, contrary to the situation in the United States, where there was a radical division over the question of slavery, everyone in Brazil said that they were opposed to slavery and that the institution survived as a sin inherited from the Portuguese. We can infer that in the imagination of Brazilian society there was an intuitive understanding that this pro-abolitionist stance served as a mechanism to restrain and nullify whatever potential existed for revenge to be carried out by the slaves.

Even with the risk of an uprising by the slave population, as confirmed by innumerable documents, what existed in reality was an accommodation. In the same way that society understood that the simple acknowledgment of the injustice of slavery already served as penitence and repentance for the sin committed, it also recognized that black slaves would never represent any sort of concrete threat to whites. In this regard, *Imprensa Evangélica* commented that the evidence of this peculiar characteristic of Brazilian society ought not serve as justification for the perpetuation of slavery. On the contrary, emancipation ought to be sought with greater calmness, without fear of repercussions like those in the United States. Meanwhile it was necessary to consider that "delay in justice for the oppressed brought danger for oppressors." This delay could contribute to the rise of insurrectionist movements. [175]

Such proof, apparently revealing a positive idiosyncrasy in Brazilian society, did not succeed in awaking and mobilizing the population to take a more radical and urgent position. What happened in Brazil was a simple acknowledgement of its reality, and a consequent deduction that, by way of such acknowledgement, society could redeem itself for the sin committed.

In the mid-1880s, when the abolitionist movement was already taking shape as a large popular urban movement, the basic question given priority by Protestantism continued to be opening up space for its acceptance and, consequently, its successful implantation. Participation in the movements favoring abolition was above all an essentially religious concern, and the opening given for discussions and defense of abolition revealed, in large measure, specific interests and functions. On the one hand, there was confirmation of the Protestants' interest in progress, in opposition to the conservatism represented by the Catholic Church; on the other hand, an effort was made to spread Protestantism as acceptable among the classes that were fighting for the abolition of slavery.

THE BRAZILIAN LAZARUS BREAKS THE STONE OF THE TOMB TO THE SOUND OF THE REDEEMING WORD: PROTESTANT THEOLOGY AND SLAVERY

> On the 27th of the present month, a black by the name of José ran away. He is a Benguela, thirty-some years of age, average height, an ugly face, a very large nose, and missing the ends of two fingers on his left hand.[176]

In Brazil there is much slavery beyond that of Africans and their descendants—Manichean theology.

In his bombastic affirmations against the two missionaries Daniel Kidder and Justin Spaulding, the radical Ultramontane Father Luis Gonçalves dos Santos, known as Father Perereca, was seen to exaggerate in his denunciation of them as messengers of a secret project aimed at abolishing slavery. "Beyond the ravaging of souls, which Methodism premeditates and has already set in motion, there is much to be feared with regard to slavery. From one fragment in the First Report of the Head of the Mission of Rio de Janeiro, it is easily seen that the Methodists have secret plans regarding our slaves." [177]

Father Perereca was mistaken. Indeed, the two Methodist missionaries, Kidder and Spaulding, came from the North of the United States and were supporters of abolition. However, at no time during their stay in Brazil did they show any interest in the struggle for abolition of slavery, nor did the Methodist Church have any plans on this issue. In the two-volume work *Sketches of Residence and Travels in Brazil*, which describes in detail all the activities undertaken there, Kidder mentions slaves innumerable times only from the perspective of a dispassionate observer of the social reality of the country.

He spoke, for example, of a large group of slaves swarming around a fountain in order to collect water, blacks gathered in certain public squares, pointing out that such crowds always ended up in fights and confusion. Kidder pointed out their physical strength and their dexterity in carrying bags of merchandise. He commented that they carried heavy bags on their heads and used one hand to balance the merchandise and the other to hold some rustic musical instrument. He remembered their love for music and singing, mentioning that at one time an effort was made to prohibit them from singing so as not to disturb the public peace. This order was followed, but the capacity for work dropped so much that the decision was soon reversed and they were allowed to sing once more.[178] Kidder commented as follows regarding the house of correction.

> The house of correction is located on the brow of a high hill between Catumbi and Mata Porcos. . . . This is the place to which slaves are sent to be corrected for disobedience, or common misdemeanors. They are received at any hour of the day or night, and retained free of expense as long as their masters choose to leave them. It would be remarkable if scenes of extreme cruelty did not sometimes occur here.

It is a melancholy sight, but one which in passing I often witnessed, to see several scores of convicts, chained together in platoons, marching under a guard of soldiers from the walls of this institution to the barracks of Mata Porcos, where they slept after the day's labor. Some of these individuals—like others met daily within the streets—wore a huge ring of iron around their necks, with an extremity projecting upwards by the side of the head. This mark is generally understood to designate a runaway slave who had been recaptured.[179]

Alongside these reports, free of any political abolitionist intentions, there is another group of depictions that strive to show that slavery in Brazil brought trouble not only to slaves but also to slave owners. The book written by Kidder with James T. Fletcher relates the following stories.

A lady of high rank in Brazil declared that she had entirely lost her health in the interesting occupation of scolding negresses, of whom she possessed some scores, and knew not what occupation to give them in order to keep them out of mischief. A lady of a noble family one day asked a friend of mine if she knew of anyone who desired to give out washing, as she (the senhora) had nine lazy servants at home for whom there was no employment. She piteously told her story saying, "We make it a principle not to sell our slaves, and they are the torment of my life, for I cannot find enough work to keep them out of idleness and mischief." [180]

Probably Kidder's strongest commentary relating to the Brazilian social situation involving black slavery, was his description of the home for found-lings, a place where newborns were left, mainly the female children of slaves. It is a long text, but it warrants transcription.

The Foundling Hospital is sometimes called *Casa da Roda* in allusion to the wheel in which infants are deposited from the streets, and by a semi-revolution conveyed within the walls of the building. The wheel occupies the place of a window, facing a public square, and revolves on a perpendicular axis. It is divided by partition into four triangular apartments, one of which always opens without; this inviting the approach of any who may be so heartless as to wish to part with their infant children. They have only to deposit the foundling in the box, and by a turn of the wheel it passes within the walls, they themselves going away unobserved.

That such institutions are the offspring of a mistaken philanthropy is as evident in Brazil as it can be in any country. Not only do they encourage licentiousness, but they foster the most palpable inhumanity. Out of 3,630 infants exposed in Rio during ten years anterior to 1840, only 1,024 were living at the end of that period. In the year 1838-39, 449 were deposited on the wheel, of whom six were found dead when taken out; many expired the first day after their arrival, and 239 died in a short period. By means of all possible endeavors, and the expense of all the wet-nurses to be procured, it has only been possible to save about a third of all that are received. Well might one of the physicians of the establishment, in whose company I visited several departments of the institution, remark, "Sir, it is carnage!"

From thirty to fifty children are brought here every month in the year. What must be the moral condition, or the human feelings of these numerous individuals who deliberately contribute to such an exposure of infant life! One peculiar circumstance connected with this state of things, consists in the alleged fact, that many of the foundlings are the off-spring of female slaves, whose masters, not wishing the trouble and expense of endeavoring to raise the children, or wishing the services of the mothers as wet-nurses, require the infants to be sent to the "engeitaria" (refuse heap) where, should they survive, they of course, are free.[181]

The Protestant missionaries established in Brazil—from the pioneering incursion of the Methodists achieved by Kidder and Spaulding, to that of the Baptists who settled in Brazil in the 1880s—were influenced by a strong theological inclination to distinguish the spiritual from the temporal. The article "Fechamento das Portas" [Closing the Doors], published in *Methodista Cathólico* and proposing to address the problem of conducting business on Sundays, makes clear this idiosyncratic position. The article claimed that while it was wrong to enslave a fellow being, taking from him what is most precious to him, "it is even more iniquitous to compel a class acknowledged to be free to work on the day that the King of kings, the Lord of lords, the Ruler of the people ordered work to cease."

This article, written anonymously by "C.G.S.S.," compared working on Sundays with the slavery of blacks and argued that working on "the Lord's Day" was much more iniquitous.[182] The Presbyterian newspaper *Imprensa Evangélica*, in the article "Sois escravos ou livres?" [Are you slaves or free?], displays some of the same characteristics, presenting an exegesis of the biblical text Galatians 5:1 and the question, "What makes a man or child free, and what makes him a slave?" The reply is that "Every man is a slave when, instead of believing upon Christ for his salvation, he is obedient to God's commandments, observes the rituals and ceremonies of the Church and keeps holy days and weeks. Oh! What hard slavery!" [183]

The newspaper *O Novo Mundo*, on a separate occasion, maintained the same ideological bias: "Slavery in Brazil extends beyond Africans and their descendants. The real political slavery from which we suffer is the child of the moral slavery which in its turn is generated by the lack of the Gospel in our hearts."[184] This distinction, where greater weight should be given to the motivations guiding Christianity as a whole, was studied by North American Protestantism. This theological Manichaeism sought to establish the limits of the action of the Church, and was based on Jesus' statement, "Give to Caesar what is Caesar's, and give to God what is God's." (Mark 12:17)

This biblical text served as a motto exclusive to a conservative branch of the Church and as a vouchsafe for separating socio-political questions from spiritual/religious ones. Matters linked to the political and social sphere belonged to "Caesar," while "spiritual" considerations, such as conversion and moral conduct, were the real concerns of the Church.[185] Consistent with this thinking, the realm of the Church's activities was already defined by the Bible, which was considered the Constitution of the Church.

The principle that aimed at establishing the limits for the Church's activity developed quite fully within the conservative wing of North American Protestantism, more specifically in what was called the 'Old School' of Presbyterianism, which in turn wielded great influence in the southern United States. The 'Old School' came to defend the social system of slavery, claiming it to be a civil institution and therefore beyond the purview of action by the Church.

The theology of the 'Old School' was also transplanted into other Protestant denominations established in the South. A very interesting article published in the April 1870 issue of the *Methodist Quarterly Review* spoke of the General Methodist Council of 1844. It related the history of the beginning of the Methodist Church in the United States with the arrival of Coke and Asbury, the first elected bishops, and the occurrence of a theological about-face that resulted in the acceptance of slavery. From its beginnings, the Methodist Church encountered great success in the southern United States and the gospel was preached by pastors who followed the Wesleyan tradition and were, consequently, abolitionists. At the beginning, there was some concern for condemning the institution and expelling from the bosom of the Church those members who did not submit to this doctrinal directive. Meanwhile, out of the many movements of spiritual revival, there was quite a growth in membership in the Methodist Church, the majority of those people being supporters of slavery.

Thus, in a region in which slavery had become a valued domestic institution interwoven with the structure of society and protected by innumerable laws, the new Methodist leaders came to take a more indulgent position. The Methodist supporters of slavery came to show strong evidence of genuine piety, weeping and struggling in prayer for mercy, rejoicing in the pardon they received and offering their slaves more humane treatment, believing that they were thus satisfying the demands of the Christian faith. Following this approach, and in accordance with the increase in the number of slave owners in the Church, there arose a strong conservative movement, with its own theology, diminishing any possibility of slave emancipation. For this movement, such a measure would be possible only when God himself, in his providence, clearly showed this to be his desire.[186]

The same path followed by the Methodists marked the other Protestant denominations established in the southern United States. In the period from North America's independence until 1830, anti-slavery feelings began to dissipate under pressure from the slave owners who dominated the fundamental institutions of representative democracy. Shortly after the Nat Turner Revolt, proselytizing among the slaves became more intense, as the masters concluded that the conversion of their slaves could serve as an important instrument of social control. At this time laws and campaigns arose that contributed noticeably to the decline in anti-slavery sentiment in the southern churches. There were laws against black preachers and prohibiting slaves from learning to read and write, and there were campaigns promoting the oral teaching of the Christian faith and a more humane treatment toward slaves.[187]

It was not possible for the Methodists to remain united, since it was extremely difficult to acknowledge and reconcile the anti-slavery laws inherited from Wesleyan Methodism with the new reality of the southern United States. Likewise, divisions occurred within the other churches. At the beginning of the 1830s, an ever broader consensus began to build, with the important support of even these Protestant churches. As doubts of conscience with respect to slavery were overcome, greater room was made for the progress and growth of these churches, since they "were securing the conditions for carrying out proselytism among the slaves, counting on the approval and support of the owners." [188]

Further reinforcing this tendency to distinguish between the *spiritual* and the *non-spiritual*, a characteristic of Protestant missions in Brazil was a Manichaean view of the world. According to this viewpoint, the present world is bad and mankind struggles and suffers like a pilgrim until arriving in a happy land, and this happy ending depends on the type of lifestyle he selects. This notion of pilgrimage was always, without a doubt, an inheritance common to the life of the Protestant denominations established in Brazil with a missionary origin. According to this doctrine, the individual is induced to resign himself to his situation since his stay here is short-lived in comparison with the happy eternal future. [189]

Even though it is in a text that is clearly intended to address important political questions, Eduardo Carlos Pereira, a Presbyterian pastor and "noted Brazilian preacher" (according to José Carlos Rodrigues), revealed a little of this Protestant Manichaean idiosyncrasy.

> People who, for certain, observe events and facts affirm that we are living in a time of transition; and this is fortunate, for the present state of our society pleases no one. A criminal indifference manifests itself everywhere, and an egotism seems to print its seal on everything that is happening. Where only patriotism should be heard, self-interests fearlessly arise. The parties take turns in power, and then fall impotent when faced with those obstacles, real or imagined, that work against the achievement of their programs. And the people shrug their shoulders, caring little about the outcome of the most vital and momentous questions. Faced with such a discouraging spectacle, a chill enters the hearts of true patriots, and they too succumb to the soporific influences of the environment in which they live. Faith grows lukewarm and there is an increase in desertion among noble champions; political skepticism seizes hold of citizens; and moral decadence prevails. This is the hallmark of the day. And who can be blamed for all this? We will not engage in a purely political discussion: partisan recriminations are completely irrelevant to our goals. If we raise this question, it is to address it from a cosmopolitan point of view, if we can express ourselves in this way. We do not wish, far from it, to offend partisan sensibilities. [190]

In the text of this Presbyterian pastor there is no objective question, no explanation or detail about what he called "a discouraging spectacle." We do not even come to know the meaning of "a criminal indifference" to which he makes reference. Close to the end, he insists on pointing out that political discussions are "completely irrelevant to our goals" and in no way does he intend to "offend partisan sensibilities." Sidestepping the socio-political points, he concludes:

Hope remains for us in some religious system; to this let it be reserved the glorious mission of raising the people to the heights of a true and permanent civilization. Religion has always been and will always be the most powerful agent of social movements. A nation's religious principles greatly influence its political and social destiny. This is history's constant lesson, and also the experience of our times. It would be possible, perhaps, to project to a certain extent the future history of a people, knowing its religious principles. If this is the case, if religion so greatly influences the route taken by a society, it follows that religion will lead a people to the heights of glory or to the depths of the abyss, in accordance with the elements that it holds in its bosom. And we believe that faced with history, faced with the events that are taking place in our own and other countries, faced with the immortal Syllabus, we can assert that Ultramontanism is the terrible barrier that stands in the way of progress, impeding the passage of the people.[191]

Why should these men who cannot sing a song, sing psalms and hymns?—Strategy of avoiding controversial subjects

Since the beginning of its establishment in Brazil, Protestantism understood that discussions of slavery could gradually become dangerous, in addition especially to enormously increasing the difficulties of the top priority, implantation. This was the conclusion of Ashbel Simonton in September 1859, shortly after his arrival in Brazil, following a conversation about slaves and slavery. The Presbyterian pioneer lamented having expressed his anti-slavery position to someone who was "absurdly pro-slavery." He concluded that this inopportune conversation had prejudiced his position, had created barriers and had caused him to lose any possibility of influencing his partner in conversation in the future.[192]

There is a very clear example confirming that the Protestantism implanted in Brazil had as a basic strategy for the achievement of its implantation the rule of avoiding the discussion of controversial topics not linked directly to religion. This is the article "Liberdade do corpo e escravidão do espirito" [Freedom of the body and enslavement of the spirit], published in the newspaper *Imprensa Evangélica* in March of 1879.

> Years ago it was considered opportune to incorporate into Brazilian law a decree declaring the womb free from a specified date forward. "No longer will anyone be born a slave in Brazil" merited the applause of the civilized world; and newspapers spun eulogies to the Emperor and his government for the measure that assured a slow but certain death to the system that gave the government, and even a man, power over the body of a fellow human being, like a businessman selling a field of cotton or trading a horse, without asking the farm or the horse whether it wanted to change owner. Today another question is being discussed that seeks to graft onto the original legislation another decree that would give freedom to the Brazilian spirit. At issue is finding out whether, while we boast of the free body in Brazil, we will have to bow our heads and confess that we have not reached the time of a free spirit.[193]

As can be seen, there was no concern for discussing the Law of the Free Womb and its repercussions in Brazilian society. There was only a succinct commentary about the publication of the law and then an affirmation that the basic concern, the most important demand, is not the freedom of the body but of the spirit, religious freedom.

A willingness to confront conflicts and foster arguments was accepted emphatically by Protestantism in Brazil. But this commitment was focused only on the religious aspects, with the goal of contributing directly to facilitating the implantation of Protestantism. The most protracted commentary made by the Methodist newspaper *O Expositor Cristão* was published in 1889 and reprinted the results of the Eighth Meeting of the Methodist Mission, held in the city of Buenos Aires with the purpose of discussing evangelization in the missionary field of Rio Grande do Sul. The newspaper, in circulation since 1886, reported the news that approximately fifty thousand former slaves were living in the Province of Rio Grande do Sul. It recommended the creation of a Sociedade Protectora dos Libertos do Brazil [Society for the Protection of the Free in Brazil] with the intention of collecting funds for the evangelization of the aforesaid group.[194]

The spiritual theology of missionary Protestantism in Brazil was satisfactorily suited to a prudent distancing from the Church regarding the serious problems faced by society, among them black slavery. The missionary Ashbel Simonton, who was openly against slavery, accompanied Mr. H. in the purchase of two slaves at an auction and lamented finding himself "again in the middle of the horrors of slavery." Although he was opposed to the institution, his theology was adapted to separate political matters from those that were essentially religious and spiritual. Above all, his top priority was the work of safeguarding the implantation of Presbyterianism in Brazil. Simonton was willing to put all his energy into achieving this task, so he ignored even the advice of Robert Kalley, which was based on his own experiences and recommended more prudence and less exposure. Simonton argued that his presence in the country and his purpose there could not be disguised, and he trusted in God's protection and was willing to use all possible means to carry out his work.[195]

The conduct of the Methodist missionary Martha Watts was identical to that of Simonton. While also opposed to slavery, she nevertheless avoided addressing the issue. Upon her arrival at the city of Piracicaba in 1881, she created a school and hired as its cook Flora Maria Blumer de Toledo, a slave to whom she immediately granted her letter of emancipation.[196] In her innumerable letters, there are almost no references to slavery. Rare were the occasions when she took up the issue briefly, such as the letter of December 1881 in which she described the populace of Piracicaba, observing, "The people dress as well as they do in the States—that is, the better class do. The poor people and the negroes do not meet all the demands of decency at all times." [197]

Years later, Joaquim Nabuco denounced the fact that the movement working for the abolition of slavery did not include participation by the Church. Obviously, he was referring to the Catholic Church, but it is important to note that one of the examples he relates when denouncing this connivance with the slave-owning regime was that "no priest ever tried to stop a slave auction." [198]

The missionary Simonton felt horrified as he watched one of these auctions being conducted. Like the Catholic clergy, he did nothing to stop what was happening. But the question is that his role was another, quite different. In addition to being a foreigner, constantly under surveillance, especially by the Ultramontanists, he came to Brazil to implant Presbyterian Protestantism. He did not approve of the slave-owning regime, but he was already accustomed to living with it. He had learned to be tolerant in his country of origin. Many pastors made use of the services provided by slaves and even made a business of it; furthermore, much ink had been used by theologians to justify the system.

Considering the times in which Simonton began his work in Brazil, it becomes quite understandable why he wanted to give first priority to matters directly related to his religious work. There were many vigilant eyes closely watching the advance of Protestantism. The Presbyterian projects were being followed, much like in the epoch of David Kidder and Justin Spaulding, the two pioneer Methodists who had their movements rigorously controlled by the leading Ultramontanists, especially Father Perereca

When the parliamentary session opened in 1859, the item on the agenda was separating the marriage contract from the Catholic sacrament. On 20 May 1859, the Archbishop of Bahia, Count of Santa Cruz, made a long, persuasive and eloquent presentation against the proposal under discussion. Arguing that the marriage contract should not flee from the shield provided by the spiritual realm, he appealed for the necessity of maintaining religious marriage as exclusively linked to Catholic discipline, avoiding the "fatal consequences of Protestant proselytism which, as is well-known, is fighting to de-Catholicize our nation and which, unfortunately, has already achieved conquests."[199]

The missionaries Daniel Kidder and James Fletcher saw quite clearly that the question of slavery was much broader, related to several other aspects of life in the country, not only the economy. For them, "the issue of slavery was also closely tied to the survival of traditional attitudes, which maintained and protected the majority of customs and institutions that Brazil had inherited from its colonial past" [200] Questioning slavery might result in the closing of the few openings provided by the country for the preaching of the Protestant model. There emerged, therefore, the explicit decision not to involve the [Protestant] Church in the social question of slavery. The first priority was to safeguard the implantation of Protestantism, the invasion of what Father Perereca called "the closed garden." [201]

With the exception of Robert Kalley, author of a very important text on the use of slave labor who expelled from his church a member who refused to free his slaves, there was no other more radical behavior during the initial phase of implantation of Protestantism. The newspaper *Imprensa Evangélica* came to recommend prudence in discussing the subject of abolition. "Malevolent and malign passions are easily excited when conflicting interests come into play. That is what is happening on a large scale. Therefore, all gentle responses and calm arguments on the topic of emancipation are welcome." [202] It was only at the end of the 1880s, when all of Brazilian society was already discussing the issue, that a limited number of manifestations appeared. Among these, worthy of mention are the message from Pastor Eduardo Carlos Pereira, the first important declaration from a Brazilian Protestant pastor, and the extremely argumentative position of Justus Nelson, a Methodist pastor in Belém, Pará. At the beginning of 1887, Nelson stated:

> Our words are neither a seditious cry nor an incitement to revolt. But for us, in the face of natural law, morality, and the very religion that the great God, in the person of a Nazarene rabbi, came to preach to the world, slavery is arguably a crime, an audacious and aggravated robbery; there is no violence that cannot be justified in trying to put an end to this monstrous and abominable institution. The cruelty of the slave trade drew out of the outraged conscience of the intrepid abolitionist Ruy Barbosa these eloquent words: "The slave trade . . . an immense black stain that covers a whole segment of history; the milky way blackened by the brush of a stupendous crime; like a dark cloud of demons brought low, spread across the firmament from one pole to the other. If Dante Alighieri had come in the eighteenth century, he would have placed the pinnacle of inexpressible suffering, the lowest circle of his inferno, in the hold of a slave ship, in one of those centers of infinite tortures, which only the sinister poetry of madness could portray." . . . Such are the foundations on which the gloomy edifice of slavery rests, today propped up on one side by the false apostles of the egalitarian and brotherly religion of Jesus, and on the other by jurists bribed by the tarnished money of the landowners and by the disgraceful advisors to our crown. . . . Only the Republic shall redeem us.[203]

This Protestantism brought in its belly its own contradictions and it had to adapt, assimilating and developing those elements that could make it suitable to a completely different culture and a social structure already essentially defined. The concern of Protestantism was exclusively focused on establishing its missions, and adaptation to this new reality occurred as a result of this objective. Two elements characterized the Protestant message in this task of adaptation: the polemic and the dogmatic. The polemical aspect involved the confrontation with the dominant religion, with regard to showing its falsehood when compared to the truth of Protestant Christianity. It represented an attempt to dislodge the established religion in order to open space for the new religion. Likewise, the dogmatic aspect was an attempt to inculcate the [Protestant] doctrine or theology and its respective worldview.

We were gladdened to find the children and even many younger slaves taking part in holy hymns—the question of integrating blacks.

The theology of the Brazilian Protestant mission was transplanted from the churches in the South of the United States. In southern society before the Civil War, social relations were quite well delineated and black slavery occupied a clearly defined space. According to the 1844 report of the General Methodist Council, slavery was an institution that had come to be quite valued and necessary, intimately woven into the structure of southern society and protected by innumerable laws and cultural norms. Moreover, according to the report, slave owners were pious men who were legitimately defended in the churches and protected by civil laws.

Faced with this reality, the solution was gradually to abandon the orientation of Wesleyan Methodism, leaving the topic aside as if it were foreign to the life of the Church and instead entrusting to God the "extirpation of slavery." This conniving approach found by the Methodist Church was also accepted by all the other Protestant denominations in the [southern] United States. The objective was to try and find harmony, and for this purpose the great and saving dominant political idea was embraced: "Union first, principle afterward." [204] In Brazil, missionary Protestantism also adopted, in practice, a very similar motto: instead of "Union first, principle afterward," it was "Implantation first, principle afterward."

When speaking of slavery, the theology of missionary Protestantism in Brazil revealed itself to be essentially conservative and paternalistic, and not at all libertarian or revolutionary. Concern was focused on the integration, conversion and education of blacks within Protestant culture, and not on their emancipation. To summarize, interest concentrated on regeneration, declaring that the degeneration of habits was contrary to Christian virtue. This is what was announced in the *Imprensa Evangélica*: "Let religious teaching come immediately, without delay, to inspire moral duties, honesty and the love of work in the hearts of slaves and *ingênuos* who live like slaves; let religious teaching come and show them the way of duty." [205]

Focusing on teaching a religiosity that helped slaves accept their lot, Brazilian Protestantism sought to make their lives more tolerable, consoling them and making them more patient and submissive. The theology that was preached reflected the existence of a stage of transition that offered the slaves simply a religious conversion. In addition, some justification was found for maintaining this situation: the good treatment of slaves, the agreeableness of the institution when compared to the North American example, and the paternalistic nature in which it was cloaked, seigniorial and semi-feudal.

Kalley paid attention to slaves, striving to make them an integral part of his church. He sought to evangelize them, taking care to see that they were treated with greater respect, directing a bible study class in his church composed of "men of color," and coming to intercede with a slave owner for the freedom of a female slave who had embraced the Protestant faith. [206]

The Presbyterians also held religious services with the intention of converting slaves to the Protestant faith. A year before the promulgation of the Law of the Free Womb, Júlio Ribeiro, embracing Presbyterianism, took steps for one of his slaves, named Joaquim, to be baptized. Later, he himself issued a certificate of freedom to this young slave and to his mother, who had also accepted the Protestant faith. [207]

Many slaves converted to the Protestant faith and became members in various churches. [208] However, as Henry Koster carefully observed, the number of slaves was not great, mainly because the Catholic faith served as an integrative element of support in their situation of misery. For a slave to abandon Catholicism and adhere to Protestantism was a radical and difficult step. This was because to be a part of Catholicism was something quite natural, and almost the entire society was included within that religion. To abandon Catholicism meant breaking with all that structure and accepting a life of ostracism. Koster pointed out that integration into Catholicism brought benefits for slaves:

> The slave himself wants likewise to be made a Christian for his fellow bonds-men will in every squabble or trifling disagreement with him, close their string of opprobrious epithets with the name of *pagão* (pagan). The unbaptized negro feels that he is considered as an inferior being, and although he may not be aware of the value which the whites place upon baptism, still he knows that the stigma for which he is upbraided will be removed by it; and therefore he is desirous of being made equal to his companions.[209]

From Koster's observation it can be deduced that slaves faced difficulties and discrimination that were much greater once they adhered to Protestantism.

In order to be able to better understand the depth of this symbiosis between the Catholic Church and Brazilian society and the difficulties a slave would face in order to participate in Protestantism, it is sufficient to refer to the difficulties faced by the Protestant Antônio Romualdo Monteiro Manso, who was elected deputy from Minas Gerais. On appearing before the leadership of the Chamber of Deputies to take office on 6 September 1888, he refused to take the pre-scribed oath, which included the phrase "I swear . . . to uphold the apostolic Roman Catholic religion." The president of the Chamber pointed out the neces-sity for such an oath and, faced with a second refusal, the leadership had to de-liberate the question. The following week, after long and heated discussion, the opinion of the Chamber Policy Commission was approved, "dispensing with the oath for any deputy who declared to the leadership that said oath was contrary to his beliefs." [210]

The likelihood was practically nil that a slave would adhere to Protestantism without being accompanied or indoctrinated by his master. It was probably most likely that this would happen in the cities, given that the slave would have a little more freedom, but even so there were many difficulties faced by Protestantism in its goal of winning over this segment of society.

Daniel Kidder pointed out that blacks were very devout and participated in the religious services promoted by the Church or their masters. This author re-lates that in his neighborhood there lived a Portuguese widow, quite elderly and surrounded by numerous slaves.

> She was a model of amiability, if not of piety. She treated her slaves as tenderly as though they had been her own children, and was specially punctilious in calling them together at vespers, and causing them to say their paternosters, and chant a litany of moderate length. So well trained where they to this exercise, that their voices would not have done discredit to the music of some churches.[211]

Later he recounts another experience that occurred on the farm of dona Gertrudes.

> In the course of the evening half an hour was devoted to vespers. I had observed a great number of the slaves entering, who in succession addressed us with crossed hands, and the pious salutation, "Seja louvado Nosso Senhor Jesus Christo"—blessed be the Lord Jesus Christ. Presently there commenced a chant in the adjoining room. . . . I was told that he attended these exercises merely as any other member of the family—the singing and prayers being taught and conducted by an aged black man. The devotions of the evening consisted principally of a Novena, a species of religious service including a litany, and consisting of nine parts, which are severally chanted on as many successive evenings. It was really pleasant to hear the sound of a hundred voices mingling in this their chief religious exercise and privilege. This assembling the slaves, generally at evening, and sometimes both morning and evening, is said to be common on plantations in the country, and is not infrequent among domestics in the cities. Mistress and servants, at these times, meet on a level. The pleasures afforded the latter by such opportunities, in conjunction with the numerous holidays enjoined by the Roman Catholic religion, form certainly a great mitigation of the hard lot of servitude.[212]

Access to Protestant religious services was practically impossible for slaves unless their masters showed a certain interest in the new religion, or unless, in the larger cities, they were allowed greater freedom of movement. This must have happened with Leopoldina Ferreira, who became a member of Robert Kalley's Congregational Church, continued a slave, and whose mistress was not part of the church. João Gomes da Rocha said that the slave Leopoldina Ferreira, a resident in Providência Street, was nominated for membership of the church by her neighbor, José Francisco da Cunha. Kalley, the pastor of the church, visited the slave's mistress to persuade her to grant Ferreira "a certificate of freedom." This woman finally agreed to follow Kalley's advice, such that three days later she informed him that she was prepared to act on his request and even to provide all the legal documents without any recompense, provided that the slave promised to continue in her service for as long as she, the owner, should live. It happened, however, that the young woman refused to accept this condition.[213]

The records of the First Presbyterian Church of São Paulo show the first baptism of a young male slave in 1870, one year before the promulgation of the Law of the Free Womb. The slave Joaquim was brought to the church by his master, the writer Júlio Ribeiro. Both the slave Joaquim and his mother, also a slave, became Protestants, because they belonged to someone within Protestantism.[214]

Slaves continued to be enrolled by the Presbyterians, principally Rev. George Chamberlain, who displayed a special interest in this group and made a practice of preaching the Gospel to them with great regularity.[215] Of the eleven new members received by him in 1879, five were slaves, all women: Felismina, Lucinda, Benedicta Justina, Joana and Leonor. Many masters sought to prevent their slaves from participating in Protestant churches. This happened with

Felismina, who was obliged to wait four years before attaining freedom from her owner.[216]

It is true that some Protestant owners saw to freeing their slaves, but this was not the general rule. Only Kalley imposed this requirement. The Positivist Church, directed by Miguel Lemos, cannot be considered a Protestant church; however, it is important to note that at the end of 1882, there occurred an important conflict between the director and Dr. J. Ribeiro de Mendonça, founder of the Positivist Society. The issue at hand was the decision made by Miguel Lemos forbidding members of the Society from accepting public offices, "aiming to avoid contradictory and sophistical situations." The director proposed on this occasion that, "anyone wishing to enter the Society should formally promise to renounce all and any political ambition and also the ownership of slaves, whether by inheritance, purchase or gift." [217]

In the other denominations there were historical precedents that showed no incongruity between being Protestant and continuing to exploit slave labor. Even with the intention of evangelizing the slaves and allowing them to participate in the churches, no thought was given to making them free.

Developing religious missions among the slaves was already common practice in the Protestant environment in the United States. The most important example was that of William Capers, a Methodist preacher who began his missions to the slaves of South Carolina farms around 1829. The results of his first missions were judged to be extremely positive, since they brought about more cleanliness, a better attitude toward work and an improved morality among the slaves. As a consequence of this effort, the missionaries' access to the slaves was facilitated by the plantation owners themselves. Naturally, the work carried out by these missions led to the recognition that there were natural limits to this situation. Their activity would be exclusively evangelistic, focused on the religious education of the slaves, with no interest in their emancipation.

According to the article "O Brasil catholico e o protestantismo" [Catholic Brazil and Protestantism] published in *Imprensa Evangélica*, the idea was to attend to the integration of blacks. This was in response to the criticisms made of Protestantism by the Ultramontane newspaper *Brasil Católico*, which said that Protestantism "embraces and nourishes all the principles subversive to Christian morality" and that one of its missionaries had gone so far as to preach to the blacks on the farms past which he traveled. The Presbyterian newspaper affirmed:

> He was so intent on condemning that, without reflecting, he made known a noble act of charity that deserves only praise from the sensible men of this land. Will *Brasil Católico* perhaps judge that a slave does not have a soul, or that there ought not be a place for him in the Church of Jesus Christ? What then is this colleague's understanding of the Christian faith? . . . Does he think perhaps that some evil will come from whatever knowledge this unfortunate race might have of the Gospel. Quite to the contrary. If these poor people knew God's gifts, it can be said with certainty that we would not have to lament scenes of bloodshed that so many times have enveloped entire families in mourning! [218]

The text refutes the accusation of subversion and states that the conversion of blacks would not produce negative repercussions for society. On the contrary, the evangelization of slaves would result in greater docility and submission, without the spectacle of the bloody crimes committed by some slaves against their owners.

This fact reveals a concern of an essentially religious nature directed at slaves on the part of Protestantism. Without question, such dedication contributed towards the development of an organic relationship between owners and slaves, woven into the fabric of paternalism. In "Escravidão e educação popular" [Slavery and public education], José Carlos Rodrigues presents some statistical data to prove the influence that public education had on slavery. Based on the census in the United States, he concluded that knowledge and slavery cannot live together.

> The existence of slavery has exactly this effect. It hampers completely all human development, be it moral or intellectual, because it blocks the actual mechanism that starts this development moving. But since all the world's great machinery is regulated with great justice, what happens is that the ill inflicted upon the slaves is precisely the same evil that afflicts society as a whole. The slave receives no instruction: as a child, either he has no parent, or the parent is unable to teach him the rudiments of relationships in this world; as an adult, he has no teacher to teach him what he needs to know in order to pursue happiness and fulfill his role as a man, for he has no happiness to pursue, nor is he even a man. It is necessary to keep slaves ignorant. Light is the enemy of their masters, and the complete stupidity of their entire being is the only bridle by which their masters hold them subject to their hand. Thus, wherever slavery prospers, thousands of men are prohibited from developing their hearts and their minds, that is to say, thousands of creatures are cut off entirely from knowing the glories of the Creator and from rendering Him the worship inspired in them by their sense of gratitude and humility.[219]

Who will work in Brazil when there are no longer any slaves?—Protestantism and the use of slave labor

Jesus and his disciples were near the city of Jerusalem when they encountered a blind man begging by the side of the road. Knowing that the man had been born blind, the disciples asked, "Lord, who sinned, this man or his parents, so that he was born blind?" (John 9:3, NRSV) More than an open-ended question, the issue raised pointed in a specific direction, illustrating a very common belief held by that society. Someone was responsible for this situation and they wanted to know who was to blame. In his answer, Jesus sought to correct them, saying that there was no culprit and that no sin was being atoned for.

The understanding revealed by Jesus' disciples concerning the origin of physical infirmities continued to appear frequently throughout history. Black slavery was also interpreted from this viewpoint. There was belief in a precise historical cause that had given rise to black bondage. Its source was sought in Noah's curse following the flood: the farmer [Ham], who fell asleep inebriated and, upon wakening with a hangover, placed a curse on Canaan, his youngest son, making him the servant of his brothers Shem and Japeth. (Genesis 9:25)

If blacks were living subject to others, it was because there was some kernel of truth in the story of the curse. This was the hermeneutic employed by many people in an attempt to justify the institution. Blacks had sinned, they were different, guilty, and they had to expiate their guilt. Southern ideologues insanely brandished the Holy Scriptures, arguing that they recorded and confirmed the blacks' curse. And since they had been cursed, the best way of expiating their guilt would be through work, which, according to a specific biblical hermeneutic, had also been created as a means of expiating sins. Blacks ought to work for whites: this was, in short, the logic justifying black slavery.

According to Ernst Troeltsch, work was understood in two ways: punishment and the way of salvation.[220] In its medieval Catholic formulation, work was understood as punishment, resulting from the fall of man. In Lutheran doctrine, the aspect of salvation was given greater emphasis than punishment. Calvinism definitively elaborated on this question and produced a deep change in North American culture, succeeding in raising work to the level of a religious duty.

Laziness, argued Calvinism, is the most dangerous of all vices, and work became an expression of divine grace, a meritorious and agreeable means of obtaining salvation. In *Alegrias e Tristezas de uma Educadora Alemã no Brasil* [Joys and Sorrows of a German Educator in Brazil], Ina von Benzer points out the existence of marked differences between the two cultures. The North American "respects work and the worker and takes on the management of work and participates in all types of service without any shame; the Brazilian, being less shrewd and also more prideful, even though he may be less cultured, despises work and the worker." [221]

Since work, according to Catholic understanding, was understood as punishment, it came to be associated almost exclusively with slaves. Daniel Kidder commented that in Rio de Janeiro during the first half of the nineteenth century there was an infinite number of blacks wandering the streets with large wicker baskets who were willing to carry all sorts of merchandise. He describes this is a fast and very cheap service such that almost the entire populace made use of these people's labor. A white man, even if he was an employee, was unwilling to do the work of a slave. Kidder explained that a white worker would feel insulted if he could not count on having an "earning black" (*preto de ganho*) to carry a roll of calico or a watermelon.

He who has enjoyed the meat may gnaw the bones

This Portuguese saying is used by Kidder and Fletcher to comment on the scandalous situation of 1855 in which innumerable beggars dominated the principal street corners in Rio de Janeiro. These were aged and ailing slaves, some were even blind, and they had been sent out to beg by their own masters. This practice was publicly condemned and society concluded that, "the owner who had enjoyed the fruit of his labor during his days of health could well afford to take care of him when overtaken by old age and sickness." [222]

The beggars were removed from the center of the city and their owners were summoned to retrieve them. Only twelve of them were able to secure licenses to continue asking for alms in the city's streets. They were either blind or lame and "have now the monopoly of the eleemosynary sympathies of the good people of Rio." For the missionaries, they never could have found a better profession. Some of the beggars "are carried in a hammock (*rede*) by two slaves, or drawn by one, one worthy rejoices in a little carriage." [223]

In the minds of these two Protestants, black slavery in Brazil was identical to that of other countries. Leaving aside the moral and religious aspects, it represented an "expensive institution and is, in every way, very poor economy," because of the careless and listless approach of the slaves to work and the necessity of constant supervision. "One of the trials of a Brazilian lady's is the surveillance of the slaves who are sent into the streets for the purpose of marketing and carrying water." [224]

The useful life of slaves was very short; in a few years they became "bones," useless for work. The representatives of the Bible Society noted that until 1850, the official date for the end of slave trading, owners considered it much more economical to use up a slave in five or seven years and then buy another one to replace him. However, with the start of the prohibition on the slave trade and its consequent increase in the price of slaves, owners began to show greater interest in their property. From then on, they took better care of their slaves because replacing them became quiet onerous. [225]

Daniel Kidder tells of innumerable experiences that occurred in his contact with slaves, especially in Rio de Janeiro. On one occasion he went with Justin Spaulding to the port of Rio de Janeiro, where there were more than fifty noisy boatmen competing for passengers. They were jockeying for work, not only to earn a living, but especially to escape the punishment they would suffer should they fail to acquire the sum demanded by their masters. The Methodist missionary said that he was well aware of this pressure suffered by the slaves and that he wanted to help all who crowded around him, offering him aid. However, the number of slaves was so great that it proved practically impossible to help them all. In the course of time, he adapted to the situation and sought "to make selections with a mutual reference to my own convenience, and apparent claims of those who desired employment." [226] Kidder also states that,

> These blacks are sent out by their masters, and are required to bring home a certain sum daily. They are allowed a portion of their gains to buy their food, and at night sleep on a mat or board in the lower portions of the house. You frequently see horrible cases of elephantiasis and other diseases, which are doubtless engendered or increased by the little care bestowed upon them. [227]

The southern immigrants from the United States came to Brazil with the intent of benefiting from slave labor. However, many other foreigners had arrived before them and had utilized the slave system, notably the English established in Brazil. The authors of *Brazil and the Brazilians* noted that the law passed in 1843 was insufficient prohibiting the selling and purchase of slaves by Englishmen in any country of the world. It was not observed, particularly by mining companies established in Brazil that continued to maintain slave labor. The owners of these firms, who lived in the English capital, were never prosecuted.[228]

The same issue was raised by Joaquim Nabuco in a letter of 11 March 1881, in which he said that many slave owners were foreigners and even though they were subjects of nations that had abolished slavery, they were tied to the institution through great financial interests. "Not long ago I had to bring before the Chamber, of which I am a member, the question of the freedom of three hundred blacks who had been enslaved for twenty years by an audacious conspiracy by the richest and most prosperous of the English companies in Brazil, the mining company of São João del Rey." [229]

The same question was raised in an editorial in *O Abolicionista*, claiming that foreigners took advantage of Brazilian legislation and were owners of a portion of the slave population, while coming from countries that no longer tolerated this practice. "Our territory is covered by large plantations, and from the manor house issue forth orders for the control of hundreds of human animals who enrich the owner. There, neither religion, nor instruction, nor morality, nor family!" [230]

In Brazil we will be able to live with quite a bit less work

The abolitionists were obliged to respond frequently to the same question: "Who will work in Brazil when there are no longer any slaves?" The editor of *O Novo Mundo* reported that many Brazilians were terrified when faced with the prospect of slave emancipation. He suggested that it would be to their advantage to receive information concerning how the southern North Americans were adjusting to their new social model. Like the Brazilians, the whites from the United States had slaves and considered them indispensable for their material and moral interests. He concluded that it would be important to become aware of this new situation so as to be able to dispense with the fear and insecurity.[231]

Rodrigues reckoned that, before thinking about introducing immigrants, Brazil ought to do something about getting the white population to work without depending so much on slaves. Further, in the cities there was always "a legion of candidates for public work, dominated by the prejudiced mean-spirited people of a society corrupted by work as bondage." His sympathy for the blacks' cause was deep, but the central concern was with the fate of the nation "rendered barren by slavery," so that a total population of ten million depended exclusively on the forced labor of a million slaves. The slave system had "converted work into a hateful conscription." [232]

The pages of *O Novo Mundo* made plain the principal causes, tendencies and manifestations of the progress of the United States, not with the intent of 'Americanizing' Brazil or copying its institutions, but making its readers understand that "all peoples are called to attain the same perfection by means of work and faith in Providence." [233] The only way to achieve progress was by abolishing slavery and "to make the faith of the capitalist come to rest instead upon industry, the resources of intellect, and the skill of the worker, rather than upon the sweat of the brute labor of slaves." [234]

One of the strategies adopted as an incentive for immigration by southern North Americans to Brazil was to point out that in the new country there would be no need to work hard. In a letter published in August 1867 in *The Copiahan* newspaper of Mississippi, the principal stimulus used by the Richard Henington was to affirm that in Brazil prospects were much better because there were "thousands of descendants of Indians and poor people who hired themselves out at a reasonable price, in addition to being able to count on slave labor." [235] The major motivation for immigration by southern North Americans to Brazil, especially between 1866 and 1869, was the possibility of continuing to use a slave workforce. "What really gets one's attention are the black slaves, just like in our country before the war. All that existed there can also be found here." His satisfaction was very great at being able to live in a country "better than the United States," where one worked much less. [236]

Another southern immigrant settled in Brazil and, fully satisfied with his good situation, offered suggestions and observations to candidates for immigration: "Every family man who wants to set himself up in this country should attend to a few basic matters: he should first acquire a house, coming himself to purchase it or working through an intermediary agent; he ought to have enough cash to carry him through a year, and also to purchase the slaves he expects to use, or come having resolved to work with his own hands." [237] The concern of this immigrant reflected the interest of the great majority. The objectives to be attained in Brazil were clearly defined. The necessity of taking advantage of specific benefits allowed by the Brazilian political-economic system was stressed quite consistently, as they were quite agreeable to the aspirations attributed to the southern North American immigrants.

It can be said that the only ones not carrying out transactions involving blacks, slaves and lands, were those who did not have the financial means, or even some few who turned to other activities. Exceedingly few North Americans were capable of expressing themselves like Thomas Ewbank, who, after witnessing the terrible weight of work thrown on the backs of slaves, admitted, "I would rather, a thousand times, be a sheep, pig, or ox, have freedom, food, and rest for a season, and then be knocked on the head, than be a serf on some plantations." [238]

With the intention of showing the presence of southern North Americans in the interior of São Paulo in the founding of the city of Americana, Judith MacKnight Jones, in *Soldado Descansa!* [Soldier, Rest!], shows that the norm, accepted by all, was to acquire slaves, who were treated as simple objects. [239]

How a true believer ought to treat his slaves.

In the same year in which the conflict between the North and South in the United States came to an end, the question as to the use of slave labor by Brazilian Protestants was presented by a missionary settled in Rio de Janeiro. In November 1865, Robert Kalley sought to call the attention of his church on the topic. "How ought a true believer treat his slaves? What would be the desire of Jesus with respect to this question?" [240]

According to João Gomes da Rocha, author of *Lembranças do Passado* [Memories of the Past], the Congregational Church itself was uncomfortable with the fact that Bernardino de Oliveira Rameiro, a member of the church, owned slaves. In response to the questions raised above, Kalley argued that work for others could be given in three different ways: as a labor of love; for a salary or wages; or even by compulsion, which is without love, without contract or settlement by payment. For him, the resolution of this problem comes by understanding 'property rights' based on the following logic: In the same way as "to me belong my own eyes, ears, mouth, hands, feet, etc., to another individual belong his own. . . . . Just as I have the right to mine, he has the right to his; man also has the right to take possession of the fruits obtained by the exercise of these organs in an honest and just fashion." Following this, he said, "No one has the right to make him a slave, robbing him of his personal freedom, trading a human creature as if he were a machine or simply some object." [241]

Parting from this initial declaration, which was quite clear, the final exhortation made by Kalley was that anyone who made use of slave labor "cannot continue as a member of the church of Jesus." Kalley proceeded to maintain an openly anti-slavery position. Heeding the entreaty from the slave Leopoldina Ferreira, a member of his church, he visited her owner, seeking to persuade her "to grant a letter of freedom." For this missionary, black slaves also had the right to be part of his church, and he himself sought on many occasions to teach them the Protestant faith. In 1871, when the Law of the Free Womb was promulgated, he expressed his happiness, rejoicing "to learn that the plan for partial emancipation of slaves in Brazil was made into law." On another occasion, Kalley sent a letter to the Rev. J.R. Smith, a Presbyterian from the South of the United States, pointing to shortcomings in his work of evangelization, among others, "his way of dealing with people of color." [242]

In contrast to this image, which could indicate an active commitment to the abolitionist cause, Kalley was careful to maintain a fairly discreet position. An explanation for his attitude can be found in his negative experience on the island of Madeira, whence he was expelled. For this reason, in his evangelizing work, based on a concern that was essentially religious, he sought to avoid to the maximum any combative attitude toward the Brazilian authorities. He wanted to avoid any 'imprudent' publicity that could disrupt his missionary work. Kalley even goes so far as to affirm that he did not wish "to experience a lot of publicity, with its disruptive consequences for the work and its vexations for the workers." Recognizing that "all his Protestant propaganda was well watched," he surely must have limited greatly activity in defense of the abolition of slavery, restricting himself to personal positions within the narrow limits of his local church.[243]

NOTHING STRIKES FOREIGNERS MORE THAN THIS ABSENCE OF BOOKS IN BRAZILIAN HOMES: THE PROTESTANT PRESS AND THE ABOLITION OF SLAVERY

According to Silvio Romero, the decade from 1868 to 1878 was the "most notable of the entire nineteenth century in forming our spiritual lives."[244] During this time, new ideas aroused the country, with Brazilian elites embracing, among others, positivism [245] and evolution, major expressions of nineteenth century philosophical thought.

Protestantism, which at that moment was striving to establish firm roots in Brazil, sought ways of spreading its religious tenets. One of the avenues found was by way of the written word. For Kalley, who from the beginning of his ministry in Brazil paid particular attention to the publication of books and sundry pamphlets, the texts served especially the objective of guiding readers to the reformed faith. Kalley himself published a translation into Portuguese of the allegory by John Bunyan, *Pilgrim's Progress,* in the 'Tribuna livre" [Open Forum] section of Rio de Janeiro's *Correio Mercantil.* He also edited pamphlets and wrote innumerable articles, using a variety of pseudonyms - "Um Crente" [A Believer], "Devoto Sincero" [Sincere Devotee], "Um Roceiro do Mato Grosso" [A Backwoodsman from Mato Grosso], "Um dos Discípulos do Crucificado" [A Disciple of the Crucified], "O Católico Protestante" [The Protestant Catholic], "Como Fomos" [The Way We Were], "Um Cristão Verdadeiro" [A True Christian], "O Crítico" [The Critic], etc.[246]

From the first moment they established themselves in Brazil, the Presbyterians took care to translate works considered basic to the formation of the Protestant faith. They also sought to produce their own literature. They began in 1867 with *Sentença de Excomunhão e sua Resposta* [The Sentence of [His] Excommunication and His Reply], by the former priest José Manoel da Conceição. The following year the collected sermons of Ashbel Simonton were published and later other works appeared like *A Igreja Romana à Barra do Evangelho e da História* [The Roman Church against the Measure of the Gospel and History] and *A Vida de Jesus* [The Life of Jesus] by Miguel Torres, and *As Bíblias Falsificadas* [The Falsified Bibles] by Antônio Pedro de Cerqueira Leite.

The boldest stance by Protestantism during this phase of implantation came from the Presbyterians, with the creation of *Imprensa Evangélica.* For twenty-eight years it was an important vehicle for the propagation of evangelical ideas and the principal mouthpiece for Brazilian Protestantism. Founded at the end of 1864—the first issue came off the press on Saturday, 5 November—the newspaper assumed throughout this period the basic role of contributing to the establishment of Protestantism in the country. Its very creation attests to the Protestant interest in publishing. "At this time the press is a powerful weapon for good or for evil. We must work so that everywhere religious literature is produced and propagated, wherein one can drink of the pure truth taught in the Bible." [247]

It is possible to discern the actual concerns of Brazilian Protestantism during this period, since this newspaper provides rich documentation showing the tenets defended by the Protestant Church, especially by Presbyterians. Focusing exclusively on objectives of a religious nature and prepared to maintain unending arguments with the newspapers *O Apóstolo, O Thabor* and *O Católico Scientífico e Noticioso, Imprensa Evangélica* positioned itself as a mere spectator before the conflicts concerning the abolition of slavery. And in 1871 it was quite cool in its applause for the Law of the Free Womb: "The nation applauds the measure and this applause will find an echo among civilized peoples. They are perhaps few, however, who do not find the law quite defective." Seeking to avoid taking any position whatsoever, the newspaper limited itself to endorsing a plan by Councilman Souza Franco, "which seeks to offer a more favorable solution and the only one feasible without great detriment to the interests of slaves as well as their masters." [248] While acknowledging the measure as positive and likely to be supported even abroad, the paper points out that the law has its defects. The stated objective was to tolerate the maintenance and continuation of the system in effect, until a way out could be found that would not prejudice the interests of either the owners or the slaves.

After that, it was only in 1874, three years later, that the newspaper returned to the topic of slavery, doing so in a similar fashion, recalling precisely the proposals made in 1871 by the Viscount de Souza Franco. It stated that these proposals had already been tried out and had met with success, making them worthy of notice. The successful experiment referred to by the newspaper was that of the commendator José Vergueiro, who, in conversations with the newspaper's editor, related that, "he opened bank accounts for the slaves, and the most diligent of them already have a considerable balance to purchase their own freedom; he also requires the formation of families among his slaves, and he honors the family structure, he establishes schools for them, supplies books, and includes religious education." [249]

It was not until 1879 that the newspaper returned to the topic, reporting a crime committed by slaves in Itu. On this occasion the paper's most objective claim was that the crime was a consequence of slavery. At the beginning of the same year, an editorial in the newspaper noted that, "Years ago it was considered opportune to incorporate a decree into Brazilian legislation declaring the free womb from a specified date forward." Such a measure "deserves the applause of the civilized world and assures the slow and certain death of slavery," but it is explicitly less relevant than another measure that was agitating the country, namely "the freedom of the Brazilian spirit." The newspaper's emphasis was on the question of religious freedom, a more "relevant" concern, in consequence of the immediate objectives desired by Protestantism. [250]

In the April 1881 edition, a piece concerning the *ingênuos* was taken from another periodical. *Imprensa Evangélica* complained that the legislation had created a special class of persons, with no concern for the articulation of laws to address the problem. There needed to be careful planning if one did not want to run the risk of "adding more individuals to the already enormous mass that supplies guests for our prisons and Fernando de Noronha." [251] The only viable alternative for handling the matter adequately was to arrange for the *ingênuos* to receive appropriate education, the best defense against the mortal dangers of depravity and ignorance.[252]

There was an interesting debate with the newspaper *Brasil Católico* at the end of 1881. *Brasil Católico* claimed that one of the missionaries was in the habit of catechizing the slaves on the farms that he passed by. In defense not only of the missionary but also of Protestantism in general, *Imprensa Evangélica* sought to justify the activity, arguing that what was happening was a noble act of kindness, and inquiring, "Might *Brasil Católico* perhaps be of the opinion that a slave does not have a soul, or that there ought not be a place for him in Christ's Church? What concept, then, does our colleague have of the Christian religion?" The arguments listed in defense of the missionary and in the discussion of the topic did not reveal the slightest concern for abolitionist ideals. The discussion addresses only the possibility of avoiding, by way of evangelization, any potential waves of violence that could be perpetrated by the slaves. It defended the preaching of a 'gospel' that could instill in slaves the practice of submission: "If these poor people knew God's gifts, with certainty we would not have to lament all the bloody scenes that repeatedly have cloaked entire families in mourning." [253]

In 1879, *Imprensa Evangélica*, was motivated by "exceptional circumstances" to relocate to São Paulo, where it came to have new contributors. The impression was given that there would be a greater concern for social issues, especially slavery. Nevertheless, the newspaper's mission continued to focus on "spreading the truths of Christianity, fighting everything that opposed the sound doctrines of the Gospel." What was new during this phase of the newspaper was its intention to "become a more popular publication, including literary articles and others that, while perhaps alien to religion, nevertheless might be of general interest." There was no important change in the line taken by the newspaper's editorials; the change occurred due to operational problems.[254]

Eduardo Carlos Pereira was one of the new contributors during this new phase of the newspaper, and he sought to show in editorials the importance of religion as an agent for social movements. Highlighting this role for religion, his interest amounted to proving that Protestantism, as a religious system, was superior to Catholicism and could assume the "glorious mission of elevating the poor to the heights of a true and permanent civilization." [255]

The newspaper's participation in the process of the abolition of slavery in Brazil began timidly in 1884, a time when emancipation movements were proliferating in every corner of the nation. The first article in this direction was contributed by Joaquim Nabuco, who examined slavery and colonization, consequently not yet expounding the Presbyterians' views on abolition.[256] The impression left by the article is an excessive hesitation in attacking this social issue. Ideological recollections of the 'Old School,' recommending concern only for those issues within the spiritual realm, made it difficult to attack issues that were political in nature. Still present was the saying "Give to Caesar what is Caesar's, and to God what is God's." For this reason, *Imprensa Evangélica* came to address slavery using a devious strategy of speaking through third parties, Joaquim Nabuco among them.

From then on, the issue of abolition appeared more frequently in the pages of this Presbyterian newspaper. In the very same month of March 1884, *Imprensa Evangélica* reproduced a news item from *A Província* about the freeing of slaves in Ceará: "Today an entire province has liberated itself from slavery, . . grand and patriotic, this generous political action." [257]

In the following month, taking advantage of a text from *O Apóstolo*, the Protestant newspaper become more emboldened in claiming abolition as a necessity: "It is everyone's obligation to hasten it." [258] From that moment forward there is an increase in news stories, references to abolitionist articles, and demonstrations asserting the complete incompatibility of Christianity with slavery. In 1884, after almost a year's delay, the newspaper spoke of Joaquim Nabuco's book, *O Abolicionismo* [Abolitionism].[259] It also reprinted the editorial from the *Gazeta de Notícias* concerning emancipation and commented on a statistic from the *Jornal do Comércio* about the slave population in Brazil.[260] It reproduced articles from the *Gazeta da Tarde* about "the runaround on behalf of slavery" [261] and "abolition and immigration." [262] It reported the appearance of the abolitionist periodicals *A Onda*, published in São Paulo, and *Lincoln*, in Alagoas.[263] It made known the decision by the Municipal Chamber of Porto Alegre regarding the freeing of slaves.[264] It criticized the delayed interest shown by *O Apóstolo* in defense of abolition.[265]

As it did with great frequency, *Imprensa Evangélica* reprinted, at the beginning of 1885, an article published in the *Gazeta de Notícias* addressing the question of the *ingênuos*. The text sought to express solidarity with the fate of the *ingênuos*, who were made use of for the most difficult and dangerous tasks. It argued that the owners held back their slaves, who represented an investment of one thousand milréis, sending instead the free *ingênuos* to the "most risky locations, since if they die it is at their own expense." The text invites public officials to pay more attention to these workers,

> unfortunate beings who have parents but no civil rights to protect them; who are free but have masters; who are lower than orphans and abandoned children, at the mercy of a man who looks upon them with disdain or like the product of what he calls a usurpation, with no compassion to provide them shelter or protection.[266]

It was only in 1885 that *Imprensa Evangélica* took the initiative of defending the abolition of slavery without basing it on the positions adopted by other newspapers or individuals. Initially, Eduardo Carlos Pereira took a clear position on the issue, seeking to demonstrate the complete incompatibility between slavery, biblical teaching, and Christian justice. "Thank God, the national soul is in agreement with the spontaneous enthusiasm for a holy cause; the Brazilian Lazarus breaks the stone of the tomb to the sound of the redeeming word." [267] The newspaper began to question with vigor the decisions made by official authorities. It criticized the Saraiva Law,[268] claiming that it did not deserve the support of those who desired freedom for slaves.

For the welfare of the nation, as well as the relief of a cruelly oppressed race whose only crime has been to be born slaves, we sincerely desire that an effective law be adopted for their complete emancipation within the shortest time possible.[269]

It concluded that the country would receive divine punishment for the oppression practiced against "the poor and afflicted slaves, because God is offended when the most humble creatures are harmed." [270]

The closest evidence of the true passion with which the abolitionists of the period discussed the slavery issue comes from Eduardo Carlos Pereira himself. In a series of articles for the *Imprensa Evangélica* first published in pamphlet form, he told of an event from his past when, still a child, he had heard the groans of a black being tortured:

Oh! Accursed institution that arouses in mankind the instincts of a beast, obliterating the most basic human feelings! Let the blood and shattered flesh of the miserable captives be specters that come constantly to trouble the criminal dream of an egotistical and cowardly indifference. It is necessary that the printing press cry out ceaselessly, that it raise its voice like a trumpet and denounce to the people the monstrousness of this national sin. It is necessary that the press declare frankly to slave owners how offensive slavery is to the laws of God and of humanity, and how vile is the shameful exploitation of a race that has just as much right as any other to the liberty that God has given them. I will cry out and denounce to the new children of Israel this crime that still stains the bosom of the evangelical churches in Brazil, to the enormous detriment of the Gospel. . . . What should be the attitude of the pulpit regarding slavery? Why then, this reservation, this fainthearted silence before a crime of such gravity? The silence of the pulpit is not prudence, it is unfaithfulness. . . . How can the silence of the watchmen of Israel be justified? Perhaps someone will say, "Let the Gospel be preached, and the day it implants itself in the heart of a slave owner the chains of his slaves will fall to the ground." If this way of proceeding were acceptable in relation to slavery, why would it not be so with respect to lotteries, gambling, drunkenness, Sabbath-breaking, and a thousand other expressions of sin? Social apathy crushes us, and one doesn't need to be very intelligent to discern in slavery the principal cause of this sin. And is it not true that we must in general lament the same evil in our communities of believers? Nothing, then, of acquiescence or of complicity in this social sin, which already has sufficiently prejudiced the vital interests of the faith. Raise in the name of the Redeemer the same protest rise up that has already been raised in the name of reason, humanity and the country's economic interests. Safeguard the glory of the Gospel by unleashing from all the pulpits the bolt that will eliminate slavery from the bosom of the churches. Hear me, then, with patience, dear brother, if you are one who owns slaves. I am driven by my desire your own well-being, as much as compassion for the dispossessed race. If up until now you have sought bewilderingly to still your conscience with some isolated scriptural text, I believe that you already are convinced of the absurdity and sacrilege of any such attempt. You will no longer dare invoke Saint Paul as an advocate of slavery. If, then, the religion you profess condemns slavery, choose between it and the slaves you own. Either keep your slaves and continue to benefit from the sweat of the brow of your fellow man, in which case, following the example of the Gaderenes, you should ask Jesus to leave your home (Mark 5:17); if not, then restore to your slaves their stolen freedom and declare that you are not merely a hypocrite.[271]

In addition to the *Imprensa Evangélica*, the Protestant missions established in Brazil organized several other small newspapers, with frequencies of publication ranging between biweekly and monthly.

The Methodist newspaper *Expositor Cristão*, which had started as *Methodista Católico*, included in its first issue in 1886 the invitation of the Aliança Evangélica to the Annual Week of Universal Prayer. On pointing out some topics for exhortation and prayer, the invitation suggested that the 8th of January should be:

> Prayers for royalty and all those in authority for the spreading of justice and peace, for thwarting of all conspiracies and malicious plots; for the abatement of national zeal and for impediments to unjust wars; for the complete abolition of trafficking in slaves, dealing in opium and all immoral business; for Gentile governors and peoples to receive Christian missionaries favorably, and for the coming of Christ in His kingdom.[272]

With the exception of this extremely superficial treatment, there is no other occasion on which the newspaper addressed the question of slavery. In the same edition, the Methodist periodical contained a commentary about the Catholic newspaper *O Apóstolo*, saying that for some months,

> has filled its pages with the reprinting of a book written against two Methodist missionaries who were here almost half a century ago. It makes people laugh when they read that newspaper's language, language used moreover with a desire to defend what its editorial staff believe to be the truth. Since Cain killed Abel there has always been the stain of bad blood on religious arguments. If we are to argue, let us always be gentlemen, that is to say, Christians.[273]

In 1874, Rev. Emanuel Vanorden organized in São Paulo *O Púlpito Evangélico*. It had a short life, disappearing after a year, but while it survived, it was dedicated exclusively to publishing sermons focusing on questions of biblical doctrine. The issues of February and March 1875, a time when the polemic around the question of religion assumed great relevance in Brazil, noted that, given the importance of such events, the newspaper considered itself obliged to "set aside a portion of its program of sermons in order to offer its readers consideration of the topic that concerned the progress of the Gospel in Brazil." [274]

Thus, it can be confirmed that *O Púlpito Evangélico*, in the short time of its existence, never reached the point of sketching out any reference whatsoever, no matter how small, to the problem of slavery in Brazil. Naturally, for a newspaper that came to practically ask forgiveness for printing reflections on the question of religion, a topic considered quite suggestive of Protestantism, which was already accustomed to controversy, the discussion about slavery was far from being part of its agenda, since it did not "concern the progress of the Gospel in Brazil." [275]

However, after the disappearance of *O Púlpito Evangélico*, the same Emanuel Vanorden founded in 1875, almost two years after founding *O Púlpito Evangélico*, another bi-weekly published regularly for ten years. Its name, *O Pregador Cristão* [The Christian Preacher], gave an indication of the style to be followed. It was quite similar to *Imprensa Evangélica*. As for slavery and its abolition, there appeared sporadically short articles and commentaries on the laws regarding the subject. The newspaper's observation of the Saraiva proposal was quite objective, even suggesting more active participation in the future, which did not, in fact, occur. "The Saraiva proposal does not satisfy the nation's aspirations; on the contrary, it satisfies only the plantation owners." There is present in the newspaper the conviction that the curse of slavery would gradually disappear in Brazil.[276]

Even though the two newspapers created by Vanorden did not show concern for the abolitionist movement, it cannot be ignored that Vanorden participated actively in the struggle for freeing the slaves. On at least two occasions, and at his own expense, he traveled to the United States and England to protest against the use of American and British ships for transporting slaves to the north of Brazil, to the provinces, and to the coffee-growing regions of São Paulo.[277]

According to the statements of contemporary periodicals, the newspaper *O Novo Mundo*, founded and managed by José Carlos Rodrigues in New York, became quite widely read, known and influential in Brazilian society, so much so that several Brazilian newspapers of the time reproduced and commented on its articles.[278] The newspaper *Cearense*, which serves as a typical example of this influence, on several occasions praised the importance of *O Novo Mundo*, as in, for example, the issue of 11 January 1874:

> The articles in *O Novo Mundo* convey a summary of the political, financial, industrial, artistic and literary movements of all peoples. There is no notable event anywhere of which you will not find the most satisfactory report in this newspaper. But for the Brazilian reader *O Novo Mundo* is recommended for other reasons. All our domestic questions are discussed therein with a patriotic interest: well-written articles with biographical information on our most distinguished men; reviews of our books; praise for the aptness of our soil for all types of cultivation, thereby encouraging immigration to our land; our industrial activity; the liberal reforms made to our legislation, etc. fill the pages of this most useful periodical, which is essentially a Brazilian publication although printed in a foreign country. . . . The interesting articles, the sharpness of the printing, the fine engravings, the faithful portraits have reached such perfection. . . . The primary function of the newspaper would be to show the principal evidence of progress by the United States, discussing the causes and trends of this progress.[279]

Founded after the American Civil War, its emphasis was on "combating two things: slavery, or the denying of freedom; and superstition or irreligiosity, which is the direct denial of the only condition for freedom."[280]

The topic of slavery always appeared in the pages of *O Novo Mundo* during its nine years of existence. When reproducing an article by José Carlos Rodrigues that was published in the newspaper *Gazeta de Notícias*, *O Aboli-*

cionista made the following laudatory comment, "It is only our duty to remind the Abolicionista family of the outstanding services rendered to the cause of freedom in the pages of *O Novo Mundo* over a nine-year period."[281] The 'combat' proposed by the newspaper would be achieved essentially by way of argumentation, highlighting in an insistent fashion that not only slavery, but also the absence of religious freedom, was a factor that impeded the nation's progress. The argument transmitted by the newspaper that "this system of labor kills all industriousness," [282] was seen to be remarkably rational and educational, for it strove to demonstrate and make possible for slave masters the understanding that freeing their slaves would be a positive investment, since such an attitude would make possible the arrival of progress.

A very clear concern can be noted for defending dominant interests in the repeated appeals directed at slave owners. The principal audience for the discourse transmitted by the newspaper were large landowners and businessmen, in short, the representatives of capital who invested in maintaining the slavery system. It was to them that *O Novo Mundo* directed its messages and proposals, inviting them to face the new moment that, according to the newspaper, was about to arrive.

> We see drawing near, with long strides, the crisis of changes in the labor system throughout the whole country, and the many complications that come in its wake; and we believe that studies and reports and time can deliver us from the consequences of the crisis. This crisis of change is the only price that is asked of us for our sin and that of our ancestors.[283]

On innumerable occasions, the Civil War served as a justification and even as an invitation for the audience to reflect seriously on the topic. The price to be paid for the change in the labor system, for the "sin committed" ought to be accepted, since it would never be a price similar to that paid by the United States, the "blood of a million men." [284] It would not be possible for the country to escape unscathed from a question as serious as that of slavery. Some payment was necessary, a kind of penance, to redeem centuries of oppression. "The government of the United States has already wiped clean its own black page with the tremendous war to which we allude; now only Brazil remains." [285]

At the same time that it is possible to see some small corners of José Carlos Rodrigues' newspaper given over to solidarity with the black slave, what is most frequent is the defense of emancipation as a necessity for forging the road to progress. There was much insistence on presenting the United States as a historical reference. For Rodrigues, progress in that country had occurred after slavery had been cast aside. If it had worked for them, it was obvious it would also work for Brazil: "Free from slavery, the country may fail in its true path towards progress, but at least whatever attitude it adopts in the future will take it in the true direction and the country can walk in peace and trusting always in providence." [286]

In the United States, the paper continued, the task had been achieved thanks to the firm and fearless pressure of certain political leaders who had the courage to complete the required surgery. In Brazil, several exemplary opportunities arose but its timorous leaders retreated in the face of the task. An excellent opportunity occurred after the American war, when the institution [of slavery] received a death sentence as measured by displays of Brazilian public opinion. The days of slavery were numbered and the head of state himself solemnly declared that Brazil was committed to bringing it to an end.

However, with the outbreak of the Paraguay War, the question had been put off. A new opportunity arose after the conflict, but the Executive Branch did not show itself up to the task of resolving the situation. Rodrigues argued that the possibility of escaping from this institution could occur only through a quick, energetic and revolutionary measure, as had happened in nearly all the countries of the New World. With the aim of inspiring courage, he recalled that in all the countries where the emancipation of slaves had been declared, the population had not regretted it. "All the Americas have been the stage for black slavery, and all the free countries of the Americas have freed themselves of slaves, except Brazil. In none of these countries did abolition bring about risk to the owners or the public cause." [287]

In *O Novo Mundo*, there appears to be no concern for black slaves, and this is shown repeatedly in the way in which the target audience was the owner of slaves. The black slave was not considered a protagonist. Each and every dialogue was with the slave owners. They were asked to be intelligent and kind and to surrender their property in slaves. Intelligent because a great revolution was occurring in the labor system and they should not be left behind and miss out on this opportunity. As an alternative, "each plantation owner should pretend that all his slaves have died and that all that remains is his farm; without capital to buy slaves, and without credit, he must extract all possible use from his lands with hired hands." [288]

The following comment made in the article "O trabalho dos emancipados" [The Work of the Emancipated] is strong verification that the slave was not considered a partner or co-worker, and even less a protagonist, but rather an insignificant and completely disrespected individual. "There is a friendly recommendation made to slave owners, saying: We recommend that you rid yourselves of the institution of human slavery as quickly as possible." [289] As can be seen in this passage, which was also reprinted in the *O Despertador* newspaper on 6 February 1874, there was not the least concern for the common humanity of the black slave. What mattered for the newspaper was that progress was being disturbed by the slavery system.

Alongside the total disinterest in the common humanity of blacks and the conviction that they were merely disposable objects, there was also other proof, namely the view that slaves and the slavery regime were the sources of a large part of the nation's woes, mainly responsible for Brazilians' laziness and uncouth behavior. Instead of a victim, the black slave became guilty and responsible for the degradation caused in society as a whole. According to *O Novo Mundo*,

> The existence of slavery has exactly this effect. It completely hampers all human development, moral or intellectual. . . . Thus, slaves do not attend school at all. The slave owners' dependents go a little, but there is no incentive

for them to pursue their education. And as for the children of the slave owners, it is true that they go to school, but it is not so much of a moral imperative or the necessity and dignity of work that sends them there; rather, it is a desire for social standing, a title to add a little luster to those who are going to be masters of men. All of this, we repeat, is the logical result of keeping slaves.[290]

The perception that keeping slaves constituted a real threat to the material and moral interests of the large plantation owners stands out in many of the newspaper's articles. The paper highlights the new awareness adopted by former slave owners from the South of the United States who came to understand the irrationality of the former system. These former slave owners considered themselves very fortunate to be free of the scourge of the South, the "servile element" of society. For the editor of *O Novo Mundo*, proclaiming the abolition of slavery meant avoiding the repetition of the conflicts experienced in the United States and safeguarding the country's entry onto the roads to true prosperity. "Where there exists compulsory slave labor, the wealth it creates is illusory because it comes from an abnormal condition of social forces." Rodrigues added that slave owners should not fear the change in the system, "not only considering humanity's many serious moral interests but furthermore for the love of your own material gain and that of the nation." [291]

The touted irrationality of the slave system is highlighted also in keeping with the immediate concerns of slave owners. "The abolition of slavery is the only way we have of saving ourselves a lot of misery. . . . Until now, with slaves, there has been great waste in the rural economy." [292] In summary, the editor maintained that slavery ought to be abolished in the self interests of slave owners and of society in general. They should realize that morally and materially they were being harmed.

In this type of argumentation it is also possible to discern two quite distinct images that characterized and were incorporated into Brazilian Protestantism. On the one side was Protestantism, a marker of wealth, progress, free labor, "divine blessings," "truth"; and on the other, Catholicism, hindering progress, hiding the truth, stimulating superstition, and bearing the "divine curse." In summary, this stereotypical image characterized Protestantism as the bearer of a new order of progress and Catholicism as the antithesis of all this, upholding an out-dated order. *O Novo Mundo* expressed just such points of view, defining its own role as enabling Brazil to free itself from factors that had blocked the trajectory of other countries and to adopt those elements that were fundamental in determining pathways to progress. According to the newspaper, Brazil was experiencing the opportunity to "bypass stages" and arrive more quickly, without facing the problems experienced by other nations.

According to the editor of *O Novo Mundo*, the major question of the change in the labor system was inextricably linked to religious freedom. The two issues were a single entity, two sides of the same coin. To change the situation was the "remedy that can heal the nation." Thus, slavery and the absence of religious freedom, which were what truly denied life to the country, needed urgently to be repealed, making way for a revitalization of the nation. If this had not occurred up to that moment, it was because these issues were exceedingly "incandescent," touching on "the country's most vital interests." His diagnosis was that both the emancipation of slaves and religious freedom were shown to be fundamental to the nation's health. Using a figure of speech, Rodrigues explained that, "the social body needing surgery to save itself, and the operation being somewhat difficult, the physician who was called in to do it backs away in fear of taking responsibility for the procedure." Nevertheless, according to him, there was no room for weakness, since "in desperate situations concerning the salvation or ruin of the country, hesitation serves only to hasten ruin; and the more painful and difficult the surgery, the more firm must be the resolve of the person who is carrying it out." [293]

All through the pages of *O Novo Mundo*, it is possible to discern that the proposal for emancipation is supported by some foundational arguments. First, there is the conviction that points to slavery as evil because it contradicts the teaching of Christianity. This view appeared in the first issue, where the editor pointed out, "The law of Christianity, which we profess to follow, says that the black is our brother. . . . The sooner we uphold it, the closer will be the harvest of those rewards that the Father of us all has reserved for those who follow his inspiration and teaching." [294]

Mixing Calvinism with positivism, Rodrigues observed that human history develops strongly under God's absolute dominion. Events form part of divine teaching and it is necessary for men to be sufficiently intelligent to recognize that what is being asked of them is to make the sacrifice demanded, disposing of their blacks and learning the divine teachings. "If there was no slavery on Earth, God's children could not carry out, in His image, the sacred and glorious mission of freeing them, and the most exalted part of their being would not be able to be exercised." [295] In this vision, abolition and religious freedom went hand in hand. The end of slavery meant adopting a Biblical religion, represented naturally by Protestantism.

A second line of argumentation relied on the conviction that slavery formed part of a phased apprenticeship and that the path toward progress and civilization passed through the end of the slavery system. Without slavery, Brazilians would be freed of a great "inherited" evil, they would free themselves of "its immediate consequences and the moral and economic ties that it creates and develops." [296] To move on to the next stage, a transition was necessary, that is, a transitional period had to be created in which the slave owners would make the "sacrifice of selling their slaves to the nation, at the price they are worth," replacing them gradually with free laborers.[297]

While talking about the necessity of urgent and radical surgery, attention is drawn to this concept of transition. This call for compensation, which is spelled out more clearly, indicates a concern for order, public safety and especially the defense of private property, particularly that of the large plantation owners. The beginning or resumption of development, a tranquil stroll towards the new time of progress, would begin with the "sacrifice" made by the owners' sale of their slaves to the nation. In this period of transition, the irrationality of the malign slave system would be eradicated gradually, safely and without trauma, in such a way that the slaves, who were caught up by irrationality, would be replaced by new free workers who would embody the ability to perform productively and rationally.

The silence regarding the fate of former slaves beyond this period of transition finds its logic in the denial of their ability to engage in free labor, and in the conviction that they embodied something antiquated that was tied to a system that deformed society and was, therefore, unsuited to the "new system" about to be inaugurated. This silence is present from the moment it is asserted that, "convinced as we are, by reason and by history, . . . the time has arrived when Brazil must cast off slavery forever." [298]

Blacks are completely denied status as subjects in history, and they are looked upon only as objects to be freed from captivity. Those who are addressed by *O Novo Mundo*, those who would truly be able to awaken a new moment in history, would be the masters, the large plantation owners, through the "sacrifice" they would carry out. In this dialogue, the future of black slaves was not taken into consideration. There was a paternalistic attitude, encouraging slave owners to abandon any type of apprehension. The mirror that was held up to them was that of the country to the north, which had the good fortune of taking the correct steps, steps that were divinely blessed, Protestant steps.

NOTES

1. Santos, *O Católico e o Metodista*, 175.

2. According to Costa, contrary to the "myth" of the preponderance of large landowners in the southern colonies, "these societies were formed for the most part of small farmers who, alone or with the occasional help of indentured servants, cultivated their land." (A.M.S. Costa, "O destino (não) manifesto: os imigrantes norte-americanos no Brasil" (Ph.D. diss., University of São Paulo, 1985), 61.) Reily argues a different position: "From colonial times, because of the climate and related factors, in the North small farms developed which were usually worked by the owner and his family; much later commerce, navigation, and industry grew. . . . While in the South, from the beginning, agriculture was organized in large plantations where tobacco, rice, indigo and, finally, cotton were grown, mainly by manual laborers in servitude. . . . Religion in the North and in the South took different directions on this issue, slavery being the fundamental factor in this differentiation." (Reily, *História Documental do Protestantismo no Brasil*, 217-218.) Ana Maria Costa explains the reason for this myth arising and taking hold: "The large plantation owners, for their part, secured their status through the work of their possessions and the financial help of British trading houses that controlled commerce. From the moment that this minority asserted its prominence because of its favored economic position, the interests of the privileged classes pressured its members into assuming political leadership at the expense of the small landowners and yeomen. . . . The property held by large land owners, a prerequisite for the right to vote as well as political and social prestige, therefore generated the myth of the southern plantation owner, who, despite being in the minority, is reflected in history and literature as the predominant element in that society. Even more important, however, was the idealization of the plantation owner on the part of the majority which, despite holding diverse positions in the economy and society, adopted the plantation owner model,

drawing upon it for their future projects and achievements." (Costa, "O destino (não) manifesto: os imigrantes norte-americanos no Brasil," 61.)

3. Slavery in the South was naturally a legacy of British rule. It had existed since the beginning of the seventeenth century but was not the occasion of much conflict or comment until the nineteenth century. The prevailing view at the end of the eighteenth century was that slavery would disappear gradually and so the problem would resolve itself. The invention of the cotton gin in 1793 by Eli Whitney put an end to this expectation. As a consequence, the number of slaves grew enormously. About 1820, the number was already approaching four million. Between 1820 and 1830, the awareness of a distinction between the South and the North grew gradually and the catalytic element that allowed for this distinction was slavery.

4. M. Bradbury and H. Temperley, *Introdução aos Estudos Americanos* (Rio de Janeiro: Editora Forense-Universitária, 1979), 124.

5. R.F. Nichols, *Religão e Democracia Americana* (São Paulo: Ibrasa, 1963), 69.

6. It is important to note the participation of the slaves themselves in this abolitionist campaign. Eugene Genovese comments on innumerable slave revolts that were crushed. See Eugene D. Genovese, *From Rebellion to Revolution: Afro-American Slave Revolts in the Making of the Modern World* (Baton Rouge: Louisiana State University Press, 1979).

7. John Wesley, *The Works of John Wesley*, ed. Richard P. Heitzenrater, vol.18, "Journals and Diaries I (1735-38)," ed. W. Reginald Ward and Richard P. Heitzenrater (Nashville: Abingdon, 1988), 180.

8. Ibid., 181.

9. Ibid.

10. "General Conference of 1844," *Methodist Quarterly Review* 22 (April 1870): 167.

11. H.R. White, "The glory of southern Christianity: Methodism and the mission to the slaves," *Methodist History* 39 (January 2001):109.

12. Ibid., 109.

13. A. Raboteau, *Slave Religion: the "Invisible Institution" in the Antebellum South* (New York: Oxford University Press, 1978), 143.

14. D.A. Reily, "William Capers: An Interpretation of His Life and Thought" (Ph.D. diss., Emory University, 1972), 58.

15. "General Conference of 1844," 166.

16. G.S. Shockley, "Methodism, society and black evangelism in America: retrospect and prospect," *Methodist History* 12 (July 1974): 164.

17. Ibid., 160-169.

18. White, "The glory of southern Christianity," 111.

19. W.P. Harrison, *The Gospel Among the Slaves* (Nashville: Publishing House of the Methodist Episcopal Church, 1893), 145.

20. L.V. Baldwin, *A History of the African Union Methodist Protestant and Union American Methodist Episcopal Churches, 1805-1980* (Metuchen, New Jersey: Scarecrow Press, 1983), 20-21.

21. D.A. Reily, *Metodismo Brasileiro e Wesleyano* (São Paulo: Imprensa Metodista, 1981), 220-221. William Capers was elected bishop of the Methodist Episcopal Church, South in 1846, the year in which it was formally organized.

22. White, "The glory of southern Christianity," 114.

23. [Moore is described in A.M. Chreitzberg, *Early Methodism in the Carolinas* (Nashville: Methodist Episcopal Church, South, 1897), 241, as "one of the first missionaries to the slaves." Samuel W. Capers was half-brother to William Capers. Trs.]

24. White, "The glory of southern Christianity," 114.

25. "The Swamp Missionaries," *Christian Advocate and Journal* 8 (27 September 1833): 19.

26. W.M. Wightman, *Life of William Capers, Including an Autobiography* (Nashville: Methodist Episcopal Church, South, 1902), 296.

27. "General Conference of 1844," 165.

28. Ibid., 165-167.

29. White, "The glory of southern Christianity," 119.

30. J.H. Thornwell, *The Collected Works*, ed. J.B. Adgar and J.L. Girardeau (Richmond: Presbyterian Committee of Publication, 1873), 4:385.

31. W. Walker, *História da Igreja Cristã* (São Paulo: ASTE/Juerp, 1980), 684.

32. Ibid.

33. Ibid.

34. Guilhon, *Confederados em Santarém*, 133.

35. [A bill introduced to Parliament in August 1845 by the British prime minister Lord Aberdeen. The act unilaterally extended the U.K.-Brazil Abolition Convention of 1826 which expired in March 1845. The act defined the slave trade as piracy and authorized the navies of Brazil and Britain to "visit" and search each other's merchant vessels and arrest alleged offenders and put them on trial in Admiralty courts. Trs.]

36. Burton, *Explorations of the Highlands of the* [sic] *Brazil*, 1:268-269.

37. Kidder and Fletcher, *Brazil and the Brazilians*, 137.

38. [The original English source for the bracketed passage could not be located. The passage is a retranslation from the Portuguese translation. Trs.]

39. Kidder and Fletcher, *Brazil and the Brazilians*, 152.

40. J.C. Rodrigues, "Colonização nacional," *O Novo Mundo* (23 March 1871):83.

41. W. Dean, *Rio Claro, um Sistema Brasileiro de Grande Lavoura* (São Paulo: Paz e Terra, 1977), 95.

42. [*sertanejo* – a person living in the arid *sertão* of northeast Brazil but by extension used to identify any dirt-poor rural person—a backwoodsman. Trs.]

43. J.C. Rodrigues, "Notas," *O Novo Mundo* (23 March 1871): 91.

44. *Diário do Gram Pará* (1 April 1867): 31. With the intention of making the American immigration more effective, the imperial government decided to open an office in New York, naming Quintino Bocayuva as director and putting him in charge of all matters concerning immigration. Bocayuva took up his duties in October 1866.

45. An event that had great repercussions throughout the country, especially in São Paulo, was the murder of Joaquim Firmino de Araujo Cunha, police deputy for Penha do Peixe in São Paulo. Many newspapers exploited the matter and pointed out that two North Americans had collaborated in the murder. The *Revista Ilustrada* observed that James Ox Warne and John Jackson Clink had fought in the Civil War on the side of slavery and had come to Brazil because of slavery. According to the magazine, the motive behind the crime was that the police deputy had refused to pursue runaway slaves. "Thus, seeing that their desired system was in its death throes, they, in savage despair, took the initiative in this terrible crime that bloodies our annals." (A. Agostini,

"Ferocidade sem nome" [Unspeakable ferocity], *Revista Ilustrada* (18 February 1888): 2.) Page 2 of the next issue, dated 25 February, gave further information on the matter.

46. Guilhon, *Confederados em Santarém*, 32-33.

47. Ibid., 19.

48. J.J. Ransom, "Immigration to Brazil," *Nashville Christian Advocate* (22 March 1879): 25. It is important to note that Ransom stated this position in 1879, when the historical moment in Brazil, but more especially in the United States, was already quite different.

49. Ransom was in the city of Santa Bárbara on 23 May 1879, and on this occasion he received information that the Baptists had criticized his claims about immigration. Ibid., 29. The text relates still other activities undertaken by him. For example, on 22 May 1879 he was present at the head office of the newspaper *Correio Paulistano,* at the invitation of the editors.

50. Guilhon, *Confederados em Santarém*, 50.

51. Ibid., 50. [The original English source for the passage quoted could not be located. The passage is a retranslation from the Portuguese translation. Trs.]

52. Ibid., 36.

53. Letter, dated 4 June 1868, James B. Bond, U.S. Consul in Pará to U.S. State Department, U.S. Archives, Dispatches from U.S. Consuls in Pará (1831-1906), microfilm T-478, roll 2.

54. Guilhon, *Confederados em Santarém*, 45. Dunn was later denounced by the newspapers in Rio de Janeiro for speculating in land granted by the Brazilian government. (Ibid., 34-35.) It is important to note that Dunn was one of the first to become a naturalized Brazilian. This occurred on 22 June 1866. See Oliveira, *Centelha em Restolho Seco*, 53.

55. Guilhon, *Confederados em Santarém*, 47.

56. Rodrigues, "O futuro e a América," 83.

57. Guilhon, *Confederados em Santarém*, 133. [The original English source for the passage quoted could not be located. The passage is a retranslation from the Portuguese translation. Trs.]

58. ["A dry or liquid measure of capacity of widely varying dimensions" according to *A Portuguese-English Dictionary*, James L. Taylor (Stanford, California: Stanford University Press, 1958). James M. Gaston in *Hunting a Home in Brazil: The Agricultural Resources and Other Characteristics of the Country* (Philadelphia: King & Baird, 1867), 114, states that the alquerie "corresponds to our bushel." Trs.]

59. Guilhon, *Confederados em Santarém*, 133-134. [The original English source for the passage quoted could not be located. The passage is a retranslation from the Portuguese translation. Trs.]

60. J.C. Rodrigues, "A emancipação dos escravos," *O Novo Mundo* (24 October 1870): 2.

61. J. Spaulding, "Rio de Janeiro Mission," *Christian Advocate and Journal* 11:15 (2 December 1836): 58.

62. [The references are to the 1831 Nat Turner uprising among slaves in Virginia and to the so-called "Baptist War" in 1833 when slaves in Jamaica under the leadership of Sam Sharpe, a black Sunday school teacher, revolted and it appeared that the cause had been supported by Baptist missionaries. Both were accompanied by much bloodshed and proved to be a major setback for the abolition movement in the South. Trs.]

63. Rizzo, *Simonton, inspirações de uma existência*, 56.

64. Guilhon, *Confederados em Santarém*, 133. [The original English source for the passage quoted could not be located. The passage is a retranslation from the Portuguese translation. Trs.]

65. Ibid., 137.

66. Burton, *Explorations of the Highlands of the Brazil*, 1:272.

67. Bastos, *Cartas do Solitário*, 49. The position of the imperial government that highlights the question of the moment was recorded in the reply given in *O Abolicionista* on 1 November 1880, 3, in response to the message from the French Council of Emancipation dated 22 August 1866. Turmoil surrounding Tavares Bastos is discussed in the *Jornal do Comércio*.

68. C. Pontes, *Tavares Bastos (Aureliano Candido - 1839-1875)* (São Paulo: Cia. Editora Nacional, 1939), 247.

69. "Escravidão no Brasil," *O Apóstolo* (30 March 1884): 2. The Presbyterian newspaper *Imprensa Evangélica* (12 April 1884): 51, in the article "A escravidão no Brasil," reprinted several lines from the editorial by this Catholic newspaper and added several comments.

70. "A emancipacão," *Imprensa Evangélica* (7 June 1884): 81.

71. J.C. Rodrigues, "A lei de 28 de septembro (opiniões da imprensa nos Estados Unidos)," *O Novo Mundo* (24 November 1871):22, quoting from the *New York Times* (12 November 1871): 4.

72. Rizzo, *Simonton, inspirações de uma existência*, 93.

73. According to Simonton, "Another hope which did not appear too great to be supported was of "beginning of the end" of slavery. If such a stain can be removed, taking away the oppression which weighs on this country, even though the day may remain distant in which this end will come to be completely attained, this would still amount to a great event. There would be a period of trials, humiliation for the national pride, of confession of sins and calls for God's help." (Ibid., 79.)

74. J.C. Rodrigues, "A abolição e os recursos do Brasil," *O Novo Mundo* (24 April 1871): 99.

75. Both the message and the emperor's reply, signed by Martim Francisco Ribeiro de Andrada, were published in the newspaper *O Abolicionista* (1 November 1880): 3. It is important to note that the message to the emperor was sent in July 1866 and his reply came quickly, on 22 August of the same year. [The context for the message was the November 1866 decree freeing slaves for the Paraguay War. (Rozendo Moniz Barreta, *José Maria da Silva Paranhos, Visconde do Rio Branco: elogio histórico,* (Rio de Janeiro: Typographia universal de H. Laemmert & C., 1884), 82). Trs.]

76. "Sub tegmine, sobre abolição," *A República* (20 January 1887): 3.

77. "Brazilian Emancipation," *Independent* (9 November 1871): 4. It is important to note that these commentaries were made apropos the promulgation of the law of 28 September 1871.

78. "Escravidão e educação popular," *O Novo Mundo* (23 November 1870): 34.

79. Rodrigues, "A lei de 28 de septembro (opiniões da imprensa nos Estados Unidos)," 22.

80. Dom Pedro Maria de Lacerda, "Carta pastoral do bispo da Diocese do Rio de Janeiro," *Cearense* (22 November 1871):1.

81. Rodrigues, "Agora é tempo aprazado," *O Novo Mundo* (23 March 1871): 82. [Brazil was engaged in war with Paraguay from 1865 to 1870 with the outcome being a hard-won victory for Brazil and its allies. The conflict is also known as the War of the Triple Alliance—Brazil, Argentina, and Uruguay. Trs]

82. Rodrigues, "A emancipação dos escravos," 2.

83. Rodrigues, "A abolição e os recursos do Brasil," 99.

84. Ibid., 98-99.

85. "Contra a escravidão," *A República* (18 February 1887): 3.

86. C.B. Ottoni, *Imprensa Evangélica* (16 May 1885): 76-77.

87. *A Voz do Escravo* (16 January 1881).

88. J.B.A.E. Silva, "Representação à Assembléia Geral Constituinte e Legislativa do Imperio do Brasil sobre a escravatura (1823)," in *Memórias sobre a Escravidão* (Rio de Janeiro/Brasília: Arquivo National Fund, Petrônio Portela, 1988), 64.

89. [See Sérgio Buarque de Holanda, *Raízes do Brasil*, 3rd.ed. (Rio de Janeiro: José Olympio Editora, 1956), 209-219, where he introduces the concept of the "cordial man" as Brazil's gift to the world. English translation of Buarque de Holanda's treatise can be found in G. Harvey Summ, ed., *Brazilian Mosaic: Portraits of a Diverse People and Culture (Latin American Silhouettes).* (Wilmington, Deleware: Scholarly Resources, Inc., 1995), 106-108. Trs.]

90. Silva, "Representação à Assembléia Geral e Legislativa," 157.

91. *Annais da Câmara dos Deputados*, "Projeto de Lei" (9 July 1827): 3:99. At the same time that the measure pointed to the possibility of achieving gradual emancipation without trauma, the bill foresaw a way of maintaining what was desired of the former slaves: ties to respectability, recognition and, principally, a commitment to work

92. Ibid., (14 May 1830): 1:144.

93. Ibid., (18 May 1830): 1:169. See B.B.Góes, ed., *A Abolição no Parlamento: 65 anos de luta* (Brasília: Câmara dos Deputados, 1988), 1:53.

94. Seymour Drescher, "Brazilian abolition in comparative perspective," *Hispanic American Historical Review* 68 (1988): 3:444.

95. Rizzo, *Simonton, inspirações de uma existência*, 79.

96. Kidder and Fletcher, *Brazil and the Brazilians*, 133-138.

97. Ibid., 137.

98. Vieira, *Protestantism and the Religious Question in Brazil*, 227-231; George Livermore, *An historical research respecting the opinions of the founders of the republic on negroes as slaves, as citizens and as soldiers* (Boston: J. Wilson, 1862).

99. [Agassiz was a biologist at Harvard University. See J. Louis R. Agassiz and Elizabeth C. Agassiz, *A Journey in Brazil* (Boston: Tichnor and Fields, 1868). Trs.]

100. Pontes, *Tavares Bastos*, 250.

101. J.C. Rodrigues, "A base da sociedade," *O Novo Mundo* (24 January, 1871): 130.

102. Agassiz and Agassiz, *A Journey in Brazil*, 129.

103. Ibid., 120.

104. Ibid., 49.

105. Ibid., 165.

106. Lacerda, "Carta pastoral do bispo da Diocese do Rio de Janeiro." The North American John Codman, who did not sympathize with the Brazilians, argued that all who studied closely the Brazilian reality ought to agree with his observation "that [the

Brazilians] are generally kind and indulgent masters, treating their slaves with much greater leniency than has been practiced by any other people among whom the "institution" has existed in modern times." (J. Codman, *Ten Months in Brazil with Notes on the Paraguayan War*, 2nd. ed. (New York: James Miller, 1872), 201.)

107. J.C. Rodrigues, "A lavoura e o crédito," *O Novo Mundo* (23 November 1870): 56. The author emphasized that the movement in favor of emancipation stifled credit for farmers, who in turn rose up in the angriest fashion against the abolitionists.

108. J.C. Rodrigues, "O caroço do algodão," *O Novo Mundo* (23 November 1870): 67.

109. Rodrigues, "Agora é tempo aprazado," 82.

110. Ibid.

111. J.C. Rodrigues, "Grande e modesta revolução," *O Novo Mundo* (24 October 1871): 3.

112. J.C. Rodrigues, "A lei de 28 de septembro" (opiniões da imprensa nos Estados Unidos)," 22.

113. J.C. Rodrigues, "Libertação de escravos na Bahia," *O Novo Mundo* (24 December 1871): 45.

114. "A lei de 28 de septembro," *Jornal do Comercio*, seção "Publicações a pedido" (3 October 1871). See F.C. Gouvêa, *A Abolição: a liberdade veio do norte* (Recife: FUNDAI/Massangana, 1988), 57.

115. J.C. Rodrigues, "O trabalho dos emancipados," *O Novo Mundo* (23 October 1872): 3. This text was also published in the newspaper *O Despertador* (6 February 1874): 2.

116. Rodrigues, "A emancipação dos escravos," 2.

117. Even before the Law of the Free Womb, José Carlos Rodrigues was already pointing out southern society's gains after the end of slavery. He claimed that no nation regretted the action taken and nowhere "did abolition cause danger to the owners and the public good." (Rodrigues, "Agora é tempo aprazado," 82.)

118. The expression *doutrina da abolição gradual* [doctrine of gradual abolition] is used by Paulo Mercadante to describe the means taken in the Brazilian parliament aimed at real emancipation of slaves by the second half of the nineteenth century. The author identifies the appearance of the doctrine in 1871 and claimed that Dantas "resolved to take it on the road to the bosom of the parliament," providing an implementation of the policies introduced with the Law of the Free Womb. (P. Mercadante, *A Consciência Conservadora no Brazil* (Rio de Janeiro: Nova Fronteira, 1980), 157-168.)

119. J.E. Newman, "Mission to Brazil," *Nashville Christian Advocate* (12 June 1875): 2.

120. J. Nabuco, *Cartas aos Abolicionistas Ingleses*, ed. by J.S. Nabuco (Recife: Fundação Joaquim Nabuco Editora Massangana, 1985), 45.

121. Ottoni, "A emancipação," *Imprensa Evangélica* (16 May 1885): 77.

122. "O abolicionismo," *Imprensa Evangélica* (24 May 1884): 1.

123. "A Lei Saraiva," *Imprensa Evangélica* (21 November 1885): 1.

124. Discussing a report drafted by James W. Koger, superintendent of the Methodist Church. Koger, "Brazil Mission," 82.

125. Discussing a report drafted by J.J. Ransom, "Brazil Mission," *Annual Report of the Board of Missions* (Nashville: Methodist Episcopal Church, South, 1883), 73.

126. T.D. Smith, "Letter from Brazil," *Advocate of Missions* 1:3 (August 1880): 13.

127. J.C. Rodrigues, "Progresso da raça Africana nos Estados Unidos," *O Abolicionista* (1 September 1881): 6. This text was reproduced from the newspaper *Gazeta de Notícias* (27 August 1881).

128. Rodrigues, "A emancipação dos escravos," 2.

129. Koster, *Travels in Brazil*, 2:295.

130. Ibid., 2:296.

131. Davatz, *Memórias de um Colono no Brasil*, 75.

132. E.D. Genovese, *Roll, Jordan, Roll: The World the Slaves Made* (New York: Vintage Books, 1976), 76. It is important to note that the use of a scriptural defense for slavery was closely observed throughout the white South between 1840 and 1850. It was affirmed that the enslavement of blacks by whites arose from the biblical curse of Ham. (Ibid., 245-246.)

133. Ibid., 77.

134. Ibid., 203.

135. J.C. Rodrigues, "Escravidão branda e escravidão dura," *O Novo Mundo* (24 July 1871): 143.

136. Ibid.

137. Agassiz and Agassiz, *A Journey to Brazil*, 49.

138. Kidder and Fletcher, *Brazil and the Brazilians*, 133, 138.

139. Codman, *Ten Months in Brazil*, 153.

140. W. Colton, *Deck and Port: or, Incidents of a Cruise in the United States Frigate* Congress *to California, With Sketches of Rio Janeiro, Valparaiso, Lima, Honolulu, and San Francisco* (New York: A.S. Barnes & Co., 1850), 113.

141. Letter, dated 4 June 1868, James B. Bond, U.S. Consul in Pará, to U.S. State Department. U.S. Archives, Dispatches from U.S. Consuls in Pará (1831-1906), microfilm T-478, roll 2.

142. J. Nabuco, *O Abolicionismo* (London: Abraham Kingdon & Co., 1883), 22.

143. Kidder and Fletcher, *Brazil and the Brazilians*, 132.

144. "Brazilian Emancipation," *The Independent* (9 November 1871): 4.

145. Smith, "Letter from Brazil," 13. Mrs. R.E.Scarritt, a North American Protestant, concluded that the mix of races in Brazil demonstrated "a hideous excrescence of the social system." R.E. Scarrit, "Letter from Brazil.," *Woman's Missionary Advocate* 2:6 (6 December 1880): 15.

146. Genovese, *From Rebellion to Revolution: Afro-American Slave Revolts in the Making of the Modern World*, 7-25.

147. Kidder and Fletcher, *Brazil and the Brazilians*, 134.

148. "A emanicipação," *Imprensa Evangélica*, (7 June 1884): 6.

149. Lacerda, "Carta pastoral do bispo da Diocese do Rio de Janeiro," 1.

150. Rodrigues, "Escravidão branda e escravidão dura," 143.

151. Pontes, *Tavares Bastos*, 246.

152. Ibid., 247.

153. Ibid., 249.

154. [A reference to the slave revolt (1791-1804) in the French colony of Santo Domingue that led to the formation of Haiti, and the ever-present fears in other slave areas that a similar revolt would occur among blacks. Trs.]

155. J.C. Rodrigues, "Notícias," *O Novo Mundo* (24 April 1871): 102.

156. Rizzo, *Simonton, inspirações de uma existência*, 76.
157. Ibid., 92.
158. Ibid.
159. Rodrigues, "A emancipação dos escravos," 2.
160. Rizzo, *Simonton, inspirações de uma existência*, 93.
161 *Annais do Senado* (15 June 1831): 1:364.
162. Ina von Benzer, *Alegrias e Tristezas de uma Educadora Alemã no Brasil* (n.l.: n.p., n.d.), 125.
163. Rizzo, *Simonton, inspirações de uma existência*, 93.
164. Rodrigues, "O trabalho dos emancipados," 3.
165. *Annais do Senado* (15 June 1831): 1:364.
166 J.C. Rodrigues, "A mensagem e o Brasil," *O Novo Mundo* (23 December 1870): 34.
167. Rodrigues, "Progresso da raça Africana nos Estados Unidos," 6-7.
168. Ibid.
169. Ibid.
170. Rocha, *Lembranças do Passado*, 2:82. Thomas Ewbank was deeply affected when he attended a slave auction in 1846. For the first time in his life he saw "the bones and muscles of a man with everything appertaining to him, put up for sale, and his body, soul, and spirit struck off to the highest bidder—God's automata knocked down for less than Maelzell's wooden puppet." And he adds that it would be "better—yes, unspeakably better—for many to be knocked on the head in their youth, have their skins converted into glue and their bones into ivory black, than endure through life what some endure." (Ewbank, *Life in Brazil*, 284.)
171. *Aurora Fluminense* (20 March, 1835).
172. Davatz, *Memórias de um Colono no Brasil*, 76.
173. Gardner, *Travels in the Interior of Brazil, Principally Through the Northern Provinces and the Gold and Diamond Districts During the Years 1836-1841* (London: Reeve Brothers, 1846), 21.
174. "A emancipação," *Imprensa Evangélica*.
175. Ibid.
176. "Avisos," *Diários do Rio de Janeiro* (4 January 1846): 4. [The Benguela were from Portuguese West Africa. Trs.]
177. Santos, *O Católico e o Metodista*, 175.
178. Kidder, *Sketches of Residence and Travels in Brazil*, 1:39. In his work in partnership with Fletcher, *Brazil and the Brazilians*, 173-177, there are more details about these activities of the slaves.
179. Kidder, *Sketches of Residence and Travels in Brazil*, 1:99-100.
180. Kidder and Fletcher, *Brazil and the Brazilians*, 169-170.
181. Kidder, *Sketches of Residence and Travels in Brazil*, 1:83-84. Mary C. Karasch, *Slave Life in Rio de Janeiro, 1808-1850* (Princeton: Princeton University Press, 1987), 101-102, provides a detailed statistical picture of infant mortality in the Foundling Hospital between 1814 and 1851.
182. C.G.S.S., "Fechamento das portas," *Methodista Catholico* (1 November 1886): 3.
183. "Sois escravos ou livres?" 194.

184. Rodrigues, "Meio século."

185. Reily, *Metodismo Brasileiro e Wesleyano*, 222.

186. "General Conference of 1844," 166.

187. Genovese, *Roll, Jordan, Roll*, 186, 321.

188. Ibid., 188.

189. José Carlos Rodrigues, "Religiões Acatólicas," *Jornal do Comércio* (1904): 103.

190. "Editorial," *Imprensa Evangélica* (17 October 1879): 329.

191. Ibid. [The "Syllabus" is probably the Syllabus of Errors promulgated by Pope Pius IX in 1864 as a reaction to modern liberalism. The last of the eighty rejected propositions was that the "Roman Pontiff can and ought to reconcile and adjust himself with progress, liberalism and modern civilization." *The Oxford Dictionary of the Christian Church*, ed. F.L. Cross (London: Oxford University Press, 1958), 1311. Trs.]

192. It is not known with whom Simonton had the conversation since only the letter "S", the initial letter of the name of his partner in conversation, is recorded in his diary. Cf. Rizzo, *Simonton, inspirações de uma existência*, 55.

193. "Liberdade do corpo e escravidão do espirito," *Imprensa Evangélica* (27 March 1879).

194. "A evangelização dos indios e dos libertos do Brasil," *O Expositor Cristão* (15 November 1889).

195. Rizzo, *Simonton, inspirações de uma existência*, 52.

196. Flora's certificate of freedom was registered in the Second Civil Registry of Notes of Piracicaba, book 33, folio 45v, 25 November 1881, signed by Dr. Prudente de Moraes, Martha Watts' attorney.

197. Letter from Martha H. Watts, published by the *Woman's Missionary Advocate* 2 (December 1881): 5. In another letter, she tells of a scene that "left her sad for the rest of the day:" an attempted suicide by a slave woman and her child. (Martha Watts, *Evangelizar e Civilizar: cartas de Martha Watts, 1881-1908*, ed. Z. Mesquita, (Piracicaba, SP: Editora UNIMEP, 2001), 37.) It is important to note that this type of behavior, in theory disapproving of slavery but accepting its existence, was quite common. Ina von Benzer, in a letter dated 28 July 1882, describes a conversation with a couple from Rio de Janeiro whom she considered very thoughtful. They "disapproved of slavery and wanted to see it abolished, but also decried the dangers threatening the country and its most wealthy farmers, threatened with impoverishment and even complete ruination by the abolition of slavery." (von Benzer, *Alegrias e Tristezas de uma Educadora Alemã no Brasil*, 104.)

198. Nabuco, *O Abolicionismo*, 18.

199. Rodrigues, "Religiões Acatólicas," 71.

200. [The passage quoted could not be located in the English edition of Kidder and Fletcher, *Brazil and the Brazilians*. The passage is a retranslation from the Portuguese translation. Trs.]

201. Santos, *O Católico e o Metodista*, 175.

202. "A emancipação," 76.

203. Nelson, "Aos escravos," *A República* (13 February 1887): 2.

204. "General Conference of 1844," *Methodist Quarterly Review*, 167.

205. "A escravidão no Brasil," 51.

206. Rocha, *Lembranças do Passado*, 2:213-214, 3:221, 2:200.

207. Vincente Themudo Lessa tells that the slaves were freed by Júlio Ribeiro. Cf. Lessa, 1938, 81. The detailed description of torture imposed on a slave, given by Júlio Ribeira in *A Carne* after he had abandoned the Protestant church, is in itself a cry of revolt against slavery and reminds us in many ways of the description of the torture of slaves described later by Eduardo Carlos Pereira. Cf. Ribeiro, 1988, 35-37.

208. Vincente Themudo Lessa claimed that 1879 was the year of the slaves: "On the first Sunday of January in 1879, two slaves, Felismina and Lucinda, were received by the Presbyterian missionary George Chamberlain. In the month of February, another slave, Benedita Justina, also was enrolled in the book of members of the church. Within the group of founders of the Presbyterian church of Borda da Mata were included three slaves of Antônio Joaquim de Gouvea. In 1879 alone, among the eleven received into the church led by Chamberlain, five were slaves." (Lessa, *Biografia do Ex-Padre José Manoel da Conceição*, 168-169.)

209. Koster, *Travels in Brazil*, 2:239-40. Ewbank points out that even the whites avoid any contact with the missionaries. "They avoid him as one with whom association is disreputable, and they entertain a feeling toward him bordering on contempt, arising from a rooted belief in his ignorance and presumption." The bond between Brazilian society and Catholicism is so deep and indissoluble that if there was any change, "civil and social relationships would be broken up, and thousands upon thousands lose the means by which they live." (Ewbank, *Life in Brazil*, 239.)

210. Rodrigues, "Religiões Acatólicas," 77-78.

211. Kidder, *Sketches of Residence and Travels in Brazil*, 1:160.

212. Ibid., 246-247.

213. Rocha, *Lembranças do Passado*, 2:211-214.

214. These slaves were freed by Júlio Ribeiro. (Lessa, *Biografia do Ex-Padre José Manoel da Conceição*, 81.)

215. It is important to note that the missionary Chamberlain was a good friend of José Carlos Rodrigues and in 1864 in Rio de Janeiro taught him English. H.C. Tucker, *Dr. José Carlos Rodrigues (1844-1923): A Brief Sketch of His Life*, 349, contains much information on the subject.

216. Lessa claimed that within the group of founders of the church in Borda da Mata are recorded the names of three slaves belonging to Antônio Joaquim de Gouvea, a member of the church. (Lessa, *Biografia do Ex-Padre José Manoel da Conceição*, 168.)

217. Rodrigues, "Religiões Acatólicas," 117.

218. "O Brasil catholico e o protestantismo," *Imprensa Evangélica* (December 1881): 353-354.

219. Rodrigues, "Escravidão e educação popular," 35.

220. Genovese, *Roll, Jordan, Roll*, 287.

221. Benzer, *Alegrias e Tristezas de uma Educadora Alemã no Brasil*, 124.

222. Kidder and Fletcher, *Brazil and the Brazilians*, 129.

223. Ibid.

224. Ibid., 170.

225. Ibid., 132.

226. Kidder, *Sketches of Residence and Travels in Brazil*, 1: 181.

227. Kidder and Fletcher, *Brazil and the Brazilians*, 134.

228. Ibid., 137.

229. Letter from Joaquim Nabuco to the Electoral Chamber in Portugal on the occasion of his journey to Lisbon. J. Nabuco, *O Abolicionista*, (1 March 1881): 10. [For more on the activities of the British-owned mines, see Marshall C. Eakin, *British Enterprise in Brazil: The St. John d'el Rey Mining Company and the Morro Velho Gold Mine, 1830-1960* (Durham and London: Duke University Press, 1989). Trs.]

230. J. Nabuco,"A nossa missão," *O Abolicionista* (1 November 1880): 1.

231. Rodrigues, "Colonização nacional," 83.

232. Ibid.

233. Rodrigues, "A emancipação dos escravos," 2.

234. J.C. Rodrigues, "A lavoura e o crédito," 56.

235. Guilhon, *Confederados em Santarém*, 133-134. [The original English source for the passage quoted could not be located. The passage is a retranslation from the Portuguese translation. Trs.]

236. Letter from Henington, 20 May 1867 (Guilhon, *Confederados em Santarém*, 38). [The original English source for the passage quoted could not be located. The passage is a retranslation from the Portuguese translation. Trs.] In February 1888, a few months before abolition, an event with considerable repercussions occurred: the murder of Joaquim Firmino de Araújo Cunha, police deputy in Penha do Peixe, in São Paulo. The event was exploited by nearly all the newspapers, principally because two of those involved in the crime were North American immigrants. Angelo Agostini, in his *Revista Ilustrada,* brought to light that James Ox Warne and John Jackson Clink were two of the active participants in the crime and that they had provoked the farmers: "They appeared to have the blood of the cockroach," they murdered the deputy because he had "refused to pursue runaway slaves." He added that "the two fought in the Civil War in the United States on the side of the slave owners, but for those who are familiar with the story of that fratricidal struggle, there is no need to say any more. Why did they come to Brazil? Why did they become naturalized Brazilians? Why did they go to the interior of São Paulo? One simple word: "Slavery!" everyone replies. So, seeing that their desired system was in its death throes, they, out of savage desperation, took the initiative in this ghastly crime that bloodies our annals." (A. Agostini, "Ferocidade sem Nome," 2.)

237. Guilhon, *Confederados em Santarém*, 133. [The original English source for the passage quoted could not be located. The passage is a retranslation from the Portuguese translation. Trs.]

238. On a visit to a plantation in the environs of Rio Janeiro in 1846, Ewbank recognized some patriarchal customs of the old Portuguese planters. He noted the role of a ninety-year old matriarch, whose habit it was to wake everyone, white and black, at two o'clock in the morning to recite matins. An old black, complaining about the situation, said, "Work, work, work all day; and pray, pray, pray all night - no negro can stand that!" (Ewbank, *Life in Brazil*, 75.)

239. J.M.K. Jones, *Soldado Descansa!* (São Paulo: Jarde,1967), 168. The Methodist missionary J.J. Ransom, when describing his travels into the interior of São Paulo, complains of not having luggage porters in the railway stations. (Ransom, "Immigration to Brazil" (27 October 1877): 16.) Furthermore, on a journey to São Paulo he tells that two of the train's cars were occupied by blacks. (Ransom, "Immigration to Brazil" (18 November 1876): 8.)

240 Rocha, *Lembranças do Passado*, 2:79-80.

241. Ibid., 2:81-82. It is important to note that Bernardino was removed from the church roll at an extraordinary session on 20 December 1865. At this same session there

were read "two letters of freedom, given to Joaquim and Pedro by João Severo." (Ibid., 2:85.)

242. Ibid., 2:85, 2:213, 3:208, 2:227-228, 4:63.

243. Ibid., 2:34, 2:35.

244. Ribeiro, *Protestantismo no Brasil Monárquico*, 51.

245. ["Members of the Brazilian elite were deeply influenced by the writings of the French philosopher, Auguste Comte (1798-1857), . . . Known as positivism, Comte's philosophy glorified reason and scientific knowledge and rejected traditional religious beliefs. He believed that humanity had begun to overcome the superstitions and religious beliefs of the past, and, with the guidance of science (positive knowledge), it would soon enter into a new age where technicians and engineers would run an authoritarian republic to achieve true progress. Comte summed up his beliefs in a pithy epigram: 'Love as the principle. Order as the base. Progress as the Goal.'" (M. Eakin, *Brazil: The Once and Future Country* (New York: St. Martins Press, 1998), 35.) The influence of positivism is reflected in the motto of the republic, "Ordem e Progresso" [Order and Progress]. Trs.]

246. Rocha, *Lembranças do Passado*, 1:50 and 2:17. Kalley was at the center of a hotly debated incident involving a pamphlet designed and printed in England for him. On the cover the figure of a crucified man was depicted with the title "O ladrão na cruz." Tavares Bastos was the defense attorney for Kalley and he did so with the purpose of "simply denouncing an unheard of act by the authorities which appears to us deeply offensive to political freedoms. Is it not an intolerable premature censorship for the Customs House to prohibit the importation of this or that piece of writing due to this or that reason?" (Bastos, *Cartas do Solitário*, 111-117.)

247. "Imprensa evangélica," *Imprensa Evangélica* (9 October 1879): 321. The first issue of *Imprensa Evangélica* had a circulation of 450 copies and was distributed also among many Roman Catholic priests. The missionaries Ashbel Green Simonton, A.L. Blackford and George Chamberlain took turns at managing the newspaper. The first issue was printed at Tipografia Universal de Laemmert; later the printing passed to Tipografia Perserverança, after the Laemmert brothers were threatened and withdrew from the newspaper.

248. *Imprensa Evangélica* (7 October 1871):28. Beyond being a newspaper focused on the Presbyterian Church, it can be claimed that it exercised a fundamental role in the work of the implantation of Protestantism in Brazil.

249. Ibid.

250 "Liberdade do corpo e liberdade do espírito," 97.

251. [A notorious island prison off the northeast coast of Brazil. Trs.]

252. "Os ingênuos," 115.

253. "O Brasil catholico e o protestantismo," 354.

254. "Imprensa evangélica," 321.

255. Ibid.

256. J. Nabuco, "Escravidão e colonização," *Imprensa Evangélica* (29 March 1884): 46. In collaboration with the *Imprensa Evangélica*, Joaquim Nabuco defended the abolition of slavery and supported European immigration, allowing spontaneous emigration, i.e., without subsidies from the state, since only in this form would it be possible to give to the Brazilian populace priority in the free labor market.

257. Ibid., 53.

258. "A escravidão no Brasil," 51.

259. "O abolicionismo," 73.

260. "População escrava no Brasil," *Imprensa Evangélica* (21 July 1884): 94.

261. "O protestantismo no Brasil," *Imprensa Evangélica* (5 July 1884): 99.

262. "Abolição e imigração," *Imprensa Evangélica* (2 August 1884): 116.

263. "A Onda," *Imprensa Evangélica* (16 August 1884): 128.

264. "Emancipação," *Imprensa Evangélica* (20 September 1884): 143.

265. "Movimento abolicionista," *Imprensa Evangélica* (1 November 1884): 168.

266. *Imprensa Evangélica* (21 February 1885). Another article published in the *Women's Missionary Advocate* reported that there were thousands of children wandering the streets of Rio de Janeiro, living on the street, without education, and without friends, food or a place to sleep. The text raised several questions, "Shall we, with God's help, seek to save these precious souls?" It also made a practical proposal: the creation of housing that would serve as a refuge where the youngsters could be sheltered, fed and allowed to rest and, above all, trained to follow "the way of salvation." Watts, *Woman's Missionary Advocate*, (May1881): 3-4.

267. Pereira, "A escravidão," *Imprensa Evangélica* (2 May 1885): 66.

268. [The Saraiva-Cotegipe Law, or "Sexagenarian Law," of 1885, which, *inter alia*, freed slaves over sixty years of age. Trs,]

269. "A Lei Saraiva,"

270. Ibid.

271. Published in the *Imprensa Evangélica* starting on 3 April 1886. The complete text, entitled "A Religião Christã em suas relações com a escravidão," by Eduardo Carlos Pereira, was published by the Sociedade Brasileira de Tratados Evangélicos (Brazilian Evangelical Tract Society) in 1886, and is given as an appendix to this work.

272. *Methodista Cathólico* (1886): 1:3.

273. Ibid. The newspaper is making reference to the book written by Father dos Santos ("Perereca") against the Methodists Kidder and Spaulding. On this occasion the priest said that one of the proposals of the missionaries and the Methodist Church in Brazil was to bring an end to slavery. The *Methodista Católico* denounced, with irony, the salvaging of this virulent text by a radical Ultramontanist, but did not take advantage of the moment to question the matter addressing the abolition of slavery.

274. G.N. Morgan, "Revista da pastoral no bispo do Pará," *O Púlpito Evangélico* (February/March 1875): 2.

275. Ibid.

276. *O Pregador Cristão* (9 January 1886):1.

277. Vieira, *O Protestantismo, a Maçonaria e a Questão Religiosa no Brasil*, 735-737.

278. An example is the newspaper *O Despertador,* which on 21 September 1872 reprinted the article "O domicílio do imigrante," and on 22 October 1872 "As guerras civis." The newspaper *Cearense* of Fortaleza reprinted a good number of the articles. In 1872 we find articles reprinted on the following dates: 11 January (p.6); 18 January (p. 6); 22 January (p.1); 5 February (p.2); 19 March (p.2); 22 March (p.2); 2 April (p.3); 26 April (p.2); 30 April (p.3); 31 May (p.4); 28 June (p.3); and 2 September (p.3). Also, André Rebouças, in his *Diário*, cites José Carlos Rodrigues and *O Novo Mundo.* (I.J. Veríssimo, *André Rebouças: através de sua autobiografia* (Rio de Janeiro: José Olympia, 1939), 246-247.)

279. Rodrigues, "A emancipação dos escravos," 2. Also published in the newspaper *Cearense* (11 January 1874): 6.

280. Rodrigues, "A liberdade e a fé," *O Novo Mundo* (24 January 1872). Also published in *Cearense* (18 January 1874): 6.

281. Rodrigues, "Progresso da raça Africana nos Estados Unidos," 2.

282. Rodrigues, "A lavoura e o crédito," 56.

283. Rodrigues, "A emancipação dos escravos," 2.

284. Ibid.

285. Rodrigues, "Agora é tempo aprazado," 82.

286. Rodrigues, "A escravidão e a lavoura," 67.

287. Rodrigues, "Agora é tempo aprazado," 82.

288. Rodrigues, "O caroço do algodão," 67.

289. Rodrigues, "O trabalho dos emancipados," 3.

290. Rodrigues, "Escravidão e educação popular," 35.

291. Rodrigues, "O trabalho dos emancipados," 3.

292. Rodrigues, "O caraço do algodão," 67.

293. Rodrigues, "A emancipação dos escravos," 2.

294. Ibid.

295. Ibid.

296. Rodrigues, "Escravidão e educação popular," 35.

297. Rodrigues, "A abolição e os recursos do Brasil," 99.

298. Ibid.

CONCLUSION

Immediately on my arrival [in Rio de Janeiro], I opened public ser-
vice in my house. The number in attendance soon increased from
thirty to forty, so that we were obliged to procure a larger and more
convenient place. . . . We have a weekly prayer meeting besides the
monthly missionary prayer meeting. . . . We have been enabled to or-
ganize a Sunday school. . . . Through recommendation and request of
some of my friends here, I have opened a day-school. . . . It is gener-
ally believed by the most intelligent here, that the establishment of
schools of learning upon broad and liberal principles will be one of
the most direct means of access to the people of this country. . . .
Could we render them this service . . .we might approach so near as
to do them, . . . the greatest of all services, by pointing them to the
Lamb of God. . . . The storm of reproach does fall principally on [the
Roman clergy.] . . . To redeem and save the morals of the clergy and
the people. . . . What will be the final result of slavery, and when it
will end in this country is impossible to say. . . . All we can do is to
be diligent and exceedingly discreet in the use of the means, watch
the signs of the times, and enter every opening door of Providence,
however small, to do them good. [1]

Writing this report on the beginnings of his missionary work in Brazil, the Reverend Justin Spalding, a Methodist pastor, was merely describing some of the basic characteristics that imbued the imagination of American missionary Protestantism. Ignorance of the "true religion," the major source of the evils that were devastating the country, was viewed as responsible for the contemporary situation in Brazilian society. And on the basis of that assertion, the following conclusion was reached: that this irksome religious heritage, established by Catholicism and the source of immoral principles on a grand scale, ought to be contrasted with Protestantism, bearer of the virtues of liberalism, morality and progress.

The implantation of missionary Protestantism in Brazil coincided histori-cally with the period in which the difficulties associated with slavery were shaking U.S. society, cooling the enthusiasm of many for liberalism and pro-gressivism. As a function of the intensification of internal conflict in the U.S., taken to the extreme of civil war, there was a heightened effort, expressed theo-logically, to create mechanisms aimed at preserving and strengthening ecclesiastical institutions.

In Brazil, Protestantism did not go through a period of adjustment as it did in the United States. From the beginning it was seen as a "new" religion, considered radical and dangerous to traditional Brazilian society. Then came a second stage, as the possibility of implanting Protestantism was taking shape, driven by the attitude adopted by Robert R. Kalley and his Portuguese followers. The new religion began to be examined with more rigor, not only as a possible threat to Catholic hegemony, but especially because of its innovative content.

Thus, with the exception of Kalley, Protestant missionary work based its initial activity among immigrants from the southern United States, and gradually assimilated and developed a new strategy. This effort to conquer religious space in Brazilian society depended basically on a three-legged stool: education, polemics and proselytism.

Bear in mind that the Protestant denominations that strived to implant missions in Brazil carried in their bellies their own contradictions, and found as their partner in dialogue a profoundly stratified society shaped by an extremely different religious culture. It is possible, then, to identify some particular features that guided their behavior in the face of slavery.

First, we have the irrefutable testimony given by the Protestant missionaries themselves regarding the prudence that was needed in carrying out their religious work. Discussions about the subject of slavery could become dangerous and, foremost, they could greatly hamper the top priority, the work of implantation. Second, the Protestant missions established in Brazil were imbued with strong conservative tendencies that sought to make a distinction between the spiritual and the temporal. Consistent with this leaning, the focus of the preaching by Protestant missionaries was directed at the problem of religious freedom, essentially against the intransigence shown by the Catholic Church.

As a consequence of this assertion, a third fundamental element emerges regarding the position of Protestantism on the subject of slavery: its interest in moral regeneration, which appears repeatedly. Protestant missionary theology in Brazil was satisfactorily accommodated to a sensible distancing of the Protestant Church from the grave problems faced by society, black slavery among them. Their concern focused not so much on the emancipation of blacks as on their conversion, education and integration into Protestant culture. In sum, interest was directed toward moral regeneration, with the assertion that the degradation of social habits was contrary to Christian virtues.

Finally, the concept of adaptation, that is the need to keep pace with the changes occurring in Brazilian society, is the fourth element to be distinguished. Protestantism argued for itself the right to be the bearer and representative of a new era, a time of progress. In this period, the mid-1880s, when abolition was already taking the shape of a large popular urban movement, the basic question and priority for Protestantism continued to be opening up space for its own acceptance and, consequently, its successful implantation. Participating in the debate surrounding abolition was, above all, an essentially religious concern, and the opportunity given for the discussion and defense of abolition reveals, to a great extent, specific goals and interests.

NOTE

1. Spaulding, "Rio de Janeiro Mission," 98. [From the letter we see that the issue of clerical morality was provoked by a proposal before the legislature to remove mandated celibacy for Roman Catholic priests so as to bring the law into line with practices. Trs.]

APPENDIX

"THE CHRISTIAN RELIGION AND ITS RELATION TO SLAVERY"

"**A** Religião Christã em suas relações com a escravidão" [The Christian Religion and its Relation to Slavery], by Eduardo Carlos Pereira, was originally published serially beginning on 3 April 1886 in *Imprensa Evangélica*, Brazil's first evangelical newspaper, created in Rio de Janeiro. In that same year, the writings were made public in their entirety by the Sociedade Brasileira de Tratados Evangélicos.[1] This represents the first important anti-slavery declaration by a Brazilian Protestant pastor.

Ordained as a Presbyterian pastor in 1881, Pereira became one of the most important collaborators of *Imprensa Evangélica* in its early days in São Paulo, taking on the role of editor. The text reproduced here was transmitted in installments by this newspaper. The author, in relating an event that happened in his infancy when he had heard the groans of a black slave being tortured, seeks to demonstrate the complete incompatibility between slavery, Biblical teaching and Christian justice

I. A Scene from Slavery

> *Shout out, do not hold back. Lift up your voice like a trumpet! Announce to my people their rebellion, to the house of Jacob their sins. (Isaiah 58:1, NRSV)*

A mong the recollections from my past, there is one that stands out like a discordant note in a nostalgic harmony. I was being introduced to the mystery of the three "R's" on a plantation.

One day, a sound coming from a closed room right at the end of the terrace caught my attention. I approached and listened. Muffled and pleading cries could be heard in the midst of the sound of something supple falling repeatedly on a limp body. From time to time, a menacing voice replied to the humble supplications of some victim. I recognized the voice and understood the cries: here was occurring one of those monstrous and harrowing scenes of slavery that from a thousand plantations have called down a terrible curse on this wretched nation.

I felt my heart beat rebelliously; but what could I do, other than to shed an ineffectual tear of indignation and pity for the poor captive?

Suffer, miserable slave, since you committed the crime of being born in the hot climes of Africa, and inasmuch as you perpetrated another crime no less grave—that of abandoning the crops and the overseer's whip in order to seek out in the woods the freedom of the runaway! Unfortunate one who did not plan on hunger drawing you out of the shadowy forests, nor on the stigma of your color denouncing you to the half-breeds, who are greedy for your master's reward! Pay then with your blood for the harm you have caused. Suffer, groan and die in misfortune, for the day of redemption will not dawn for you! Die, because in this civilized and Christian land only death can hold back the reflexive arm of your partner before the deadly novena determined by the justice of the plantation can be completed! Meanwhile, may both you and we be consoled by the belief that your cries and your blood have been collected in the chalice of the wrath of upright and awful justice.

I remember that the following day, or several days later, I found the room open and I went in. Oh, misery! A horrifying instrument was hanging there: a short stick approximately one centimeter in diameter serving as a handle for several strips of thin, hard rawhide, all bloody at their ends and the rest spattered in blood. A ladder on the floor showed where the torture was carried out.

I left the room. It was a splendid day and undoubtedly the smiling blue sky quite quickly would have swept these sad impressions from my childish spirit had a new spectacle not come to reinforce them deeply.

I had gone out into the backyard, and there in the shade of an orange tree I saw a poor black man lying face down on the ground, and if my memory serves me correctly, he had a large iron mass restraining him at the ankles. I approached: it was that same wretched victim, seeking shelter from the heat of the sun. I shooed away the flies that were pestering him, and what a repulsive sight! Through the rags that barely covered his buttocks, I could see an open sore, deep and festering!.

Oh! Accursed institution that arouses in mankind the instincts of a beast, obliterating the most basic human feelings!

Almost twenty years have passed, and what will have become of this wretch?

Death probably will have given him the rest and hospitality that human hearts denied him. Or perhaps he is still miserably dragging through the fields whatever flesh remains from the overseer's rawhide whip, a disgraceful remnant fought over by the voracity of slavery in opposition to the freeing of sexagenarians.[2]

Meanwhile, how many wretches like him, violently deprived of their natural rights, have for three centuries been, cowardly exploited, cruelly martyred and killed by the humanitarian civilization of our cultured Empire.

The curse of Canaan has had a terrible consummation, but woe to those by whose hand Noah's terrible prediction has been and continues to be carried out!

The prophesies about the Son of Man were also terrible, but woe to the Judas who betrayed Him, woe to the god-murdering people who carried them out!

Very well then, after so much and such great suffering, may the groans and cries of pain from the victims of our avarice and greed echo like a dreadful voice of remorse in the ears of the present generation! Let the blood and shattered flesh of the miserable captives be specters that come constantly to trouble the criminal dream of an egotistical and cowardly indifference.

It is necessary that the printing press cry out ceaselessly, that it raise its voice like a trumpet and denounce to the people the monstrousness of this national sin, for the ignorance of centuries of darkness can no longer attenuate it.

It is necessary that the press declare frankly to slave owners how offensive slavery is to the laws of God and humanity, and how vile is the shameful exploitation of a race that has just as much right as any other to the liberty that God has given them.

I will cry out and denounce to the new children of Israel this crime that still stains the bosom of the evangelical churches in Brazil, to the enormous detriment of the Gospel.

And while justice is spoken from my mouth, my voice will have the same authority as the Prophet, because the voice of justice is the voice of Jehovah.

II. Slavery in light of the Old Testament

> Remember that you were a slave in the land of Egypt, and the Lord your God redeemed you; for this reason I lay this command on you today. (Deuteronomy 15:15, NRSV)

When we examine slavery in the light of reason and the noble sentiments of the heart, when we consider its disastrous social consequences, we can claim a priori with all assurance that it does not and cannot have divine sanction.

If the sentiment of justice and good, the noblest trait with which the Creator endowed us, is not a lie, then slavery cannot be sustained upon the Old or New Testament, which contain the exalted revelation of this great Creator. May His infinite justice and compassion be reflected in those souls created in His image and likeness.

Nothing, however, obscures our understanding more than the misunderstood interests of this life. It is not unexpected, but deeply lamentable that many Christians commit the sacrilege of defending their slave ownership with the Word of the God of justice and love.

It is time to open the eyes of our brothers, looking at slavery in the light of both Testaments. Today, I will examine it through the Old; in subsequent articles we will look at it in light of the New.

From the study of the Pentateuch we infer that a type of slavery was tolerated by Mosaic Law; yet this same study shows us that its character was quite different from the slavery that unfortunately reigns in our country.

Setting aside for now this type of consideration, I ask: Did the Old Testament perhaps institute or even endorse this mild slavery, which could still not fail to possess a certain degree of injustice and oppression? I reply: No, it only tolerated it.

The Divine Master, demanding God's justice, shows us the reason for this tolerance.

One day the Pharisees attempted to put Jesus at odds with Moses over divorce. Having asked if it was lawful to repudiate a wife for any reason, and being told "No," they replied, "Why then did Moses allow it?"

"It was because you were so hard-hearted that Moses allowed you to divorce your wives, but from the beginning it was not so." (Matthew 19:8, NRSV)

This reply and reason, which underscores God's wisdom and goodness, explains the tolerance among the Jews for this mild captivity and at the same time safeguards Divine Justice.

At the beginning this was not so: God did not institute divorce for any cause whatsoever; He tolerated it, preparing the people for the reestablishment of original purity and justice. Thus, for slavery of any degree, God did not create the black in order to cultivate the Garden of Eden for Adam and Eve; they cultivated it with their own hands. (Genesis 2: 6,7,18). Later, when the soil produced thorns and thistles, the Lord did not say, "You will eat your bread by the sweat of the brow of your slave." Rather, He ordained, "By the sweat of your face you shall eat bread." (Genesis 3:18-1, NRSV)

This is the original order instituted by God, but as men multiplied over the Earth, they grew in the depravity of their fallen nature. The darkness of their understanding became ever darker and wiped from their souls the traces of the original likeness of God in true righteousness and holiness. (Ephesians 4:24) Pride, cupidity and indolence gave deep root to slavery in the customs of all peoples, just as lasciviousness introduced polygamy into the personal lives of all societies.

To uproot these abominable institutions without preparing the people, without lifting up society to an awareness of justice and holiness, was to apply a patch of new cloth to an old garment, or to pour new wine into old wineskins.

To say to these benighted men that they did not have the right to kill or enslave prisoners taken by the prowess of their bows and swords in open warfare with their enemies, was to say to them something absolutely incomprehensible and completely absurd.

In the face of this hardness of hearts, we note the wisdom of Moses and the patience of God in tolerating the times of this ignorance. (Acts 17:30)

Unable to abolish slavery, the Hebrew lawgiver encircled it with such measures that he restricted its abuses and deprived it of its cruel nature, the latter being its most prominent feature in our cultured Christian society.

It is amazing to see this great Lawgiver, three thousand years ago in an eastern country, rising way above our nineteenth century legislators in his understanding of justice and his feelings of humanity.

Let us make a brief comparison, and let us be ashamed by the contrast.

Whoever kidnaps a man and sells him, says Moses, is guilty of a crime and must be executed. (Exodus 21:16)

Meanwhile, our legislators legalized the infamous robbery and hideous traffic in Africans. That is not all: Since Article 1 of the Saraiva-Cotegipe Law does not require a declaration of birthplace in the new registration, it decrees the enslavement of those who were freed by the law of 1831.

The contrast is painful! In the Old Testament is proclaimed the dignity of man created in God's image; here the work of the Creator is destroyed, reducing his rational creatures to the level of things!

If you purchase a Hebrew slave, he will serve you six years, and in the seventh year he will be freed out of kindness. And he will not be sent away empty handed. (Exodus 21:2, Deuteronomy 15:13)

The contrast is obvious. After three hundred years of horrific slavery, the glorious Dantas ministry fell for having written into its program the freeing of slaves who had already served ten times six years![3]

"If the owner knocks out a tooth of a male or female slave, the slave shall be let go, a free person." (Exodus 21: 27, NRSV)

Yet for three centuries, under the protective shield of our laws, slaves were allowed to go free from their masters when, with bloodied flesh, their whippings also stripped them of their lives!

"Slaves who have escaped to you from their owners shall not be given back to them. They shall reside with you, in your midst, in any place they choose in any one of your towns, wherever they please; you shall not oppress them." (Exodus 23:15f, NRSV)

The contrast here with the new law concerning the servile class is poignant.

If a slave, impelled by a compelling instinct, escapes the atrocities of captivity, if, says one of our eloquent tribunals, he appears suddenly ragged, cruelly treated, terrified, falling on his knees before you, among your little children who caress you and the mother who smiles at you, you must crush your heart, stifle your tears, harden your face, and throw the wretch out or tie him up to be handed him over to the authorities. If not, legal proceedings, with a fine of one thousand milreis.

Alongside these Mosaic arrangements which indicate the gentle character of the slavery tolerated among the Jews, there is a relevant admonition that could not fail to cause a deep impression in the hearts of the Israelites. It appears at the beginning of this section. Remember that you were a slave in the land of Egypt, and the Lord your God redeemed you.

Such a warning gave great strength to the liberating tendencies of the Mosaic laws and hastened powerfully the softening of the hardness of hearts and the re-establishment, within the bosom of religious families, of that order instituted at the beginning.

Therefore, it has been shown in this section:

- That Jewish slavery, or rather, servitude, was very different from contemporary slavery; consequently it is absurd to justify the latter by the former;

- That even that servitude was only tolerated because of the deep ignorance of the times and the hardness of hearts; such arguments cannot be invoked in this enlightened age under Christian dispensation;
- Finally, that whoever wishes to defend his ownership of slaves by using the Old Testament, must appeal to the order established by God in the beginning: "You will eat your bread by the sweat of your brow."

III. Slavery in Light of the New Testament

In everything do to others as you would have them do to you; for this is the law and the prophets. (Matthew 7:12, NRSV)

It is quite clear from the preceding section that the Old Testament was far from legitimizing slavery. And in the text given above, the Divine Master, infallible interpreter of the law and the prophets, synthesizing the teachings and the spirit of the Old Testament, amply confirms the conclusions of that section.

Therefore, while the Old Dispensation which Saint Paul called the "yoke of slavery" (Galatians 5:1, NRSV), might condemn bondage, does the New Dispensation, or Royal Law of liberty, as it was called by Saint James (James 2:8, 12, NRSV), sanction it?

It is indeed saddening this necessity to demonstrate to Christians that the nature of Christianity is completely hostile and deeply opposed to the institution of slavery.

In fact, He who came to preach the freeing of prisoners, as declared by the Prophet (Isaiah 61:1), could He possibly make a pact with captivity of any kind? And His noble Gospel, which announces to men the freedom of sons of God, could it possibly be reconciled with slavery? Lastly, the New Testament, which presents to us the Son of God spilling His own most precious blood to release us from captivity; the New Testament, which contains the Gospel that offers freely to all the Spirit of the Lord, which is the Spirit of Freedom (2 Corinthians 3:17), can it perhaps cover with its mantle of justice and love the most flagrant and cruel violation of love and justice?

Yet some Christians, who perhaps deserve that name, blinded by slave interests, seek to justify with certain recommendations by Saint Paul that which not only is a betrayal of the spirit of the Gospel, but also is a complete denial of the doctrines and life of that great apostle to the Gentiles.

Saint Paul recommended that servants obey their masters and that masters treat their servants with justice and fairness: hence—fatal blindness!—slavery is justified in light of the New Testament.

With eyes closed to the light of the Gospel, they disregard the monstrous blasphemy of such a conclusion. How so? Could the spirit of freedom and brotherly love bond, even harmonize, with the nature of slavery? Could Christ, the Redeemer of the world, connive in the sacrilegious destruction of the work of the Creator, in the moral assassination of thousands of creatures?

May there shine in our souls some ray of the magnificent light of Christianity, and then the madness of such a conclusion will be made manifest.

Resting the seal of His divine authority on the Law and the Prophets, the Lord enjoined his disciples, "In everything do to others as you would have them do to you." (Matthew 7:12, NRSV)

Now I ask: This commandment from the great Redeemer, understood as it is intended, is it or is it not an abolitionist commandment?

Once it has penetrated the understanding, heart and conscience of any Christian who is not a mere hypocrite, can he fail to decide compulsorily, obligatorily to free his slaves?

In addition to being an article of sound doctrine, "Do to others as you would have them do to you," is a most important truth, a moral axiom so intuitively applicable to the relationship between a master and his slaves that I need not dwell upon it further.

While others, dominated by niggardly interests, may systematically refuse to put this Golden Rule into practice in the myriad relations of life, never will this be done by the sincere Christian, because for him it is doubly holy, doubly obligatory: the Creator commands it by the means of reason, and Christ in the golden pages of His Gospel.

Saint Paul affirms that by bringing down the wall separating Israel from the other nations, Christ killed through Himself all animosities and ended the distinction between Jews and Gentiles. (Galatians 3:28) From the heights of the Galilean hills, sending out His apostles, the Savior proclaimed, by means of His cross, the equality of all men of all colors, the catholicity of the new religion, which would embrace in its maternal bosom all races, languages and conditions. In the parable of the Samaritan, He caused the scales to fall from the eyes of the doctor of the law, and in the tiny heart of this Jew He played the sublime notes of Christianity, teaching him that his fellow man is not only someone who speaks the same language or is of the same color. (Luke 10:25-37) Thus opening wide unknown horizons, Jesus ordered his people, "You will love your neighbor as yourself."

And is it not a transgression of this commandment to keep my neighbor under a yoke which under no circumstances I would ever wish for myself?

Along with Saint Paul, it is permissible for me to say with noble haughtiness, "I will never be anyone's slave." But how can there be in me any Christian reciprocity, any of Christ's charity, if I allow another man to be made my slave?

"Love your neighbor as yourself" is the ultimate condemnation of bondage.

Furthermore, when at night in your bedroom, following the commandment of the Savior, you say, "Our Father," perchance do these words not burn your lips? How do you dare to proclaim, in these sublime words of the Lord's Prayer, the brotherhood of all men, if there in the slave quarters a man on hard planks who is your slave stretches out his ragged and broken limbs? Where is your honesty? He who for a brief while is able to forget his sad misfortune, is he not in fact your brother, such that you can rightly say, "Our Father"? Do you perhaps so disdain God that you believe that your prayer will be heard?

Do you not see that the black's sweat, shed by you and for you, his tired limbs, his deformed and broken body, his brutalized mind, are terrible pleas crying out to eternal justice? Do you not hear the hypocrisy in the prayer: He is not my brother, he is my master?

The wonderful opening line of the Lord's Prayer, which reveals the divine essence of Christianity, is a most eloquent manifestation of its brotherly spirit, diametrically antagonistic to the injustices and atrocities inherent in slavery. It is, therefore, an emphatic and decisive condemnation of slavery.

The Lord's Prayer was placed by the Divine Master in the mouths of His disciples to be proclaimed like a daily protest against all the tyranny and violence of human ferocity.

"Our Father!" Three syllables that encompass the most elevated idea given to us to understand, says A. Martin, and which one day must conquer all tyranny, revive all peoples, and establish the human race in its glory and freedom.

In fact, in every time and nation in which the genuine spirit of the Gospel contained in these luminous syllables has been embodied in the bosom of communities, man has always been known to break the chains of captivity so as to say to his slave: You are my brother!

Freedom and fraternity, the human spirit's sublime utopias, are the universal fruits of true Christianity.

What has been said is sufficient to prove that the nature and precepts of the New Testament, far from being in harmony with slavery, are on the contrary the most energetic and efficacious condemnation of this transgression of natural law.

Is it to be believed, then, that the most eminent hero of the New Testament, the fullest example of evangelical kindness, the most vivid incarnation of the Christian spirit, the great Apostle to the Gentiles, would betray the mission of love, justice and freedom entrusted to him by the Savior, justifying slavery?

Impossible.

And Saint Paul's guidance?

That is what I will examine in the following section.

IV.

The law is laid down not for the innocent but for the lawless and disobedient, for the godless and sinful . . . for slave traders . . . and whatever else is contrary to the sound teaching. (I Timothy 1:9-10, NRSV)

On the basis of the preceding section, it can be claimed without hesitation that if Moses snatched the prisoners away from the serpent of slavery among the Jews, Christ killed it among the Christians.

In order to dispel any doubts about the truth of this assertion, perhaps it behooves us to observe here, as did Saint Paul, that not all that is called Jewish is in fact Jewish; in the same way, many who call themselves Christians are a disgrace to that name.

It is time, therefore, to cleanse the Apostle to the peoples of the stain of favoring slavery, undertaking an examination of his recommendations.

"Slaves, obey your earthly masters in everything. . . . Masters, treat your slaves justly and fairly, for you know that you also have a Master in heaven." (Colossians 3:22, 4:1, NRSV)

These are the words which when read through the prism of the slave traders' interests, appear to justify slavery.

When we read them stripped of preconceptions, however, in the light of the high interests of the Gospel and the circumstances of the times, we see dispersed the cloud that threatened to darken the limpid skies of Christianity.

Upon these recommendations we have already focused the intense light of the spirit and precepts of the New Testament, and we have made quite clear the madness, blasphemy and monstrousness of a conclusion supporting slavery.

In this section I will examine the reasons that suggested to the Apostle these apparent contradictions with the Gospel he preached.

Sent by the Divine Master to plant the good seeds of justice and love, the Apostle found in the gentile world the same extremely mean and wicked ideas about slavery, the same hardness of heart that Moses found among the Jews.

What to do? It would be foolish to start an immediate, unyielding and relentless war. Perhaps it would be noble, but it certainly would not be prudent for an unknown Jew to fall in open warfare, crushed under the weight of that terrible institution identified with life in pagan societies. With tearful eyes we admire John Brown, protesting in the nineteenth century from the height of the gallows against the monstrosity of slavery; but we would rightfully find fault with the great Apostle if, without considering the circumstances of the time, he had imprudently misrepresented the wise counsel of the Master, putting the new wine of sublime doctrines in old pagan wineskins.

It behooved him, therefore, to imitate Moses' prudence; it was important to renew the wineskins so that they could withstand the powerful expansion of new ideas.

The Reverend Houston offers a wise observation on this point: Saint Paul could not expect the harvest before first scattering the seed. It was first necessary to scatter the seeds of justice, kindness, absolute equality of all social conditions and positions, through Christ crucified; of universal brotherhood through the only God of all the Earth, the common Father of all humanity, so that the bright harvest of freedom could be secured. It was necessary for Christ's spirit to first penetrate the impure Gentile masses.

Slavery was symptomatic of egotism, laziness, and unbridled ambition; it was necessary to combat the source of this evil. Indeed, the physician who combats the symptoms instead of fighting the disease is either a charlatan or inexperienced.

It is not rare for a fever, for example, to be the result of an organic wound, in which case only foolishness would lead the physician to attempt to cure it without first treating the wounded organ.

Such considerations render Saint Paul's recommendations clearly understandable. Like a wise and diligent physician, he applied the powerful remedies of the new doctrines to the original diseases, with the certainty that the symptoms would disappear with the disease.

Moreover, Saint Paul was not a politician who was attempting to reform the norms of the ancient societies. Social regeneration was simply a natural consequence of the sound principles he was preaching. His mission was immediate and loftier: he sought the salvation of souls through faith in Jesus Christ crucified.

For that reason, then, would he thwart the urgent salvation of thousands by raising up in the beginning the deafening cry of earthly prejudices and profound interests of a private and political nature?

Given all these very powerful considerations, it behooved him still to overlook these times of ignorance and, like Moses, await better times, to capitulate before the hardness of hearts to the extent compatible with the dignity of his ministry.

Therefore, the words of the Apostle do not imply the legitimacy of slavery at any time, much less in the century in which we live. The truth of this can be expressed in the following paraphrase:

Have patience, oh Christian servants, you are Christ's slaves, which demands that you abide the injustice of bondage for a little longer, so that the premature revolt of thousands of slaves does not throw society into a terrible confusion, thus disrupting the dissemination of the New Faith, raising up a blasphemy of powerful societal prejudices and causing political and temporal designs to be attributed to it rather than the spiritual goals, that are its exclusive aim.

Have patience; the seed of the Gospel is germinating, and soon you will harvest the sweet fruits of freedom.

When we consider that the number of slaves in Imperial Rome was almost twice that of the free population and made up almost the whole of active society, we can imagine the horrific prospect of a social conflagration if Christianity had not assumed the prudent position it adopted.

Approximately six years after Saint Paul wrote these recommendations, the terrible revolt led by the heroic Spartacus came to fully justify the great Apostle's prudence.

Cesar Cantu, on page 51 of the fourth volume of his *História Universal da Escravidão no Império Romano* [Universal History of Slavery in Imperial Rome], provides evidence of the accuracy of what has been said regarding the motives that guided Saint Paul's foresight in the face of this fearful problem.[4]

Like Moses, he rose way above his time and in his epistles drew up the death sentence of slavery without, however, sparking the civil conflagration that later, in 133 C.E., would shake the Empire terribly.

In view of the explosive state of society, revealed by this fearful slave revolt and by the heroic gladiators' insurrection in 71 C.E., let us admire the skill with which the Apostle reproved servitude, advising slaves to free themselves: "Were you a slave when called? Do not be concerned about it. Even if you can gain your freedom, make use of your present condition now more than ever. For whoever was called on the Lord as a slave is a freed person belonging to the Lord, just as whoever was free when called is a slave of Christ. You were bought with a price, do not become slaves of human masters." (1 Corinthians 7:21-23, NRSV)

These words certainly do not show great enthusiasm for slavery.

Saint Paul did not forget about the owners in this sticky matter. Not only does he remind them that they and their slaves are slaves of the same Lord, for whom there is no favoritism; he also orders them to desist from threats and to do with their slaves what is just and equitable.

And now that the sweetest light of the Gospel has dissipated the clouds from reason, what is it, I ask the most ardent supporters of slavery, what is it, in the face of the immutable principles of justice, that ought to be done with those who were iniquitously deprived of their rights?

The words with which Saint Paul defended a runaway slave are still relevant. The owner is Philemon and the slave is Onesimus. ". . . though I am bold enough in Christ to command you to do your duty, yet I would rather appeal to you on the basis of love. I am appealing to you for my child, Onesimus. So that you might have him back forever, no longer as a slave, but more than a slave, a beloved brother." (Philemon 8-10, 16, NRSV)

Such a request certainly does not come from an enthusiast for slave ownership, for when understood correctly, it amounted to an order to free the convert Onesimus.

Finally, the excellent Apostle declared that God's Law was set for the condemnation of robbers of men. (I Timothy1:9-10, NRSV)

To make such a declaration is to blast slavery at its origins, especially in Brazil, because of those who benefit from this robbery under the terrible curse of divine law.

It must be believed that they will no longer impiously invoke Saint Paul to cover with his venerable authority that which is a flagrant contradiction of the spirit and doctrines of Christianity. His advice can be explained in the light of the times and it cannot be raised up in conflict with the invincible force of the Gospel, which has proclaimed throughout the globe, "freedom to the captives."

V. The Pulpit as regards Slavery

> But if the sentinel sees the sword coming and does not blow the trumpet, so that the people are not warned, and the sword comes and takes any of them, they are taken away in their iniquity, but their blood I will require at the sentinel's hand. (Ezekiel 33:6, NRSV) [5]

Slavery is a sacrilegious robbery because freedom is a fundamental gift from God, essential to the full achievement of the highest destiny of human nature

In the light of our century, this proposition is established with intuitive clarity as an axiomatic truth. Let it be said, in homage to the Brazilian intellect, that even the most intransigent supporter of slavery dare not deny the brilliance of its unequivocalness.

The abolitionist position is, therefore, very strong in this, the last quarter of the century; unfortunately the same did not happen in Apostolic times. It is hard to believe that the ignorance of the pagan spirit was so great that even their philosophers fought in support of slavery as a natural right, saying that it was a social necessity.

Society certainly cannot be sustained without manual labor and industriousness; however, the morally blind of those times preached that citizens should not be dishonored with labor and work, which naturally were reserved for those whose bodies bore the brand of captives. Xenophon said that a man condemned to manual work became useless to the Republic, only a half-defender of the fatherland, and then a bad one. Cicero considered any profession requiring labor as shameful and unworthy of a free man, and he hardly made an exception for architecture and medicine.[6]

With such absurd and unfortunate prejudices, it was not to be expected, claimed the same historian, "that slavery, as a natural right, should be considered a political dogma by slave owners and philosophers, who could not imagine a society without this sinister condition. Furthermore, the slaves themselves, when they revolted, did not contest the principle of their status but limited themselves to protesting the excesses whereby their masters made them victims."

This brings a new light to bear on the prudent attitude of the Apostle to the Gentiles, and greatly corroborates the considerations in the previous section. For more than one reason it behooved him first to broaden the moral horizons and demonstrate as foolishness the wisdom of that age. An intransigent and immediate abolitionism would be a crime of offence against society, the violation of a social right!

Today after nineteen centuries of enlightenment, the brilliant rays of Christianity have swept away the dark shadows of the human spirit; today there is no longer the need for the Apostle's reservations, since it is as clear as the midday sun that slavery is a violation of natural law, a crime of offence against humanity, a sacrilegious attack upon the work of the Creator.

In the light of these irrefutable truths, what should be the attitude of the pulpit regarding slavery?

Should it be the negative attitude of reservation?

Why? Might there be a danger that a spark from the pulpit will produce a social conflagration? Over eleven million free men, might there be one hundred million slaves in this empire whose trembling, inflamed state might be eagerly awaiting the first incendiary spark?

It would be ridiculous to suppose that Saint Paul's position in Imperial Rome is identical to that of today's preachers of the Gospel in Imperial Brazil.

Why, then, this reservation, this fainthearted silence before a crime of such gravity?

Might our listeners still not understand that slavery is unlawful and extremely offensive to God, claiming it necessary to overlook the times of this ignorance and first prepare the wineskins to receive the pure wine of Christian justice, mercy, equality and brotherly love?

To assert such a claim would be to ignore the work of nineteen centuries.

If none of the circumstances persists today that so fully justified Saint Paul's somewhat reserved posture, then the silence from the pulpit is not prudence, it is unfaithfulness.

More than robbery in the face of reason, captivity is a flagrant violation of the Christian spirit, a conscious neglect of the most holy principles of the adorable Redeemer.

If this is true, as I have shown it to be, how can the silence of the watchmen of Israel be justified?

Perhaps someone will say, "Let the Gospel be preached," and the day when it is planted in the heart of the owner, the chains of his slaves will fall to the ground.

If this way of proceeding were acceptable in relation to slavery, why would it not be so regarding lotteries, gambling, drunkenness, Sabbath-breaking, and a thousand other expressions of sin?

In this manner of proceeding there is, therefore, a false apprehension regarding pastoral duties, which unfortunately the attitude of many families of believers presumes to demonstrate.

"The eyes of the Lord God," says Amos, "are upon the sinful kingdom, and I will destroy it from the face of the earth." [Amos 9:8 NRSV]

And the ruins that litter the deserted soil of the old world lie there in the eloquence of their silence, bearing witness to the veracity of the Prophet.

Thus, will it not be an urgent duty for the sons of Aaron to grasp the censer and raise upon the altar the incense of His intercession before the Lord's anger is kindled against this national sin.

But the smoke of this incense will provoke God's righteous indignation if the priests are participants in this sin. And even if we do not practice the anathema in our homes, does it not exist perchance in our churches?

If the injustice of slavery must bring down some other whip on this nation, does it not say in the Holy Scriptures that it will begin with the house of God?

Social apathy crushes us, and one doesn't need to be very intelligent to discern in slavery the principal cause of this great evil. And is it not true that we must, in general, lament the same evil in our communities of believers? Why then not attribute to the same cause the source of this religious atrophy, this premature aging which threatens the churches?

Is it not then time to cry out with Joshua, "Anathema is in the midst of you, O Israel"? [Joshua 7:13]

Out of the bosom of the evangelical churches in the United States there went up the cry that shattered the shackles of four million unfortunate souls. If the punishment was tremendous that the South received for its resistance, most rich were the blessings that followed from the redemption of the captives.

The ministers of the Lord addressed appeals to the Government of the Republic; the pulpit launched the thunderbolts of divine condemnation against the abominable institution.

Thus, the national conscience was raised and, with the sole of Lincoln's foot, the head of the accursed serpent was crushed..

And when the slave ships boldly crossed the seas, as an affront to the Creator's justice, it was again the Christian spirit which, taking possession of Wilberforce, Buxton, and Lamartine, gave satisfaction to Providence by blasting the hideous traffic in Africans with the fiery word of justice and charity.[7]

Did this powerful word perhaps die on the lips of the Lord's ministers? The holy fire of the Gospel that gave an unbreakable hardness to the persevering courage of Garrison and Brown, and made a generous heart beat in the ample breast of Wilberforce and Buxton,[8] will it no longer have the virtue of inculcating the same dedication in the hearts of believers and producing the same heartbeats in the face of the iniquitous oppression of an unfortunate race?

The extinction of this social iniquity is providentially linked to effective protests by eminent Christians. If society deprives itself of this fruitful protest, is it not perhaps impeding Providence's designs or, at least, bringing upon itself the threat printed as the heading of this section?

Even if there are doubts about the power of the word of the Gospel, in this vast country, can the pulpit observe this heart-wrenching spectacle in silence, indifferent, without violating its most holy responsibilities, as rights, justice and charity are trampled in the most holy shadow of the faith of the Crucified?

Nothing, then, of acquiescence or complicity in this social sin, which has sufficiently prejudiced the vital interests of the Faith.

Raise in the name of the Redeemer the same protest that has already been raised in the name of reason, humanity and the country's economic interests.

Safeguard the glory of the Gospel by unleashing from all the pulpits the bolt of lightning that will eliminate slavery from the bosom of the churches.

VI. The Believer and Slavery

Having called attention in the previous sections to the fact that slavery is highly offensive to the laws of God and humanity, as I conclude the task I set for myself, I am obliged to impress upon the sincere Christian's conscience the truths that I have expounded.

Hear me, then, with patience, dear brother, if you are one who owns slaves. I am driven by my desire for your own well-being, as much as compassion for the dispossessed race.

1. You profess to be Christian and consequently a respecter of God's laws, whether they be written in the pages of the Scriptures or engraved on the tablets of your heart.

Very well then, have you never noted the manifest incompatibility that exists between your profession of faith and the captivity that stains your home?

If up until now you have sought bewilderingly to still your conscience with some isolated scriptural text, I believe that you already are convinced of the absurdity and sacrilege of any such attempt. You will no longer dare to invoke Saint Paul as an advocate of slavery.

If, then, the religion you profess condemns slavery, choose between it and the slaves you own. Either you keep your slaves and continue to benefit from the sweat of the brow of your fellow man, in which case, following the example of the Gaderenes, you should ask Jesus to leave your home; if not, then restore to your slaves their stolen freedom and declare that you are not merely a hypocrite.

"But this is hard," you will say. "Noone has the right to propose to me such a harsh alternative."

That it is hard, I will not deny; however, that I have no right, even more, no duty, to bring to your attention this difficult choice, that is something that might be true if you and I lived in the time of Saint Paul.

In the full light of Christianity, which has illuminated the moral sphere of humanity, I am simply complying with a duty that unfortunately has been neglected.

In the face of what has been put forward in the previous sections, answer me: Is or is not slavery an injustice that directly offends the spirit and precepts of the Gospel? If it is, unless you dare to deny it, it cannot fail to be a sin profoundly distasteful to the God of mercy proclaimed by the great Redeemer.

And can a Christian, with a clear conscience and without ipso facto losing the right to that sacred name, uphold in his home something sinful and distasteful to his God, under any pretext?

You are aware that slavery is an injustice and therefore a sin, and yet you continue voluntarily to commit this sin?

You certainly will not deny Saint Paul and Saint John the right to present to you, in your circumstances, the terrifying alternative. Listen:

"For if we willfully persist in sin after having received the knowledge of the truth, there no longer remains a sacrifice for sins, but a fearful prospect of judgment, and a fury of fire that will consume the adversaries." (Hebrews 10:26-27, NRSV)

"Little children, let noone deceive you. Everyone who does what is right is righteous, just as he is righteous. Everyone who commits sin is a child of the devil." (I John 3:7-8, NRSV)

Therefore, in bringing to your awareness this terrifying fork in the road, I did nothing more than offer to you the teaching of these illustrious Apostles. But fear not, for I have offered you a touchstone so that you can show your brothers the fine gold of your beliefs and convince yourself of the sincerity of your faith.

2. You will perhaps object, "And what about my interests, how will I live afterwards?"

Your interests are the interests of justice and truth, they are the interests of the Gospel, and the life of your soul is worth a thousand times more than the life of your body.

"But strive first for the kingdom of God and his righteousness," (Matthew 6:33, NRSV) this is the ultimate commandment from your Divine Master. Who, then, will dare to disobey the Lord of Lords? What possible interests could there be on Earth or in hell capable of supplanting the supreme interests of the Kingdom of God?

Moreover, who told you that your temporal interests would suffer? Is God's blessing not worth more than the labor of a thousand slaves?

A few days ago, I heard from a farmer who had expected to harvest a hundred alqueires of rice and collected only four. Honor the Lord's precepts and He will "open the windows of heaven for you and pour down for you an overflowing abundance." (Malachi 3:10, NRSV)

The southern states of North America believed that ending slavery would kill "King Cotton," destroy farming and, consequently, the wealth and prosperity of the nation. On 1 January 1863, with one violent blow, the great Lincoln made four million slaves into citizens. After this terrible jolt, and more than four years of a dreadful civil war, the wealth and prosperity of the United States has no rival in the world and the southerners have no reason to envy the North's prosperity. When contrasted with our own country, this picture provides an eloquent confirmation of the following truth affirmed by the Scriptures, a truth that naturally is proved in the individuals who in aggregate constitute the nation. "Righteousness exalts a nation, but sin is a reproach to any people." (Proverbs 14:34, NRSV)

In addition, He who said, "But strive first for the kingdom of God and his righteousness," added, "and all these (temporal) things will be given to you as well." (Matthew 6:33, NRSV)

3. In the egotistical desire to preserve your property, perhaps you will say, "But the law of my land allows me to own slaves."

Even though such a law might exist, it is invalid when confronted by your conscience, even if it were promulgated by an assembly of angels. For you no law is valid if it contradicts God's laws.

This supposed law concedes to you the possession of another man's freedom; nevertheless, an older and higher law confers on this man the control over his own freedom. The two laws contradict each other; it is necessary to choose between them, and here again the harsh alternative rises up before you: Either the law of men or the law of God. You decide.

4. Those who, through trickery and by force, took possession of free men on the African coast in order to sell them to plantation owners in Brazil, clearly committed a heinous robbery. And none of the laws of our legislators are able to legitimize a robbery. God's law, declared Saint Paul, is against the robbery of men. (I Timothy 1:9-10)

But you will object, "The guilty are those who did the robbing, I owned slaves in good faith."

True, and for this you are guiltless; however, that good faith no longer exists.

You know they were stolen, how then can you consent to upholding the robbery?

Being the accomplice is as good as being the thief. Applying this maxim is hard in your case, and I sincerely hope you can be cleared of this finding.

Moreover, this maxim is the popular consecration of what the apostle said, "Those who practice such things deserve to die - yet they not only do them but even applaud others who practice them." (Romans 1:32, NRSV)

You did not steal, that is true, but you benefit from the theft that others carried out and so you are complicit, becoming one with them before God.

When we buy a stolen object and the owner lays claim to it, it would be absurd and ridiculous to demand of him the value of the object before being willing to turn it over to him. Our only recourse is to go and beat on the door of the robber to demand our money. But the robber has died and there are others living in his house. What to do? Demand reparations from the new occupants? Incensed, they would slam the door in our face.

There is no solution: Either we hand over the stolen object or we weep uselessly over our imprudence or bad luck. The alternative is to fail in our honesty and lay claim to the right to be equals of the robber.

Very well then, the slave is the owner who demands of you his freedom. Should you require him to pay you the sum that by natural law belongs to him?

"The thief is the government," you say. Very well then, demand money back from the robber. But the government, which according to your reasoning was the robber, has already died, and even if it had not died, it would not have money to pay you, since the government is only the administrator of public funds. By what right, then, do you demand reimbursement from the current government?

Acknowledge your mistake in the face of these eternal principles of justice. You have no right to speculate with the freedom of your fellow man, and as a Christian you ought to leave the fund for emancipation to those who are not guided by the sublime rules of the Gospel. Suffer the loss and return stolen freedom to its rightful owner, as is demanded by honesty, justice, humanity and God.

5. Read the story of Achan told in the seventh chapter of the book of Joshua. . . . Take note of how man's greed brought trouble to the whole of Israel. It was only after the flames of the Valley of Achor[9] consumed his body and everything that belonged to him that the blessing of Jehovah could fall on the congregation of his people. (Joshua 7:18-26, NRSV).

Very well then, by preserving the curse of slavery, not only do you call the displeasure of God upon your home, but also upon the Church of which you are a member. The Church, however, will protest vigorously and in everything demonstrate that it shares no guilt in this matter. Therefore, the curse will fall only on the heads of those who are found to be stained with this crime.

6. I confess: Great is my shame and great is the bewilderment of Christ's Church in Brazil, upon seeing unbelievers release their slaves out of simple love for humanity; while those who profess faith in the Redeemer of captives fail to break the fetters of impiety nor set the oppressed free! Reader, if perchance you see an unbeliever reading this article, I beg you, for the honor of our Lord's Church in Brazil, that you not allow his eyes to peruse this sixth paragraph.

7. If, in order to free the slaves of the Israelites, Moses recalled their slavery and liberation from the land of Egypt (Deuteronomy 15:15), would you, Christian, not have in the story of your own life an even stronger and more moving argument to free your slaves?

Has not the blood of a compassionate Redeemer liberated you from a bitter and degrading captivity? And now, as you look upon your slave, do you not hear your Lord's terrible rebuff?

"You wicked slave! I forgave you all that debt. . . . Should you not have had mercy on your fellow slave, as I had mercy on you?" (Matthew 18:32-33, NRSV)

8. As you can well see, unfortunately it is hard to "do to others as you would have them do to you," because, "the way to heaven is narrow." The slave is "your eye which serves as a scandal." And "your right arm that made you sin." Very well then, tear them out, says the Master, it is the violent who rage against the Kingdom of Heaven. [Matthew 7:12-13, 5:29-30]

In the person of your slave, honor the image of your God. Do not assault the inviolable right to a holy property.

In the name of the justice that smote Achan, in the name of the mercy that was preached by the Crucified Redeemer of captives, do not continue to cloak in mockery the disgraced Church of our Lord Jesus Christ. Restore inalienable freedom to its rightful owner.

NOTES

1. *A Religião Christã em suas relacões com a escravidão.* São Paulo: Sociedade Brasileira de Tratados Evangélicos, 1886.

2. [Reference is to the Saraiva-Cotegipe Law of 1885 which, *inter alia*, freed slaves over sixty years of age. Trs.]

3. [In 1884 the administration of Manoel Pinto de Souza Dantas proposed a reform program including the immediate freeing of all slaves over sixty years of age. The proposal was lost when the administration did not survive a no confidence vote in 1885. See note 2 above. Trs.]

4. [Cesar Cantu, c.1804-1896, was an Italian historian and author of the multi-volume *Universal History.* Trs.]

5. [Verse 9 is also relevant to the argument, "But if you warn the wicked . . .and they do not turn from their ways, the wicked will die in their iniquity, but you will have saved your life." Trs.]

6. [In *Oeconomicus* Xenophon (431-354 B.C.E.) has Socrates observe to Critobulus, "Hand in hand with physical enervation follows apace enfeeblement of soul: while the demand which these base mechanic arts makes on the time of these employed in them leaves them no leisure to devote to the claims of friendship and the state. How can such folk be other than sorry friends and ill defenders of the fatherland?" (Xenophon, *The Works of Xenophon*, trans. H.G. Dakyns, vol..3 (London: Macmillan & Co., 1890-1897), ch. IV.) It has not been possible to trace the reference to Marcus Tullius Cicero. Trs.]

7. [William Wilberforce (1759-1833) and Thomas Fowell Buxton (1786-1845) were leaders in the abolitionist movement in Britain, while Alphonse de Lamartine (1790-1869) was a French poet and writer partly responsible for the abolition of slavery in the French empire in 1849. Trs.]

8. [William Lloyd Garrison (1805-1879) occupied a radical position in the antislavery movement and was openly critical of what he saw as indifference on the part of most mainline clergy. John Brown (1800-1859) was an abolitionist who argued that a massive slave uprising was the only way to end slavery in the United States. He saw such an event as provoking the northern states into military action. Trs.]

9. ["Achor" can be translated as "trouble" (NRSV). Trs.]

BIBLIOGRAPHY

"Abolição e imigração." *Imprensa Evangélica* (2 August 1884): 116.
"O abolicionismo." *Imprensa Evangélica* (24 May 1884): 1.
Agassiz, J. Louis R. and Elizabeth C. Agassiz *A Journey in Brazil*. Boston: Tichnor and Fields, 1868.
Agostini, Angelo. "Ferocidade sem nome." *Revista Ilustrada* (18 Feb 1888): 2.
Avé-Lallemant, R. *Viagem pelo Norte do Brasil no anno de 1859*. 2 vols. Rio de Janeiro: Instituto Nacional do Livro, 1961.
Baldwin, L.V. *A History of the African Union Methodist Protestant and Union American Methodist Episcopal Churches, 1805-1980*. Metuchen, N.J.: Scarecrow Press, 1983.
Barreta, Rozendo Moniz. *José Maria da Silva Paranhos, Visconde do Rio Branco: elogio histórico*. Rio de Janeiro: Typographa universal de H. Laemmert & Cia., 1884.
Bastide, R. *As Religiões Africanas no Brasil*. 2 vols. São Paulo: Pioneira, 1971.
Bastos, A.C. Tavares. *Os Males do Presente e as Esperanças do Futuro*. São Paulo: Cia. Editora Nacional, 1939.
———. *Cartas do Solitário*. São Paulo: Cia. Editora Nacional, 1938.
Benzer, Ina von. *Alegrias e Tristezas de uma Educadora Alemã no Brasil*. n.l.: n.p., n.d.
Bergad, Laird W. *Comparative Histories of Slavery in Brazil, Cuba, and the United States*. New York: Cambridge University Press, 2007.
Bethell, L. *A Abolição do Tráfico de Escravos no Brasil*. Rio de Janeiro and São Paulo: Expressão e Cultura/Edusp, 1976.
Biard, F. *Deux années au Brésil*. Paris: Libraire de L. Hachette et Co., 1862.
Boeher, George C.A. "José Carlos Rodrigues and O Novo Mundo, 1870-1879." *Journal of Inter-American Studies* 9 (January 1967): 127-144.
Bradbury, M. and H. Temperley. *Introdução aos Estudos Americanos*. Rio de Janeiro: Editora Forense-Universitária, 1979.
"O Brasil cathólico e o protestantismo." *Imprensa Evangélica* (December 1881): 353-354.
"Brazil." *The Gospel in All Lands* (20 July 1882).
"Brazilian Emancipation." *The Independent* 23: 1197 (9 November 1871): 4.
Burlamaqui, F.L.C. "Memória analítica acerca do comércio de escravos e acerca dos males da escravidão doméstica" (1837). In *Memorias sobre a Escravidão*. Rio de Janeiro and Brasília: Arquivo Nacional/Fund. Petrônia Portela, 1988.
Burton, Richard Francis. *Explorations of the Highlands of the* [sic] *Brazil*. 2 vols. London: Tinsley Brothers, 1869.
Cardozo, Manoel. "A escravidão no Brasil, tal como é descrita pelos americanos: 1822-1888." *Revista de História* 43 (July-September 1960): 139-163.
———. "Slavery in Brazil as described by Americans, 1822-1888." *The Americas* 17 (January 1961): 241-260.
"Catecismo Evangélico." *O Presbiteriano* (March 1908): 3
César, W. *Para uma Sociologia do Protestantismo Brasileiro*. Petrópolis: Vozes, 1982.
C.G.S.S. "Fechamento das portas." *Methodista Catholico* (1 November 1886): 3.

Chreitzberg, A.M. *Early Methodism in the Carolinas*. Nashville: Methodist Episcopal Church, South, 1897.

Codman, John. *Ten Months in Brazil with Notes on the Paraguayan War*. 2nd. ed.New York: James Miller, 1872.

Colton, Walter. *Deck and Port; or, Incidents of a Cruise in the United States Frigate* Congress *to California, With Sketches of Rio Janeiro, Valparaiso, Lima, Honolulu, and San Francisco*. New York: A.S. Barnes & Co., 1850.

Conrad, Robert Edgar. *Children of God's Fire: A Documentary History of Black Slavery in Brazil*. University Park, Pennsylvania: The Pennsylvania State University Press, 1984.

———. *The Destruction of Brazilian Slavery, 1850-1888*. Berkeley: University of California Press, 1972.

———. *Os Últimos Anos da Escravatura no Brasil*. Rio de Janeiro: Civilização Brasileira/INL, 1975.

"Contra a escravidão." *A República* (18 February 1887): 3.

Costa, A.M.S. "O Destino (não) manifesto: os imigrantes norte-americanos no Brasil." Ph.D. diss. University of São Paulo, 1985.

Crabtree, A.R. *Baptists in Brazil*. Rio de Janeiro: The Baptist Publishing House of Brazil, 1953.

Davatz, Thomas. *Memórias de um Colono no Brasil: 1850*. Belo Horizonte/São Paulo: Itatiaia/Edusp, 1980.

Dean, W. *Rio Claro, um Sistema Brasileiro de Grande Lavoura*. São Paulo: Paz e Terra, 1977.

"Deportação." *A República* (17 November 1886): 3.

"O domicílio do imigrante." *O Despertador* (21 September 1872).

"Os dous systemas." *Imprensa Evangélica* (1 September 1877): 132.

Drescher, S. "Brazilian abolition in comparative perspective." *Hispanic American Historical Review* 68:3 (August 1988): 429-460.

Dunn, Ballard S. *Brazil, The Home for Southerners*. New York: George B. Richardson, 1866.

Eakin, Marshall C. *British Enterprise in Brazil: The St. John d'el Rey Mining Company and the Morro Velho Gold Mine, 1830-1960*. Durham and London: Duke University Press, 1989.

"A Emancipação."*Imprensa Evangélica* (7 June 1884): 6.

"Escravidão no Brasil." *O Apóstolo* (30 March 1884): 2.

"A escravidão no Brasil." *Imprensa Evangélica* (16 April 1884): 51.

Etzel, E. *Escravidão Negra e Branca*. São Paulo: Global, 1976.

"A evangelização dos indios e dos libertos do Brasil." *O Expositor Cristão* (15 November 1889).

Ewbank, Thomas. *Life in Brazil, or a Journal of a Visit to the Land of the Cocoa and the Palm*. New York: Harper & Brothers, 1856.

Feijó, Diogo Antônio. *Resposta às Parvoices, Absurdos, Impiedades e Contradições do Sr. Padre Luís Gonçalves dos Santos na Sua Obra Intitulada "Defesa do Celibato Clerical Contra o Voto em Separado pelo Padre Diogo Antonio Feijó*. Rio de Janeiro: n.p.,1827.

Ferreira J.A. *História da Igreja Presbiteriana no Brasil*. São Paulo: Casa Editora Presbiteriana, 1959.

Franca, Pe.L. *A Igreja, a Reforma e a Civilização*. Rio de Janeiro: Livraria Agir Editora, 1958.

Franco, M.S.C. *Homens Livres na Ordem Escravocrata*. São Paulo: Ática, 1976.

Frase, R.G. *A Sociological Analysis of the Development of Brazilian Protestantism: a study in social change.* Ann Arbor: Xerox University Microfilms, 1988.

Gammon, S.R. *The Evangelical Invasions of Brazil or a Half Century of Evangelical Missions in the Land of the Southern Cross.* Richmond: Presbyterian Committee of Publications, 1910.

Gardner, George. *Travels in the Interior of Brazil, Principally Through the Northern Provinces and the Gold and Diamond Districts During the Years 1836-1841.* London: Reeve Brothers, 1846. Reprint, Ams Press, Inc. 1970.

Gaston, James McFadden. *Hunting a Home in Brazil: The Agricultural Resources and Other Characteristics of the Country.* Philadelphia: King & Baird, 1867.

Gauld, Charles Anderson. "José Carlos Rodrigues, o patriarca da imprensa carioca." *Revista da História* 4 (October-December 1953).

"General Conference of 1844." *Methodist Quarterly Review* 22 (April 1870): 165-188.

Genovese, Eugene D. *From Rebellion to Revolution: Afro-American Slave Revolts in the Making of the Modern World.* Baton Rouge: Louisiana State University Press, 1979.

————. *The Political Economy of Slavery: Studies in the Economy and Society of the Slave South.* New York: Vintage Books, 1967.

————. *Roll, Jordan, Roll: The World the Slaves Made.* New York: Vintage Books, 1976.

————. *The World the Slaveholders Made: Two Essays in Interpretation.* New York: Pantheon, 1969.

Góes, B.B. ed. *A Abolição no Parlamento: 65 anos de luta.* Vol. 1. Brasília: Câmara dos Deputados, 1988.

Goldman, F.P. *Os Pioneiros Americanos no Brasil.* São Paulo: Pioneira, 1972.

Goulart, M. *A Escravidão Africana no Brasil.* São Paulo: Alfa-Ômega, 1976.

Gouvêa, F.C. *A Abolição: a liberdade veio do norte.* Recife: FUNDAI/Massangana, 1988.

Grahan, R. "Escravidão e desenvolvimento econômico: Brasil e sul dos EUA no século XIX." *Revista de Estudos Econômicos.* 13 (1983): 223-257.

————. *Escravidão, Reforma e Imperialismo.* São Paulo: Perspectiva, 1979.

————. *Grã-Bretanha e o Início da Modernização no Brasil.* São Paulo: Brasiliense, 1973.

"As guerras civis."*O Despertador* (22 October 1872).

Guilhon, Norma A. *Confederados em Santarém: saga Americana na Amazônia.* Rio de Janeiro/Brasília: Presença/INL, 1987.

Hamilton, Charles Granville. "English-speaking travelers in Brazil, 1851-1887." *The Hispanic American Historical Review* 40 (November 1960): 533-547.

Harrison, W.P. *The Gospel Among the Slaves.* Nashville: Publishing House of the Methodist Episcopal Church, 1893.

Herberg, W. *Protestantes, Católicos e Judeus.* Belo Horizonte: Itatiaia, 1962.

Hollanda, Sérgio Buarque de. *Raízes do Brasil.* Rio de Janeiro: José Olympio, 1977.

Ianni, O. *As Metamorfoses do Escravo.* São Paulo: Difel, 1962.

————. *Raça e Classes Sociais no Brasil.* Rio de Janeiro: Civilização Brasileira, 1972.

"Imprensa evangélica." *Imprensa Evangélica* (9 October, 1879): 321.

"Os ingênuos." *Imprensa Evangélica* (April 1881): 115.

Jones, Judith MacKnight. *Soldado Descansa! Uma epopéia norteamericana sob os céus do Brasil.* São Paulo: Jarde, 1967.

Karasch, Mary C. *Slave Life in Rio de Janeiro 1808-1850.* Princeton: Princeton University Press, 1987.

Kennedy, J.L. *Cincoenta Annos de Methodismo no Brasil.* São Paulo: Imprensa Metodista, 1928.

Kidder, Daniel Parish. *Sketches of Residence and Travels in Brazil, Embracing Historical and Geographical Notices of the Empire and its Several Provinces.* 2 vols. Philadelphia: Sorin & Ball, 1845.

Kidder, Daniel Parish and James Cooley Fletcher. *Brazil and the Brazilians, Portrayed in Historical and Descriptive Sketches.* Philadelphia: Childs & Peterson, 1857. University of Michigan Reprint Series.

Koger, J.W. "Brazil Mission." Annual Report Board of Missions. Nashville: Methodist Episcopal Church, South, 1884.

———. "The country and people of Brazil." *The Gospel in all Lands* (20 July 1882).

Koster, Henry. *Travels in Brazil.* 2nd. ed. 2 vols. London: Longman, Hurst, Rees, Orme, and Brown, 1817.

Lacerda, Pedro Maria de. "Carta pastoral do bispo da Diocese do Rio de Janeiro." *Cearense* (22 November 1871): 1.

"A lei de 28 de septembro." *Jornal do Comercio*, seção "Publicações a pedido." (3 October 1871).

"A Lei Saraiva." *Imprensa Evangélica* (21 November 1885): 1.

Léonard, E.G. *O Protestantismo Brasileiro.* São Paulo: Aste, 1963.

Lessa, Vincente Themudo. *Annaes da Primeira Egreja Presbyteriana de São Paulo (1863-1903): subsídios para a história do protestantismo.* São Paulo: Edição da Primeira Egreja Presbyteriana Independente de São Paulo, 1938.

———. *Biografia do Ex-Padre José Manoel da Conceição.* São Paulo: Gráfica Cruzeiro do Sul, 1955.

"Liberdade do corpo e escravidão do espírito." *Imprensa Evangélica* (27 March 1879): 97.

Livermore, George. *An historical research respecting the opinions of the founders of the republic on negroes as slaves, as citizens and as soldiers.* Boston: J. Wilson, 1862.

Long, E.K. *Do Meu Velho Baú Metodista.* São Paulo: Junta Geral de Educação Cristã da Igreja Metodista, 1968.

Luccock, J. *Notas sobre o Rio de Janeiro e Partes Meridionais do Brasil.* São Paulo: Livraria Martins, 1942.

Luz, F. *et al. Esboço Histórico da Escola Dominical da Igreja Evangélica Fluminense: 1855-1932.* Rio de Janeiro: n.p., 1932.

Luz, N.V.A. *Amazônia para os Negros Americanos (as origins de uma controvérsia internacional).* Rio de Janeiro: Saga, 1968.

Mattoso, Katia M. de Queirós. *To Be a Slave in Brazil 1550-1888.* Trans. Arthur Goldhammer. New Brunswick, New Jersey: Rutgers University POress, 1986.

Mendes, M., ed. *Simonton, 140 anos de Brasil.* São Paulo: Mackenzie, 2000.

Mendonça, A.G. *O Celeste Porvir: a inserção do protestantismo no Brasil.* São Paulo: Paulinas, 1984.

———. "Incorporación del protestantismo y la cuestión religiosa en Brasil en el siglo XIX: reflexiones e hipótesis." *Cristianismo y Sociedad* 92 (Mexico, 1987).

Mennucci, S. *O Precursor do Abolicionismo no Brasil (Luiz Gama).* Rio de Janeiro: Cia. Editora Nacional, 1938.

Mercadante, Paulo. *A Consciência Conservadora no Brazil.* Rio de Janeiro: Nova Fronteira, 1980.

Mesquita, A.N. *História dos Batistas no Brasil de 1907 até 1935.* Rio de Janeiro: Casa Publicadora Batista, 1940.

Mesquita, Zuleica, ed. *Evangelizar e Civilizar: cartas de Martha Watt, 1881-1908.* Piracicaba, São Paulo: Editora UNIMEP, 2001.

Moog, V. *Bandeirantes e Pioneiros: paralelos entre duas culturas.* Rio de Janeiro: Civilização Brasileira, 1967.

Morais, E. *A Campanha Abolicionista (1879-1888)*. Rio de Janeiro: Leite Ribeiro, 1924.

Morgan, G.N. "Revista da pastoral no bispo do Pará." *O Púlpito Evangélico* (February/March 1875):2.

"Movimento abolicionista." *Imprensa Evangélica* (1 November 1884): 168.

Nabuco, Joaquim. *O Abolicionismo*. London: Abraham Kingdon & Co., 1883.

———. *Abolitionism: the Brazilian antislavery struggle*. Trans. and ed. Robert Conrad. Urbana: University of Illinois Press, 1977.

———. *Cartas aos Abolicionistas Ingleses*. Ed. José Thomaz Nabuco. Recife: Fundação Joaquim Nabuco, Editora Massangana, 1985.

———. "Escravidão e colonização." *Imprensa Evangélica* (29 March 1884): 46.

———. "A nossa missão." *O Abolicionista* (1 November 1880): 1.

Nelson, Justus. "A redenção da Amazônia." *A República* (23 January 1887): 3.

———. "Aos escravos." *A República* (13 February 1887): 2.

———. "A festa de Nazareth e o jogo." *A República* (11 November 1886):3.

Neves, M. *Digesto Presbiteriano, Resolução do Supremo Concílio da Igreja Presbiteriana do Brasil, de 1888-1942*. São Paulo: Casa Editora Presbiteriana, 1950.

Newman, Junius E. "Mission to Brazil." *Nashville Christian Advocate* (12 June 1875): 2.

Nichols, R.F. *Religão e Democracia Americana*. São Paulo: Ibrasa, 1963.

"Noticiário." *Methodista Catholico* (1 April 1887): 4.

Oliveira, B.A. *Centelha em Restolho Seco*. Rio de Janeiro: Published by the author, 1985.

"A Onda." *Imprensa Evangélica* (16 August 1884): 128.

Ottoni, Christiano Benedicto. "A emancipação." *Imprensa Evangélica*, (16 May 1885): 76-77.

Pereira, Eduardo Carlos. "A escravidão." *Imprensa Evangélica* (2 May 1885): 66.

———. *O Problema Religioso da América Latina: estudo dogmático-histórico*. São Paulo: Empresa Editora Brasileira, 1920.

———. *A Religião Christã em suas relações com a escravidão*. São Paulo: Sociedade Brasileira de Tratados Evangélicos, 1886.

———. "O romanismo e o progresso." *Imprensa Evangélica* (21 November 1885): 170.

Pereira, J. dos R. *Breve História dos Batistas*. Rio de Janeiro: Casa Publicadora Batista, 1972.

Pereira, J.C. "Os meios próprios para plantar o reino de Jesus Christo no Brasil." *Imprensa Evangélica* (25 January 1881): 7.

Pitts, Fountin E. "A Call for Missionaries." *Christian Advocate and Journal* 10:15 (4 December 1835): 58.

Pontes, C. *Tavares Bastos (Aureliano Candido - 1839-1875)*. São Paulo: Cia. Editora Nacional, 1939.

"População escrava no Brasil." *Imprensa Evangélica* (21 July 1884): 94.

"O protestantismo no Brasil." *Imprensa Evangélica* (5 July 1884): 99.

"Que lugar deve ocupar a escola no trabalho de um evangelista?" *Imprensa Evangélica* (19 December 1878): 401.

Raboteau, A. *Slave Religion: the "Invisible Institution" in the Antebellum South*. New York: Oxford University Press, 1978.

Ramalho, J.P. *Prática Educativa e Sociedade*. Rio de Janeiro Zahar: 1976.

Ransom, J.J. "Brazil Mission." Annual Report Board of Missions. Nashville: Methodist Episcopal Church, South, 1883.

———. "Immigration to Brazil." *Nashville Christian Advocate* (22 March 1879).

———. "Immigration to Brazil." *Nashville Christian Advocate* (27 October 1877).

———. "Immigration to Brazil." *Nashville Christian Advocate* (18 November 1876).

Rebouças, A. *Diário e Notas Auto-biográficas*. Rio de Janeiro: José Olympio, 1938.

Reily, Duncan Alexander. *História Documental do Protestantismo no Brasil.* São Paulo: Associação de Seminários Teológicos Evangélicos (ASTE), 1984.

———. *Metodismo Brasileiro e Wesleyano.* São Paulo: Imprensa Metodista, 1981.

———. "William Capers: An Interpretation of His Life and Thought." Ph.D. diss. Emory University, 1972.

Ribeiro, B. *O Padre Protestante.* São Paulo: Casa Editora Presbiteriana, 1950.

———. *Protestantismo e Cultura Brasileira.* São Paulo: Casa Editora Presbiteriana, 1981.

———. *Protestantismo no Brasil Monárquico.* São Paulo: Pioneira, 1981.

Ribeiro, J. *A Carne.* São Paulo: Círculo do Livro, 1988.

Rizzo, M.A. *Simonton, inspirações de uma existência. Diário do ver. Ashbel Green Simonton.* São Paulo: Rizzo, 1962.

Rocha, J.G. *Lembranças do Passado.* 4 vols. Rio de Janeiro: Centro Brasileiro de Publicadade, 1941, 1944, 1946, 1956.

Rodrigues, José Carlos. "A abolição e os recursos do Brasil," *O Novo Mundo* (24 April 1871).

———. "Agora é tempo aprazado." *O Novo Mundo* (23 March 1871): 82.

———. "A base da sociedade." *O Novo Mundo* (24 January, 1871): 130.

———. "O caroço do algodão." *O Novo Mundo* (23 November 1870): 67.

———. "Colonização nacional." *O Novo Mundo* (23 March 1871):83.

———. "Egreja official e egreja livre." *O Novo Mundo* (23 September 1873): 194.

———. "A emancipação dos escravos." *O Novo Mundo* (24 October 1870): 2.

———. "A escravidão e a lavoura." *O Novo Mundo* (21 February 1871). 67.

———. "A escravidão e educação popular." *O Novo Mundo* (23 November 1870).

———. "Escravidão branda e escravidão dura." *O Novo Mundo* (24 July 1871): 143.

———. "O futuro e a América." *O Novo Mundo* (23 March 1871): 83.

———. "Grande e modesta revolução." *O Novo Mundo* (24 October 1871): 3.

———. "Idéias de religião." *O Novo Mundo* (23 October 1873): 3.

———. "A lavoura e o crédito." *O Novo Mundo* (23 November 1870): 56.

———. "A lei de 28 de septembro (opiniões da imprensa nos Estados Unidos)." *O Novo Mundo* (24 November 1871): 22.

———. "A liberdade e a fé." *O Novo Mundo* (24 January 1872): 6.

———. "Libertação de escravos na Bahia." *O Novo Mundo* (24 December 1871): 45.

———. "Meio século." *O Novo Mundo* (23 August 1872): 186.

———. "A mensagem e o Brasil." *O Novo Mundo* (23 December 1870): 34.

———. "A multiplicidade de seitas." *O Novo Mundo* (23 March 1874): 98.

———. "Notas." *O Novo Mundo* (23 March 1871): 91.

———. "Notícias." *O Novo Mundo* (24 April 1871): 102.

———. "Progresso da raça Africana nos Estados Unidos." *O Abolicionista* (1 September,1881): 6.

———. "Religiões Acatólicas." *Jornal do Comércio* (1904).

———. "Uma tarefa gloriosa." *Imprensa Evangélica* (23 April 1872): 115.

———. "O trabalho dos emancipados." *O Novo Mundo* (23 October 1872): 3.

Romero, Sílvio. *Estudos Sobre a Poesia Popular do Brasil.* 2nd ed. Petrópolis: Editora Vozes Ltda., 1977.

Salvador, J.G. *História do Metodismo no Brasil.* São Paulo: Imprensa Metodista, 1982.

Santos, Luiz Gonçalves dos. *Memórias para Servir a História do Reino do Brasil.* Belo Horizonte and São Paulo: Itatiaia/Edusp, 1981.

———. *O Católico e o Metodista; ou Refutação das Doutrinas Heréticas que os Intitulados Missionários do Rio de Janeiro, Metodistas de New York tem vulgarizado nessa Corte do Brasil por meio de Huns Impressos Chamados Tracts, com o Fim de Fazer Proselitos para a sua Seita, &c.* Rio de Janeiro: Imprensa Americana de I.P. da Costa & Co., 1838.

————. *O Celibato Clerical e Religioso Defendido dos Golpes da Impiedade e da Libertinagem dos Correspondentes da Astréia, com um Apêndice em Separado do Sr. Padre Feijó.* Rio de Janeiro: n.p., 1827.

————. *Desagravos do Clero e do Povo Católico Fluminense; ou Refutação das Mentiras e Calúnas do Impostor que se entitula Missionaionário do Rio de Janeiro, e Enviado pela Sociedade Metodista Episcopal de New York para Civilizar e Converter ao Cristianismo os Fluminenses.* Rio de Janeiro: Imprensa Americana de I.P. da Costa, 1837.

————. *A Voz da Verdade da Santa Igreja Católica, Confundido a Voz da Mentira do Amante da Humanidade para Sedativo da Efervecência Casamenteira dos Modernos Celibatários.* Rio de Janeiro: n.p., 1829.

Scarrit, R.E. "Letter from Brazil." *Woman's Missionary Advocate*, 2:6 (6 December 1880): 15.

Schwarcz, L.M. *Retrato em Branco e Preto.* São Paulo: Companhia das Letras, 1987.

Shockley, G.S. "Methodism, society and black evangelism in America: retrospect and prospect." *Methodist History* 12: 4 (July 1974): 145-182.

Silva, J.B.A.E. "Representação à Assembléia Geral Constituinte e Legislativa do Imperio do Brasil sobre a escravatura (1823)." In *Memórias sobre a Escravidão.* Rio de Janeiro and Brasília: Arquivo National Fund. Petrônio Portela, 1988.

Silva, S.T.D.G. "A religão dos pioneiros americanos no Brasil, na região de Santa Bárbara d'Oeste, Estado de São Paulo." Mimeograph copy, 1997.

Simmons, Charles Willis. "Racist Americans in a multi-racial society: Confederate exiles in Brazil." *The Journal of Negro History* 67 (Spring 1982): 34-39.

Simonton, A.G. "Os meios próprios para plantar o reino de Jesus Christo no Brasil." *Imprensa Evangélica* (25 January 1881): 6.

————. "A morte e o futuro estado dos justos." *Imprensa Evangélica* (1868).

————. *Sermões Escolhidos.* New York: G.L. Shearer, 1869.

Smith, T. D. "Letter from Brazil." *Advocate of Missions* 1:3 (August 1880): 13.

"Sois escravos ou livres?" *Imprensa Evangélica* (20 June 1878): 194.

Spaulding, Justin. "Rio de Janeiro Mission." *Christian Advocate and Journal* 11:15 (2 December 1836): 58.

Stewart, Charles Samuel. *Brazil and La Plata: the personal record of a cruise.* New York: G.P. Putnam & Co., 1856.

"Sub tegmine, sobre abolição." *A República* (20 January 1887): 3.

Summ, G. Harvey, ed., *Brazilian Mosaic: Portraits of a Diverse People and Culture* Wilmington, Delaware: Scholarly Resources, Inc., 1995.

"The Swamp Missionaries." *Christian Advocate and Journal* 8 (27 September 1833): 19.

Tarsier, P. *Histórias das Perseguições Religiosas no Brasil.* São Paulo: Cultura Moderna Sociedade Editora, 1936.

Tawney, R.H. *La Religión en el Origen del Capitalismo.* Buenos Aires: Editorial Dedala, 1959.

Testa, M. *O Apóstolo da Madeira (dr. Robert Reid Kalley).* Lisbon: Igreja Evangélica Presbiteriana de Portugal, 1963.

Thornwell, James Henley. *The Collected Works.* Ed. J.B. Adgar and J.L. Girardeau. 4 vols. Richmond: Presbyterian Committee of Publication, 1871-73.

Toplin, Robert Brent. *The Abolition of Slavery in Brazil.* New York: Atheneum, 1972.

Torres, J.C.O. *História das Idéias Religiosas no Brasil.* São Paulo: Editora Grijalbo, 1968.

Tucker, H.C. *Dr. José Carlos Rodrigues (1844-1923): A Brief Sketch of His Life.* New York: American Bible Society, n.d.

Tupper, H.A. *The Foreign Missions of the Southern Baptist Convention.* Philadelphia: American Baptist Publication Society, 1880.

Venâncio, F. *Contribuição Americana à Educação.* Rio de Janeiro: Edição Lições de Vida Americana, 1941.

Veríssimo, I.J. *André Rebouças: através de sua autobiografia.* Rio de Janeiro: José Olympio, 1939.

"Viagem imperial." *O Methodista Catholico* (1 December 1886): 3.

Vieira, Davi Gueiros. "Liberalismo, masonería y protestantismo en Brasil: siglo XIX." *Cristianimo y Sociedad* (Mexico) 25 (1987): 9-47.

———. *Protestantism and the Religious Question in Brazil: 1850-1875.* Ann Arbor, Michigan: University Microfilms International, 1977.

———. *O Protestantismo, a Maçonaria e a Questão Religiosa no Brasil.* Brasília: Editora Universidade de Brasília, 1980.

Walker, W. *História da Igreja Cristã.* São Paulo: ASTE/Juerp, 1980.

Watjen, H. *O Domínio Colonial Hollandez no Brasil: um capítulo da história colonial do século XVII.* São Paulo: Companhia Editora Nacional, 1938.

Watts, Martha H. *Evangelizar e Civilizar: cartas de Martha Watts, 1881-1908.* Z. Mesquita, ed. Piracicaba, São Paulo: Editora UNIMEP, 2001.

———. "The Homeless Children of Rio de Janeiro." *Woman's Missionary Advocate* (May 1881): 3-4.

Weaver, Blanche Henry Clark. "Confederate Immigrants and Evangelical Churches in Brazil." *The Journal of Southern History.* 18 (November 1952): 446-468.

Weber, M. *A Ética Protestante e o Espírito do Capitalismo.* São Paulo: Pioneira, 1967.

Wedemann,W.A. *A History of Protestant Missions to Brazil:1850-1914.* Ann Arbor, Michigan: Xerox University Microfilms, 1988.

Wesley, John. *The Works of John Wesley.* Ed. Richard P. Heitzenrater. Vol. 18. "Journals and Diaries I (1735-38)." Ed. W. Reginald Ward and Richard P. Heitzenrater. Nashville: Abingdon, 1988.

White, Heather Rachelle. "The glory of southern Christianity: Methodism and the mission to the slaves." *Methodist History* 39 (January 2001): 108-121.

Wightman, William M. *Life of William Capers, Including an Autobiography.* Nashville: Methodist Episcopal Church, South, 1902 [original edition, without autobiography, 1858].

Willems, E. *Assimilação e Populações Marginais no Brasil.* São Paulo: Cia. Editora Nacional, 1940.

Williams, E. *Capitalismo e Escravidão.* São Paulo: Americana, 1975.

Wright, A.F.P.A. *Desafio Americano à Preponderância Britânica no Brasil: 1808-1850.* São Paulo: Cia. Editora Nacional, 1978.

INDEX

ABOUT THE AUTHOR AND TRANSLATORS

JOSÉ CARLOS BARBOSA was born in Rio das Pedras, São Paulo, in 1957. He studied social communication at the Methodist University of Piracicaba (UNIMEP) and theology at the Methodist University of São Paulo (UMESP). Dr. Barbosa earned his master's degree in history at the University of Brasília and his doctorate in American History at the University of Seville, Spain. At the time of the publication of *Negro não Entra na Igreja. . .* Dr. Barbosa was the Coordinator of the Center for Research on Methodist Education at UNIMEP. He is author of *Entrevista com o Profeta Jeremias* and *Levar as Cargas uns dos Outros - ética crista* (Piracicaba, SP: Gráphica UNIMEP, 2001), *Frutos do Espírito e Outras Virtudes* (Campinas, SP: Hortograf Editora, 2001), and *Encontros no Antigo Testamento* and *Encontros no Novo Testamento* (Brasília: Vinde Editora, 2000). Dr. Barbosa currently teaches history at the Centro Universitário Metodista, Izabela Hendrix, in Belo Horizonte, Minas Gerais.

FRASER G. MACHAFFIE is Professor of Management and Accounting and Assistant to the President and Provost at Marietta College, Marietta, Ohio. He has visited Brazil many times and lectured at several universities and colleges. He has published in the area of Brazilian studies.

RICHARD K. DANFORD is Associate Professor of Spanish and Portuguese at Marietta College, Marietta, Ohio, and Director of Latin American Studies. Dr. Danford has visited Brazil several times and delivered presentations at professional meetings there and in the USA.